Competitive Political Regime and Internet Control

Competitive Political Regime and Internet Control: Case Studies of Malaysia, Thailand and Indonesia

By

Liu Yangyue

CAMBRIDGE SCHOLARS

PUBLISHING

Competitive Political Regime and Internet Control:
Case Studies of Malaysia, Thailand and Indonesia
By Liu Yangyue

This book first published 2014

Cambridge Scholars Publishing

12 Back Chapman Street, Newcastle upon Tyne, NE6 2XX, UK

British Library Cataloguing in Publication Data
A catalogue record for this book is available from the British Library

ISBN (10): 1-4438-5694-0, ISBN (13): 978-1-4438-5694-2

TABLE OF CONTENTS

LIST OF ILLUSTRATIONS

List of Maps

LIST OF TABLES

ACKNOWLEDGEMENTS

This book appears in its current form due to the assistance and guidance of a great many people, though some of them may not be mentioned here. I owe my deepest debt of gratitude to my PhD supervisor, Professor William Case, who brought me into this fascinating field and guided me with great patience and valuable insights. Every conversation with him (as well as the occasional debates about a number of conceptual and theoretical issues) is of extraordinary value for me. I also enjoyed a lot when he kindly showed me around the historical sites in Jakarta during my field trip.

Numerous colleagues and friends provided comments and suggestions on various parts of the manuscript. Graeme Lang and Jonathan London in City University of Hong Kong carefully read my annual reports and gave me important advice. He Zhou and Jason Abbott offered valuable advice and criticism, and I have worked hard to implement their suggestions. Many teachers in the Department of Asian and International Studies (CityU) helped me in various ways. I am indebted to Paul Cammack, Chan Yuk Wah, Federico Ferrara, Kyaw Yin Hlaing, Lee Tae-dong, Justin Robertson, Nicholas Thomas, Mark Thompson and Robert Taylor. David Zweig at Hong Kong University of Science and Technology also supported my study at various stages, for which I'm extremely grateful. I also received useful feedback from audiences at seminars or conferences where I presented material from the book. These include talks at CityU, the Chinese University of Hong Kong, the Shue Yan University and Massey University. My new institution at the National University of Defense Technology (NUDT) in China provided generous support and encouragement.

For financial support, I wish to acknowledge the CityU and AIS which generously supported my field trips as well as other research-related activities. Center of International Studies and Group of Cultural Security Studies at the NUDT also provided support in this publication. My editor at the Cambridge Scholars Publishing offered substantive feedback, guidance, and encouragement, for which I am grateful.

This book would not have been possible without the cooperation of my interviewees in Malaysia, Thailand and Indonesia, who were so generous with their time and information, and made my field research so rewarding and enjoyable. Special thanks to Elok Robert Tee who treated me cordially in Kuala Lumpur.

As always, my parents, Liu Jifeng and Yang Baifang, and other family members have given me their unequivocal support throughout my life. My wife, Wu Haijing, has stayed with me throughout the years. This book would not have been completed without her love, patience, and support. For their love and sacrifice, I dedicate this book to them.

CHAPTER ONE

INTRODUCTION

Politics in the Information Age

When Malaysia became the first country in Southeast Asia to offer Internet access to the public in 1994, the aim of transforming Malaysia into a global IT hub and building an Asian Silicon Valley was considered so important and strategic by its Prime Minister Mahathir Mohamad, that his government pledged in 1996 that there would be no censorship of the Internet (Rodan 2004). However, as the Internet penetration rate increased exponentially in the following decade, not only was Malaysia's social-political structure dramatically affected by the unequal empowerment of Internet communications, but the ambitious and attractive rhetoric by the government also changed. On the one hand, flexible yet effective use of the Internet in the 2008 electoral campaign by opposition parties forced Mahathir's successor, Abdullah Badawi, to admit afterwards that the de facto single dominant party-alliance BN (Barison Nasional) "lost the Internet war" (*New York Times* 2008). On the other hand, in addition to increasing surveillance of Internet content and harassment of dissident bloggers and online activists, an Internet filtering project, similar to China's proposed "Green Dam", was under consideration by the Malaysian Ministry of Information (Koswanage 2009).

Meanwhile, another story in China is noteworthy. On 13th January 2011 the Internet giant, Google, announced on its blog that it would end its operations in China since it was no longer willing to censor, as the government required, its Chinese version of the search engine, google.cn (BBC 2010). Although the Chinese government attempted to depoliticise this discord and label it as a pure business event, US Secretary Hilary Clinton's remark supporting Google, together with the worldwide public discussion and debate on the Internet, sovereignty, and security, has endowed the Google issue with much political significance. Much speculation has been made on whether this transnational magnate should coordinate with China's regulatory system, or vice versa. Nonetheless, these two stories are just the epitome of various conflicts and struggles between ever-rising Internet developments and diverse political systems.

The last two decades have witnessed a tremendous expansion of the Internet all over the world, especially in Asia where economies experienced the most rapid growth. It was reported that the number of global users of the Internet in 2009 climbed to 1,734 million in total, and the average penetration rate has reached 25.6%, with 74.2% in North America and 52.0% in Europe (Internet World Stats 2009). By contrast, Internet user distribution in East Asia mapped a striking discrepancy between extremely high levels of Internet penetration in countries such as Japan (75.5%), South Korea (77.3%), and Singapore (72.4%), as compared to some latecomers such as Cambodia (0.5%), Laos (1.9%), and Burma (0.2%). As a rising player in the international arena and one of the most influential powers in Asia, China has expanded its Internet user number from around 17 million in 2000 to 591 million in 2013, and is currently the largest population in the world with Internet accessibility (CNNIC 2000; 2013).

As information technologies evolved gradually and accessibility to the Internet increased dramatically, this newly developed technical system is reshaping people's life style and habits, restructuring economic structures, and most importantly, reforming politics all over the world. The era of the Internet has at least a fourfold political implication: first, national governments all over the world have to deal with a technological system which is, to some extent, internationally uniform and standardised by several leading companies and organisations; second, almost every state seeks to promote Internet development as a symbol of modernisation and globalisation, and as a means to obtain political legitimacy and public support for its leadership; third, the Internet has greatly influenced the political and social systems both domestically and globally by empowering different social groups and political parties, giving rise to the changing nature of political participation and the flexible expression of dissident, even extremist outlooks; last, Internet development has been distorted by persistent efforts by governments to control it politically. Such methods of control vary from specific content filtering to a general regulatory framework.

This phenomenon of Internet politics, or more precisely, the political Internet, reflects underlying conflicts and interactions between two systems: the socio-technological Internet system and the political regime. The primary objective of this book is to investigate and explain these conflicts and interactions. More specifically, it focuses on the last of the four aspects discussed above — political control of the Internet. This aspect has particular importance not only because Internet controls often mirror the political impact the Internet can have as well as strategic choices of national development (and is, thus, strongly related to other aspects of Internet politics) but also because discussions on Internet controls increasingly resonate with those on authoritarian resilience and democratic transition, subjects in which political scientists have long been engaged. Therefore, it highlights the relationship between a type of political regime, as the most distinct feature of a political system, and Internet control practice. It is interesting and important to investigate whether regime type (especially among democratic and semi-authoritarian regimes) affects the intensity of Internet controls, and if not, to identify the major factors that cause Internet controls. To narrow it to a viable scope, this book focuses on the region of Southeast Asia, where diverse political regimes exist and are frequently transitioning and transforming. It further narrows its focus on competitive political regimes, thus excluding fully authoritarian regimes which are conventional subjects in the study of Internet control. It hopes that, by studying Internet control practices, it would not only enhance and substantiate our understanding of politics in an Internet-dominant era, but also help to explain the role of technology in political analysis.

What is Internet Control?

Probably the most influential technology over the past two decades, the Internet has its roots "in the darkness of the Cold War" (Rosenzweig 1998, 1533). The first computer network, Advanced Research Projects Agency Network or ARPANET, was invented in 1969 against a backdrop of US–USSR technological competition (Carr 2009), enabling the research scientists working for US defence agencies to exchange data and information through a "packet-switching"[1] process (Abbate 2000). Due to the fact that the access to ARPANET was initially limited to defence, science and academia, it is possible that security and authoritative control of the network was not the priority of those engineers and technicians, and thus the anarchical nature was embedded into the Internet from its inception. As Jayne Rodgers (2003, 42) put it, "whether by design or default, the result was an inherently decentralised communications technology which could be used to establish direct or indirect links between individuals and institutions".

Because of the history of Internet development, the essential technologies and infrastructures of the Internet have, for decades, been under the tight monopoly of the United States. The root servers, which store the addresses and technical standards databases and serve as the crucial nucleus of the international networking system, consist of 13 sets of colossal computer systems, 10 out of which are located within the United States (Cukier 2005). As for the overall administration of, and supervision over, the Internet system, Jon Postel, a computer science professor at the University of Southern California, oversaw the relevant affairs almost exclusively until 1998, when his role was superseded by a private-sector non-profit organisation called the Internet Corporation for Assigned Names and Numbers (ICANN). Nonetheless, the United States has retained much power over Internet governance, as ICANN was established under the law of the state of California and responsible only to the US Department of Commerce (Mathiason 2009). While the United States has dominated the global structure of the Internet at an international level, the *Pax Americana*, anticipated by many Internet enthusiasts, did not occur since cyberspace, instead of being entirely free and borderless, was further controlled by various means at a national, domestic level. The subordinate servers deployed by national governments, functioning as transshipment stations that deliver and exchange packets between internal users and external destinations, make it feasible and effective that nation states can claim sovereignty over their cyberspace.

The nature of the Internet is not as borderless and anarchical as many early users had anticipated. In fact, governments, no matter whether authoritarian or democratic or somewhere in between, have at their disposal a large pool of various feasible methods and policies for Internet control. This diversity of control strategies is perhaps best illustrated by Zittrain and Palfrey (2008, 31) in the following words:

> Sometimes the law pressures citizens to refrain from performing a certain activity online, such as accessing or publishing certain material. Sometimes the state takes control into its own hands by erecting technological or other barriers within its confines to stop the flow of bits from one recipient to another. Increasingly, though, the state is turning to private parties to carry out the control online. Many times, those private parties are corporations chartered locally or individual citizens who live in that jurisdiction.

In general, the various methods that compose the overall repertoire of Internet control can be divided into four groups: methods that (1) censor the Internet content, (2) exploit legal framework, (3) monopolise network infrastructure, and (4) enforce psychological self-censorship. The first method involves restraining netizens from accessing certain kinds of content. The most direct and economical control of online content always involves technological means through which sensitive content is filtered and "detrimental" websites blocked. However, the exact mechanisms of filtering or blocking content may vary from case to case, depending upon the motivation and capability of the organisation deploying them. Common types of technical blocking/filtering include TCP/IP address blocking, Domain Name System (DNS) tampering, Uniform Resource Locator (URL) filtering (Murdoch and Anderson 2008), and keywords filtering. Besides the conventional blocking mechanisms, websites can also be made inaccessible by overloading the target server or network connection. For instance, it was reported that ahead of Myanmar's national elections in November 2010 — which had not been held since 1990 — a massive Distributed Denial of Service (DDoS) attack occurred that almost crippled the Internet traffic throughout the country (BBC 2010). The technical report from Craig Labovitz (2010), an expert in Arbor Networks, showed that the sudden influx of Internet traffic was "several hundred times more than enough to overwhelm" the country's network capacity. Similar incidents occurred in Malaysia — this time, DDoS attacks on several prominent newssites — before the critical Sarawak state election in April 2011 (Reporters without Borders 2011). None of these attacks could be traced directly to any government agency, but the timing has proved beneficial principally to governments in Myanmar and Malaysia.

In the second method, in order to rationalise and legitimise the supervision of online content as well as to moderate the radical, provocative, and oppositional voices of Internet users, legal and regulatory frameworks are necessary for governments who attempt to politically control the Internet. In general, three types of regulations can be identified. The first involves rules stipulating under what conditions and in what manner Internet Service Providers (ISPs) could be organised and websites registered. The second strand of regulations addresses different types of web-based activities, including online posts, emails, and blogs and so on, which are not permitted on the Internet. For instance, in Thailand, the law against lèse-majesté is broadly used in the online regulation that prosecutes behaviours insulting, defaming, or threatening the Thai royal family. The last type stipulates how illegal online activities are penalised. In Myanmar for example, the State Peace and Development Council demanded that all network-ready computers must be registered with Myanmar Posts and Telecom (MPT), with fines and prison sentences of between seven and fifteen years if the requirement was not met. The actual punishment for online Burmese activists and dissidents is even tougher: Nay Phone Latt, a famous blogger who was nominated for a "Cyber-Dissident or Blogger" Award, was arrested by the Burmese authorities for posting information about the September 2007 demonstrations on his personal website and sentenced to twenty years in jail. Incidents like this are almost ubiquitous across the whole region.

Apart from targeting infringing content online, nation states also attempt to control the overarching infrastructure that creates and supports the Internet fundamentally. On this score, states could purposely deploy Internet accessibility geographically and manipulate the Internet service when necessary. A more direct and effective way is to "switch off" (part of) the entire network. Referring to the Internet shutdown in Burma in 2007, researchers in the OpenNet Initiative (2007) explained that "a switch off could therefore be conducted at the top by shutting off the border router(s), or a bottom up approach could be followed by first shutting down routers located a few hops deeper inside the AS (Burmese Autonomous System)". The fourth method of Internet control occurs psychologically. On the one hand, states may use intimidatory actions of monitoring and punishing "untamed" online activities, encouraging an atmosphere of "self-censorship". For example, as Terence Lee (2010) argued, the Singaporean government was continuously seeking to create a "culture of self-censorship" in its cyberspace that could govern the mindset and conduct of Internet users. Moreover, governments may actively participate in online activities for propaganda and ideological purposes. Political leaders as well as hired commentators attempting to (re)shape online public opinion have been a crucial part of the "cyber troopers" in many Southeast Asian countries.

The discussion above illustrates how Internet control is technically feasible and empirically practiced. Internet control takes various forms, ranging from content censorship to the chilling effect of psychological manipulation. In this book, the level of Internet control is measured by observing the occurrence, frequency, and scale of these various forms. Meanwhile, different forms of Internet control share a common feature. They point to state repressive actions particularly associated with Internet usage that threatens established interests in the political system. Therefore, it is reasonable to conceptualise Internet control as a component or form of political repression, which broadly refers to "government regulatory action directed against those challenging existing power relationships" (Davenport 1995, 683), or "the systematic violation of the civil liberties and human rights of groups and/or individuals" (Regan and Henderson 2002, 120). The importance of this conceptualisation is that it allows us to draw lessons from political repression studies (which is reviewed in the next chapter) to identify the key factors behind Internet control policies.

Internet control has been a hotspot in the study of Internet politics. Based on the belief that the Internet poses an insurmountable threat to authoritarian rule, most of the work in this aspect reflects Internet control in authoritarian countries. On this score, Garry Rodan (1998; 2004) revealed how the ruling party of Singapore, as well as that of Malaysia, promoted Internet development while seeking to control it politically. Even more studies cite the case of China (Kalathil and Boas 2003; Wacker 2003). Meanwhile, several studies have found that political control of the Internet occurs not only in authoritarian regimes, but also in democratic states. Lessig (1999) argued that governments everywhere can regulate the Internet both by controlling its underlying code and by shaping the legal environment in which it operates. Furthermore, a study by Giacomello (2008) indicated that the different types of Internet control in democratic countries, such as the US, Germany, and Italy, were determined by the different relations between governments and societies.

However, current studies on Internet control suffer from several weaknesses. Firstly, although these studies often provide detailed accounts of *how* Internet controls are designed and implemented, especially technically (see, for example, Goldsmith and Wu 2006; Murdoch and Anderson 2008), they give few answers as to *why* political control of the Internet occurs. While the forms, processes, and techniques of Internet control have been carefully examined, allowing us to assess the intensity and diversity of Internet controls, we still need theoretical explanations that identify the driving and constraining forces behind Internet control. Secondly, much literature is devoted to the single case study which aims to only examine the impact of the Internet and government responses in a given circumstance (see, for example, Rodan 1998; Wacker 2003; Hill and Sen 2005; Zheng 2008; Morozov 2011a). By contrast, comparative research, built on an explicit and coherent theoretical framework that highlights the major determinants of Internet control, is infrequent and inadequate (see, for example, Kalathil and Boas 2003; Howard 2010).

More importantly, most studies, though sometimes implicitly, attribute Internet control practices to the resistance, or inherent nature, of authoritarian political regime, thus implying a linear relationship between Internet control and regime type (see, for example, Rodan 1998; Kalathil and Boas 2003; Wacker 2003; Gomez 2004; Morozov 2011a). This presumed relationship, however, has been made without careful examination. Some empirical evidence has revealed that democratic countries also implement Internet control policies, while some authoritarian states leave their cyberspace uncensored (Giacomello 2008; Deibert and Rohozinski 2010; Howard 2010). These deviant cases necessitate re-examination of the supposed "regime–control" relationship. To what extent can regime type determine the level of Internet censorship? Addressing this question, the following section will evaluate the "regime–control" thesis and present the major puzzle that renders an alternative framework necessary.

Presenting the Puzzle

As previously mentioned, Internet control strategies have been widely considered as a natural, inevitable response of authoritarian political regimes, thus implying a linear relationship between Internet control and regime type. While deploying this relationship as the underlying premise of their analyses, these studies seldom question the validity of this relationship per se. This section provides a brief examination of this relationship which is more complicated than a simple linear dependence.

We first test the correlation between the level of Internet control and the degree of democracy. Although so far a comprehensive index of Internet control (covering a large sample of countries as well as a full repertoire of Internet control measures) is barely available, Freedom House (2011) has made an important effort to quantify the level of Internet freedom, recording and measuring governmental regulations in 37 countries. Despite using only a small number of samples (already a sharp increase from the 15 countries in the previous version), this report has covered countries at varying levels of political and economic development. It is therefore, to some extent, representative. The scoring system contains three sub-groupings: "obstacles to access," "limits on content," and "violations of user rights". Countries are scored from 0 (best) to 100 (worst) to describe a "free" (0–30), "partly free" (31–60), or "not free" (61–100) Internet environment (Freedom House 2011, 386–388). To enable comparison between Internet freedom and democraticness, scores on the democraticness of these same countries are extracted from Economist Intelligence Unit's Democracy Index 2010 and Polity IV Country Reports 2010 respectively.[2] Under EIU's index, a score of 10 represents the highest level of democracy and 0 the lowest. Meanwhile, Polity IV's scheme envisages a regime spectrum ranging from -10 (most autocratic) to +10 (most democratic).[3]

The results are shown in Fig.1-1 and 1-2. Despite slight differences, the two figures demonstrate similar relations between variables. There are two major observations to be made from the data. Firstly, a statistical correlation can be observed between the level of democracy and that of Internet freedom, indicating that regime types do matter. As democraticness increases, countries in these surveys have higher probability of allowing greater Internet freedom, and vice versa.

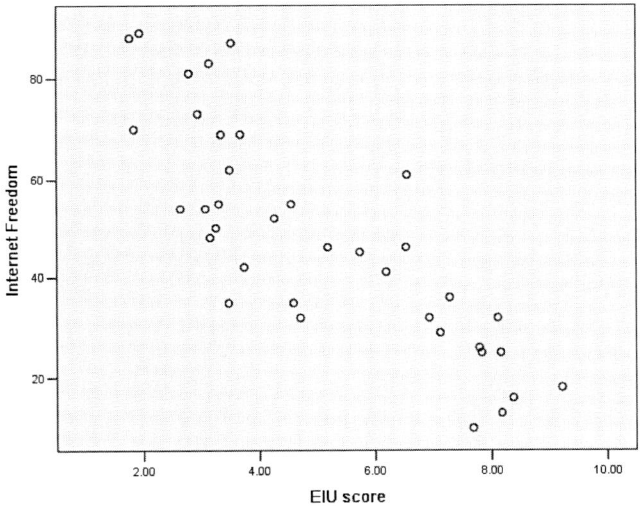

Fig. 1-1: Correlation between political regime and Internet freedom
Source: EIU 2010

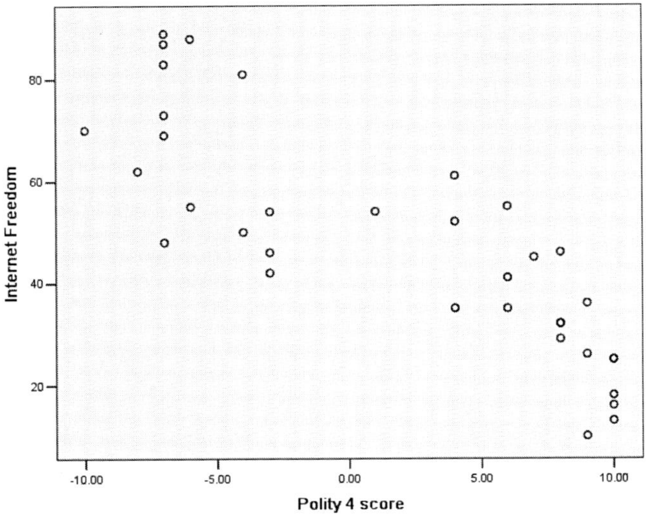

Fig. 1-2: Correlation between political regime and Internet freedom
Source: Polity IV 2010

Nonetheless, the correlation is much stronger at either end of the equation than in the middle. In general, fully democratic regimes impose far fewer restrictions on Internet freedom, while politically closed regimes control the Internet system in a pervasive and systematic way. But among those intermediate political regimes, the level of democraticness appears inadequate in explaining Internet control outcomes. With similar degree of democracy, countries may substantially vary in their respective level of Internet freedom. For instance, scored in the range of 4–5 under EIU's index, Pakistan (with a score of 55 in Internet freedom), Russia (52), Georgia (35), and Kenya (32) appear quite different in protecting Internet freedom. Similarly, the same score under Polity IV's classification produces dissimilar results — a score of 4 (indicating "open anocracy") leads to a "partly free" status (Nigeria and Russia) as well as a "not free" status (Thailand) in Internet freedom. Such mismatch persists when we move along the regime continuum. Contrary to our expectations, one degree of increase in democracy may be accompanied by a decrease in Internet freedom, and vice versa. Therefore, the purported relationship between regime type and Internet control turns out to be much more complicated and confusing than originally assumed, at least within the intermediate range of regime types.

In fact, it is recognised that the role played by political regime type in shaping repressive actions is highly ambiguous (Davenport 2007). On this score, Davenport and Armstrong (2004) have found that above a certain level of democracy the relationship between democracy and repression is linear, but below that threshold state coercive actions are not influenced by regime type. The significance of their finding is that "the level of democracy thus retains its importance for theory as identified within most of the literature relevant to the topic, but only at the very end of the democratic continuum" (Davenport and Armstrong 2004, 551–552). This finding corresponds to what we have observed above. Therefore, it is possible that regime type is not the direct determinant of Internet control. In this sense, we should look at other factors in addition to regime type to better understand Internet control, especially in semi-democratic and semi-authoritarian contexts.

Based on the discussion above, this study proposes two major hypotheses. The first relates to the relationship between regime type and Internet control. The other presents an alternative model of Internet control that underscores the role of online transgression and civil society. Theoretical framework used in these hypotheses will be further elaborated in Chapter 2.

Hypothesis 1 (H1)

In the intermediate range of political regimes between democracy and authoritarianism, regime type does not correlate closely with the level of Internet control. Online transgressiveness and the power or capacity of online civil society better account for Internet control outcomes than do regime types.

Hypothesis 2 (H2)

While online transgression encourages the state to respond with Internet controls, online civil society capacity enables society to resist and overcome such control.

Selecting the Case

This research is designed to address the "regime–control" puzzle and identify the major factors that better account for Internet control practices among intermediate political regimes. It also attempts to illustrate the trajectories in which different countries develop their Internet control strategies. Instead of taking a cross-regional approach which risks facing not only divergent outcomes, but also a great variety of potential causes, this study focuses on the region of Southeast Asia, distinguished by its "remarkable range of political forms" (Hewison 1999, 224). The various types of semi-democratic and semi-authoritarian regimes that Southeast Asian countries have would enable us to identify the major determinants of Internet control among intermediate political systems. Moreover, by narrowing our focus on a specific region, we may better control potential differential factors such as cultural and geographical differences, level of development, and historical legacies (Slater 2008).

A comparative in-depth case study methodology is used as the main approach for several reasons. Firstly, since Internet politics is a relatively new research subject, there are few established theories of Internet control to be tested. In this sense, this study is as much about generating new hypotheses as about confirming or disconfirming existing theories, a task that case study techniques better address (Lijphart 1971). By closely examining the internal political dynamics of a few cases, this study attempts to develop a grounded theory upon which further large-scale, quantitative investigations can draw.

Secondly, although case study techniques, unlike statistical testing, cannot quantify precise causal relations, they are able, as a first step, to identify and investigate casual mechanisms. On this score, case studies allow us to see how different variables interact and thus better understand the causality between them (Gerring 2004). In addition, case study techniques enable us to trace the historical development of Internet control institutions and strategies in selected countries. Last but not least, there are also some practical reasons for avoiding a large-N research design. The most critical reason is the unavailability of comprehensive, large-scale data sets on Internet control. As noted above, the first report quantitatively measuring Internet freedom, released by Freedom House in 2009, only covered 15 countries, while its 2011 updated version, despite its valuable and path-breaking effort, merely boosted the sample size to 37. Other important efforts in this regard either remain small-scale and qualitative (such as reports released by Reporters Without Borders), or concentrate only on a particular strategy of Internet control without taking into account the full repertoire (such as Open Net Initiative's Internet filtering reports). All these factors provide rationale for a comparative case study approach. The validity and weakness of this approach will be further examined in the final chapter.

As mentioned above, the "regime–control" puzzle is most evident in the intermediate range of regime types. Therefore, the usual dichotomy between democracy and non-democracy needs modification. This book utilises existing regime typologies that treat political regime as a continuum ranging from liberal democracy at one end to politically closed regimes at the other (Diamond 2002). In between these two ends are different types of hybrid regimes, including — according to their levels of democraticness — electoral democracy (Diamond 1999), competitive authoritarianism (Levitsky and Way 2010) and electoral authoritarianism (Schedler 2006). These hybrid regimes are labelled competitive political systems so that we can distinguish them from either full democracies or full autocracies. This intermediate area is the focus of our research interest. Since this study focuses on competitive political regimes in Southeast Asia, six countries fall into our sample list: these are Cambodia, Indonesia, Malaysia, Philippines, Singapore, and Thailand.[4] None of them can be further qualified as liberal democracies, but democratic traits do exist to different extents (see Freedom House 2012; Economist Intelligence Unit 2011; Polity IV 2010).

Malaysia, Thailand and Indonesia have been selected as in-depth case studies because these countries represent an evident mismatch — their regime types do not correlate with their respective extent of Internet control. Competitive authoritarianism in Malaysia, although amounting to less democratic politics than in the other two countries, is accompanied by low-medium intensity of Internet control practice. Electoral democracy in Thailand is associated with the most repressive environment for the Internet. Meanwhile, electoral democracy in Indonesia, currently the most democratic state in the region, implements Internet controls at a medium level. Freedom House's (2011) recent report quantified the level of Internet control in these countries by establishing an index of Internet freedom. It showed that Thai people enjoyed much less Internet freedom, with a score of 61 (a status of "not free") compared with 46 ("partly free") in Indonesia, and 41 ("partly free") in Malaysia. In other words, regime type in Malaysia would lead us to expect Internet controls there to be more intense than they actually are, while regime types in Thailand and Indonesia would suggest that Internet controls should be less intense than they are.

Moreover, we take a closer look at one specific controlling method — the extent to which governments in Southeast Asia censor sensitive websites. On this score, the Open Net Initiative has technically tracked the Internet filtering situation across the world. In a recent research report, they scrutinised, among other countries in Asia, the filtering and blocking practices in Burma, Indonesia, Malaysia, Thailand, and Vietnam (Deibert et al. 2012). The results show that Burma and Vietnam represent two of "the most pervasive regimes of Internet filtering in the region, primarily targeting independent media and content related to politically sensitive issues, human rights, and political reform" (Deibert et al. 2012, 226). However, while both Indonesia and Thailand adopted selective filtering on websites with political content and websites for Internet tools (such as those websites offering circumvention software), no evidence of filtering practices was found in Malaysia (see Fig.1-3). Again, the democraticness of political regime and the level of Internet filtering did not match in the intermediate zones of the political regime spectrum.

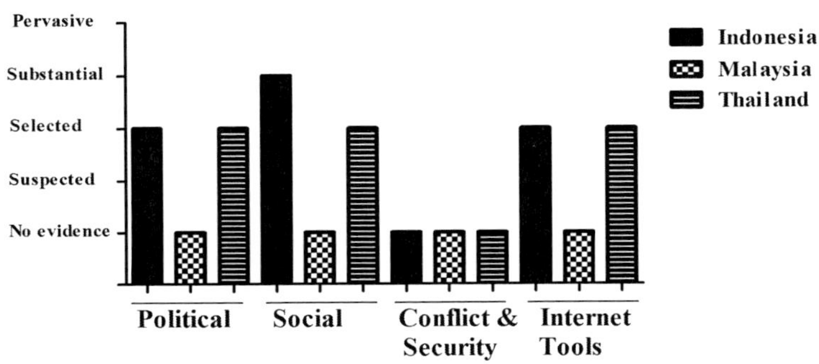

Fig. 1-3: Internet filtering in hybrid regimes
Source: Deibert et al. 2012

This mismatch refutes the commonly perceived "regime–repression" causal relationship, and thus, necessitates in-depth examination of alternative explanations of Internet control in these countries. By closely exploring the abnormal cases that negate the "regime–repression" model, this book attempts to construct an alternative model of Internet control.

By contrast, the remaining three Southeast Asian countries, Cambodia, Singapore, and the Philippines, operate authoritarian and democratic regimes within the competitive spectrum that correlate, as would be expected, with the level of Internet control. These country-cases are given less attention, since it is the anomalous cases that this book has sought most to explain. But they are worthy of at least cursory examination, due to the possibility that in these cases, regime types mask other factors that are more fundamentally at work. Therefore, while this research chooses three countries as case studies for in-depth analysis, the remaining three countries will be briefly investigated in Chapter 6 to see whether our alternative model can still be applied.

In order to obtain first-hand information on Internet controls, field research has been conducted in Malaysia, Thailand and Indonesia. Appendix A details the process, rationale, and strategy of interviewee selection, and provides the question lists.

Overview of the Book

This book is structured as follows. Chapter 2 theoretically constructs the alternative model used in this study. It draws insights from existing studies on political repression to find out which factor(s) truly affects Internet control outcomes. Specifically, it identifies two major variables — intensity of online transgressiveness and capacity of online civil society — that are most important in explaining Internet control in competitive political systems. This alternative model argues that online transgressiveness serves as the impetus which defines the necessity of Internet controls, while online civil society represents an inhibiting force, the cohesiveness of which determines the extent to which societal resistance against Internet control might succeed. Criteria of measuring these variables are developed, supplemented by a detailed measurement scheme in Appendix B. In addition, the theoretical model also highlights the role of historical and contextual conditions.

Chapters 3, 4 and 5 apply the alternative model to in-depth case studies, investigating Internet control practices in Malaysia, Thailand, and Indonesia respectively. These case studies present first-hand information collected through several field trips, including interviews with relevant government officials, politicians, scholars and activists. Each case starts with a brief summary of the historical development of the political system in question as well as the Internet system in that country, followed by a discussion on how the Internet facilitates political change and how governments respond by controlling it politically. These cases reveal that it is the intensity of online transgressiveness and the capacity of online civil society, instead of regime type, that collectively affect the level of Internet control.

In Malaysia, although a moderate-high level of transgressiveness has provided a stimulus for the government to suppress online activism and opposition campaigns, the online civil society, which often coordinates with opposition parties and other social forces, has effectively prevented the government from upgrading its Internet control arsenal. In Thailand, the combination of a high level of transgressiveness and a fragmented online civil society gives rise to extensive and systemic Internet control measures. Meanwhile, Indonesia faces moderate online transgression and modest civil society capacity. Internet control there operates, accordingly, at a moderate level. The findings from these country-cases bear out this study's theoretical framework.

Chapter 6 deals with other democratic and semi-democratic countries in Southeast Asia. Internet control practices in Cambodia, Singapore, and the Philippines are explored to supplement our inquiry of why competitive political regimes control the Internet. This chapter uses mainly secondary but reliable information obtained from scholarly research and NGO reports. The concluding chapter synthesises the insights drawn from case studies and makes comparison across these cases. It then raises and briefly tests several alternative explanations of Internet control, including the rate of Internet penetration, media environment, and foreign investment dependency. These factors are found to be much less decisive in Internet control practice. Finally this chapter also discusses how these insights make theoretical contributions to political science as well as Internet studies.

CHAPTER TWO

TRANSGRESSION, CIVIL SOCIETY AND INTERNET CONTROL

This chapter attempts to construct an alternative framework that better accounts for Internet control outcome. In previous chapter we conceptualised Internet control as a form of political repressive action. Analysis in the following section returns to this theme, drawing upon existing literature on political repression to identify the major factors that determine Internet control policies.

What do Studies on Political Repression Say and Not Say?

Agency-level explanations: The central role of threat

How should we use existing knowledge about political repression to explain Internet control? What are the factors leading to political repression in general? Are these factors the same as those that lead to Internet control? Perhaps one of the most significant relationships that has withstood rigorous investigation is between domestic threats — the challenges made to existing authorities in the form of political dissent — and political repression. This suggests that when political threats are present, government authorities frequently use repression as a means to restrict or eliminate these threats in order to preserve their interests (Davenport 2000). More importantly, the nature of political threats strongly affects how governments respond (Gurr and Lichbach 1986; Davenport 1995; 2007; Gartner and Regan 1996; Moore 2000). Political dissent that involves large-scale mobilisation and uses unconventional or unconstitutional tactics is more likely to provoke government repression than the contentiousness that involves smaller populations and is confined within conventional strategic options. On this score, McAdam, Tarrow, and Tilly (2001) distinguish between two types of political contentiousness — a transgressive one and a contained one. While conflicts in the former type involve almost exclusively parties "previously established as constituted political actors", the latter brings in at least some "newly self-identified political actors", and exhibits some innovative collective actions (McAdam et al. 2001, 7–8). Transgressive contention is generally considered as larger, systemic political threats while contained contention is associated with less critical, and often individual or organisational-based threats. Besides scale and intensity, threat can also be measured by the political content of dissenting groups (Gartner and Regan 1996). The opposition's demands indicate the concession that the political leadership is called upon to make. Therefore, political claims to replace the current political system are more threatening than claims to redistribute resources or challenge individual politicians/institutions.

Based on the observation above, this book will measure political threat in terms of the trangressiveness of political dissent. To transgress is to cross the limits or boundaries that the political establishment has prescribed for conducting political activities. Transgressiveness refers to the extent to which political contentiousness and activities stand in contradiction, inversion, or as alternatives to the status quo (Stallybrass and White 1986). It includes, in general, two attributes: (1) to what extent the dissent (contentiousness) mobilises new political players that were previously tranquil and employs new strategies and (2) whether its political demand is targeted at the systemic level or at the individual/organisational level. The adoption of transgressiveness in measuring Internet threat will be explored in a later section.

As an independent variable, transgressiveness, or the level of threats, should be effectively separated from other plausible factors such as regime type. It would be tempting to argue that democracies are less likely to experience political threats than autocracies are, and thus the level of threats merely reflects the degree of democracy. In this sense threat is only a secondary factor, unworthy of special attention. However, studies on political repression acknowledge the distinction between political threat and regime type and argue that the conventional perception of a linear relationship between them is misleading (Regan and Henderson 2002; Davenport 2007). Instead, empirical findings reveal an inverted-U relationship, with semi-democracies facing the highest level of threats, due to the fragility of state institutions and the limited range of available options (Regan and Henderson 2002, 124). Therefore, it is not the regime type, but other factors embedded in the political system instead, that directly affect the level of threat. If the linear covariance of threat and regime type does not exist empirically, it is reasonable to treat the level of threat as an independent factor. In fact, it has been argued that the level of threat is more useful than regime type in explaining the likelihood of repression (Regan and Henderson 2002; Earl 2003). In a similar vein, this study considers transgressiveness and regime type as separate variables, while recognising their complicated, non-linear connections.

Meanwhile, related to the "threat" factor is the capacity of civil society to resist repression. A strong civil society often leads to better human rights protection, and thus less state repression (Neumayer 2005; Hathaway 2007). When substantial (or potential) violation of civil rights occurs, civil society organisations could exert pressure upon governments to withdraw repressive actions. They do so through promoting public deliberation, mobilising social movements, and allying with media and oppositional forces. As Dan Slater (2012, 27) recently argued, restraints on coercive actions "may well depend, in turn, on the capacity of opposition forces to muster a sufficient challenge to press leaders to reconsider their patterns of rule". Particularly in competitive political systems, the political costs of repression would exponentially heighten if civil society is well institutionalised, consolidated, and coordinated within itself. On the other hand, the fragmented civil society (or highly isolated from elite politics) brings far less pressure against state repressive actions. Factional conflicts among civil organisations may even exacerbate political repression as some repressive policies are in accord with the interest of a particular civil group. Under such circumstances, an "uncivil society" occurs that ails rather than heals democratic institutions and practices (Thompson 2008). In other words, government authorities could garner greater public support in their coercive (regulatory) measures when the attitudes of civil society towards such policies are divided or antithetic. Therefore, I hypothesise that the capacity of online civil society in its diverse forms, such as new media, the blogger community, and online movements, also affects government decisions on Internet control.

These variables — the level of threats and the capacity of civil society — underscore the strategic interaction at the agent level. This model considers state repressive actions as cost-benefit calculations concerning the necessity as well as repercussions of government decisions. However, this agency-level discussion is still insufficient in two aspects. Firstly, while government behaviour may stem directly from agency-level interactions, it remains unclear how a particular form of political threat is shaped and what governs the state–society relationship. In other words, we have to investigate why transgressiveness of online contentiousness is much greater, and why the capacity of online civil society is higher, in one country than another. In this sense, it is necessary to identify the conditioning factors that frame the character of agency-level variables. Secondly, while threat and online civil society may be sufficient in explaining current Internet control outcomes in Southeast Asia, it appears to be inadequate in explaining initial government decisions at a time when Internet technologies were beginning to develop region-wide. At that time, due to the infancy-state of Internet development, the political threat of the Internet was insignificant and online civil society lacked organisational cohesiveness and muscle. To some extent, the contrasting initial responses from Southeast Asian governments in the 1990s deviate from a strict "threat–response" correlation. For instance, in the last days of "New Order" Indonesia, the government did little to control information flows even though it threatened regime survival. In contrast, the Singaporean government practiced early Internet censorship well before substantial threats emerged online. Although this inconsistency may partly be explained by the difference between the stormy "People Power" movement in Indonesia — an indicator of the weakening state power vis-à-vis the society — and the tamed societal force in Singapore, people still wonder what contextual conditions may have affected government choices in regulating the Internet.

Historical institutionalism and contextual factors

How should we move from agency-level explanations to historical and contextual factors? First of all, instead of treating Internet control as a static outcome, perhaps we should trace the historical processes through which Internet control institutions are formed and developed. This argument borrows insights from historical institutionalism as well as studies in political repression. Taking an analytic approach, historical institutionalism emphasises "historical process" rather than "equilibrium order", regarding "institutions as the legacy of concrete historical processes" instead of merely "coordinating mechanisms sustaining these equilibria" (Thelen 1999, 381–382). It looks at the particular sequencing of events to explain divergent outcomes. On the one hand, "institutions emerge from and are sustained by features of the broader political and social context" (Thelen 1999, 384). On the other hand, once established, institutional configuration and arrangement can be difficult to change, and the initial pattern of institutional formation can be influential upon its future development (Orren and Skowronek 1995; Skocpol and Pierson 2002).

Some studies in political repression have adopted such an approach and borne fruit. On this score, examining the political origin and development of military courts, Anthony Pereira (2005) analyses how political trials and legal manipulations were employed differently in the military regimes of Brazil, Argentina, and Chile. In a similar vein, this book pays attention to the historical development of Internet regulation institutions (such as government agencies and legislations). Besides this process-based focus, another useful lesson drawn from these theoretical and empirical works is that we should differentiate between an initial stage of institutional formation and later development. In this sense, factors that generate initial governmental response towards Internet regulation could be different from factors that affect government control in the later period when the Internet has penetrated more deeply into the society. In the 1990s, when the Internet became popular in much of the developing world, it embodied few visible threats. It was in this particular political and social context — which I summarise as liberalising and democratising conditions — that governments had the opportunity to take preemptive actions against the potential danger of Internet politics. These actions, or inactions, have shaped the early pattern of Internet control institutions (in terms of rules and norms), which have had further impacts on their own development.

This approach thus highlights the issue of timing. Governments that practiced Internet control at an early stage — due to the lack of liberalising or democratising conditions in the 1990s — would probably have more technical and intellectual resources on Internet control, breed a more cautious and quiescent online community culture, and enjoy a broadened repertoire of control strategies at a later stage. Meanwhile, governments that missed the initial opportunity for contextual reasons might find themselves enjoying fewer options and resources when they decide to control the Internet later. In fact, the importance of timing has been elaborated in Gerschenkron's (1962) classic discussion on economic development. This study stresses that different conditions at the outset of development determine the future trajectory of that development.

It is necessary, then, to identify those conditions that frame the initial pattern of Internet control. Such conditions may vary according to different types of repression. For instance, Krain (1997) argues that variables such as civil wars, extra-constitutional changes, and decolonisation, increase the probability of the onset of genocides and "politicides", while Pereira (2005) underscores the features of the previous political regime and the degree of military-civilian consensus as important framers for "authoritarian legalities". What these conditions have in common is the way they constrain or broaden the range of options available to the elites, thus diminishing or enlarging state capacity for repression. As Krain (1997, 335) points out, "major structural changes [...] create 'windows of political opportunity' during which the elites may and must more freely act to consolidate power and eliminate the opposition".

By the same token, contextual changes can also generate openings for political opportunity that make it difficult for elites to impose repression. These openings may occur when major democratisation processes emerge that bring about substantial change in state–society relations and a liberalising discourse, or when dominant modes of political economy are reshaped based on external resources, especially when Western foreign investment increases, which also drives up the price of political control. These changes share a common feature in that they all empower the liberal framers vis-à-vis the authoritarian practitioners or introduce into the political arena new liberalising forces. This study categorises these openings in the political opportunity structure as liberalising and democratising conditions. Such grouping underscores the cumulating long-term rather than one-off effects of contextual changes and therefore highlights again the importance of historical process.

Reviewing political repression studies, Christian Davenport (2007, 3) has observed that "the theoretical orientation of most researchers of repression has evolved from a hard structuralism to a soft rationalism". The framework of this book, however, underlines both agency-level factors — in terms of political threats and civil society capacity — and context-level conditions that serve as external sources for agents' behaviours. The following section is accordingly divided into two parts: the first part addresses the main independent variables — the level of transgressiveness and the capacity of online civil society — that directly shape Internet control; the second part traces the historical and contextual sources that have shaped initial government strategies in the 1990s and subsequently caused agency-level variations.

Transgressiveness, Civil Society and Government Responses

Online transgressiveness

For students of Internet politics, controlling the Internet is primarily the response of governments towards Internet-related political (Kalathil and Boas 2003; Zheng 2008), social (Noman 2011), or security (Gomez 2004) challenges. The political threats of the Internet, however, vary in different settings and times, ranging from the more systemic (such as an Internet-mobilised uprising) to the more personal (such as the exposure of a particular corrupt politician). In this book, online transgressiveness is used to describe the level of threat that the Internet poses to a particular government. It is defined as the extent to which online political contentiousness and activities contradict, invert, or alter established political interests. As discussed in the previous section, two dimensions are involved in affecting the level of transgressiveness: scale and content.

Scale refers to the size and composition of participants in transgressive online contentiousness. An important indicator in this regard is the number of people involved in social movements[5] that have been mobilised largely by the Internet technologies. Massive social movements often reflect strong, deep social grievances about government policies or performance. Especially in competitive political systems where political elites are, to varying degrees, accountable to the electorate, these movements, once having garnered considerable societal support, exert enormous pressure on the government to reverse, rescind, or reform its decisions. As a movement expands, the government may have less space to negotiate a concession and minimise the cost of policy change. Moreover, the expansion of social movements may lead to uncontrollable riots, causing political instability and violence (Wilkinson 2009). All these indicate the large political threats that the government has to address. In fact, the magnitude of social movements, riots and rebellions has been widely used in repression studies to measure the degree of threats (Davenport 1995; Regan and Henderson 2002). Although online political contentiousness involves forms other than Internet-mobilised movements, such as critical discussion and online petitions, it is when online contentious activists take to the street that the ruling elites face direct and explicit challenges. Therefore, this study stipulates that high and moderate levels of online transgressiveness require the occurrence of massive social movements (involving at least 10,000 participants) that are largely facilitated by Internet technologies, while low level of transgressiveness does not meet this criterion.

The second indicator of scale is the involvement of new political actors — political groups that were previously inactive, marginalised, or politically restricted. As a new platform for information and communication, the Internet enables political actors to voice political contentiousness in an otherwise restricted context. In some semi-democratic or semi-authoritarian regimes, political participation through formal institutions has been calibrated to allow for only a small number of players, who are often corrupt. Certain segments of society (based particularly on ethnicity, class, or religion) are discriminated against systematically when trying to participate in high level politics. And the government authorities monopolise public information by tightly controlling all kinds of media outlets. The Internet makes it possible for some leaders in certain social/political groups to mobilise previously marginalised or inactive social forces. They do so by setting up numerous kinds of websites and personal blogs, and by building email lists and online circles. The greater involvement of new actors brings higher costs for the government, since it indicates the need to redistribute and reorganise existing power structures (McAdam et al. 2001). Examples on this score can be found when marginalised separatist groups in Aceh, Pattani, or Tibet increase their presence in cyberspace and mobilise followers through new technologies. If a major proportion of participants in Internet-empowered social movements come from these new political groups, cases are coded as having a high level of transgressiveness. If they do not fulfil these conditions fully, the level of transgressiveness is coded as low to medium.

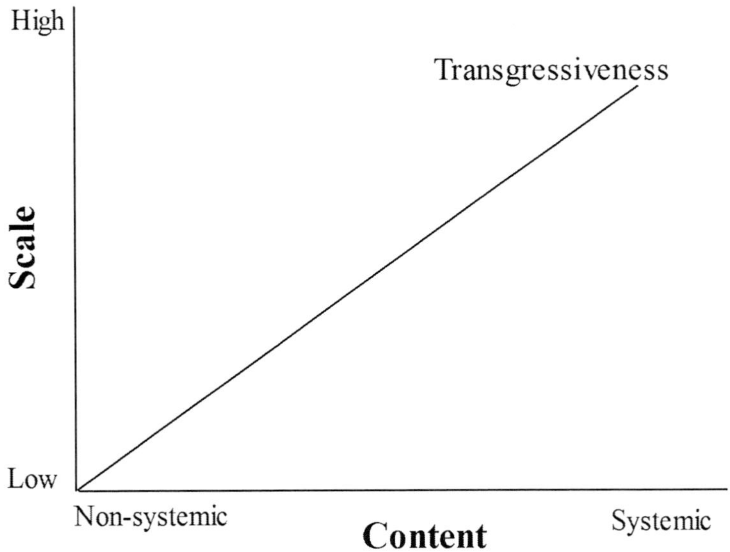

Fig. 2-1: Measuring Transgressiveness

In addition, content refers to the nature of political claims embedded in online contentiousness. Systemic political claims target the fundamental dimensions of the socio-political order. Often calling for radical changes, they demand the dismantling of current political regimes, the unravelling of state-promoted ideologies and beliefs, or the total transformation of current political and economic models. For example, the Red Shirt movement in Thailand, facilitated by new information technologies, has strong system-based claims. It criticises the alleged involvement in political affairs of the monarchy which, over the past decades, has been elevated to a position that supersedes the constitution and Thai-style democracy (Ferrara 2011). By contrast, such fundamental challenges to the monarchical system seldom occur in cyberspace of other constitutional monarchies in this region, such as Malaysia and Cambodia. Meanwhile, less systemic claims made by online activists target discrete features of the regime, such as a particular political process or institution. For example, online contentiousness may call for reform of the electoral process, which undoubtedly affects the status quo, but not to the extent that fundamental, systemic claims do. Elsewhere, it has been argued that the content of political contentiousness has a great impact on government responses (Regan and Henderson 2002; Davenport 2007). This book contends that online contentious performance with systemic political claims increases the level of transgressiveness and thus has a greater probability of inducing government control. Fig.2-1 illustrates the scale and content dimensions of online transgressiveness.

Based on these criteria, high level of transgressiveness is achieved when: (1) massive social movements (involving at least 10,000 participants) occur which are (widely believed to be) largely facilitated by Internet technologies (SCALE); (2) a major proportion of participants of these movements come from political groups that are previously inactive, marginalised, or politically restricted (SCALE); and (3) core political claims raised by online contentious groups seriously contradict the fundamental socio-political order (such as monarchy, religious authority, and so on), or major ideological or cultural norms, upon which political system of a given country relies (CONTENT). The same criteria are used to measure medium and low levels of transgressiveness. Details of measurement are provided in Appendix B.

In Southeast Asia, Internet politics in Thailand so far possesses the highest degree of transgressiveness. Massive demonstrations of red, yellow, and multi-colour shirts (representing different political attitudes), facilitated by the use of information technologies, prevailed in Thai politics in recent years. The backbone of red shirts consisted of the rural and urban poor who were politically important, yet, remained under-represented groups in Thailand. The Internet also enabled exiled political leaders to effectively communicate with their domestic supporters. More importantly, the Internet opened up a unique space for an anti-monarchy discourse, thus envisioning fundamental changes to the Thai socio-political order. This high level of transgressiveness has led to traditional Thai elites fighting tooth and nail to restrict online information flows and activities.

In contrast, Malaysia, Indonesia and Singapore demonstrate a medium level of online transgressiveness. Internet-empowered social movements did galvanise hundreds of thousands of people into collective actions, such as the Bersih movements in Malaysia and the demonstrations supporting Indonesia's Corruption Eradication Commission (KPK). While new political actors emerged from these movements, such as Malaysia's alternative media and blogger community, the main strength of online political contentiousness (especially in Indonesia and Singapore) still came from established political forces, including political parties and the critical elements of civil society. Moreover, the political claims embedded in these political struggles are much less systemic than in Thailand. Fundamental dimensions of the socio-political order, such as the monarchy system (in Malaysia), religious orthodoxy, and ethnic relations, were seldom the core targets of online contentiousness. Instead, such contentiousness focused on particular features of political regime and asked for gradual reform, rather than radical change, of the system. For instance, in these countries, online communities struggled to improve the undemocratic parts — lack of political competitiveness, clientalism, money politics and so on — of their political regimes, while leaving the fundamental pillars of these regimes intact.

In Cambodia and the Philippines, the transgressiveness of Internet politics appears much weaker. The underdeveloped status of the Internet in Cambodia has meant that political threats, in terms of scale and content, will not emerge from cyberspace in the short term. Transgressiveness remains low in the Philippines, mainly because after the second "People Power" movement in 2001 that ousted Joseph Estrada from presidency, nation-wide movements with strong political demands have been infrequent. In addition, the Philippine civil society has already been vibrant and institutionalised since the country's democratic transition in 1986 (Boudreau 2009). Therefore, the empowering-effect of the Internet is much less notable. In both cases, controlling the Internet would provide only marginal benefits for the incumbent governments.

As previously discussed, transgressiveness is not the direct product of regime type. This argument also applies to online transgression. Firstly, transgressiveness could be intensified in democratic contexts. For example, under Thaksin's rule, online contentiousness dramatically boiled over into gigantic demonstrations against the democratically-elected prime minister, while online transgressiveness remained intense even after the Pheu Thai Party regained power through a generally free and fair election. Secondly, countries with similar regime type may exhibit different levels of transgressiveness. On this score, the difference in transgressiveness between electoral democracies in Indonesia and the Philippines mainly results from the divergent trajectories their respective regime transition features (Boudreau 2009). As a result, while transgressiveness and regime type may have mutual impact and, indeed, demonstrate a complex relationship, causality between them (in either direction) remains ambiguous, and thus it is reasonable to separate them as independent factors.

Capacity of online civil society

The second, yet related, factor of Internet control is the capacity of online civil society. In this book, the capacity of online civil society refers to the bargaining power that online communities have to forestall, restrain, or resist government repression. While transgressiveness provides rationale for government authorities to control the Internet, online civil society serves as a major constraint for regulatory policies. As Internet technologies gradually penetrate society, more and more studies have paid attention to the forming of an Internet-based, Habermasian public sphere (see Yang 2003; Castells 2008; Azzizuddin Sani 2009). In that public sphere, online civil society stands for the "organized expression of the values and interests" (Castells 2008, 78) of various online communities. Attempts to control the Internet would disturb the interests of (at least part of) the online civil society, since this endangers freedom of expression. Through collective actions such as online petitions and boycotts, or offline demonstrations and electoral feedback, the online communities could effectively increase the costs of Internet control. In this sense, the capacity of online civil society to resist repression becomes critical in levering government decisions, especially in political contexts where democratic procedures are institutionalised.

This book evaluates the capacity of online civil society by considering four major elements. The first dimension relates to the vibrancy of online civil society, indicated by the size of online community. In this regard, this book follows Philip Howard (2010) by looking at the Internet *penetration* rate in concerned countries. In general, as online communities expand in size, the prospect for collective resistance against government repression would increase accordingly. Meanwhile, the government has to be more cautious and less arbitrary in planning Internet regulation policies in places where Internet users account for a substantial part of the electorate. Low level of Internet penetration unavoidably weakens online civil society's capacity for presenting a cohesive force.

Secondly, the capacity of online civil society increases when it is well connected to offline politics. If Internet-based movements and organisations have strong offline *political linkage* with political parties, politicians, or other organisations, they are expected to have greater leverage over government policies. For instance, a coalition between online communities and opposition parties could exert considerable pressure upon governments when the latter plans Internet control schemes, as Malaysian opposition forces showed after the 2008 elections. In fact, the importance of political linkage in strengthening civil society has been underscored in a number of studies (see, for example, Ainsworth 2001). This research gauges political linkage by examining the extent to which major online social movements possess political backing (in the form of receiving funding from or being organised by political groups, especially political parties). Similar to the function of political linkage is the existence of *critical media* in cyberspace. New media based on the Internet over the world is becoming an increasingly important component of civil society. When major domestic online media are critical of and independent from the government, have substantial share of readership, and have equal or higher credibility over traditional media, they represent a new political force that governments would take into account when planning Internet regulations. In this sense, the existence of critical online media strengthens the capacity of online civil society.

While the three elements above affect the capacity of online civil society in an indirect way, a more direct indicator is the *cohesiveness* of online communities. The capacity of online civil society is undermined if the online communities are highly divided and mutually antagonistic. Fundamental splits between online groups offer the government opportunities to restrict information flows and thwart online activism in the name of protecting one group against another. For instance, when online information about ethnic clashes became magnified in one state of India and caused widespread panic within the threatened group, the Indian government banned users from sending mass messages. In this study, such splits are evaluated by evidence of major counter-movements — movements that are antagonistic to each other in terms of political or ideological orientations — in cyberspace. In countries where online communities are polarised along social or religious lines, the capacity of online civil society would be weak and the cost of government repressive actions low. Table 2-1 shows how different levels of online civil society capacity are measured. It should be noticed that since cohesiveness is the indicator directly relevant to civil society's capacity in resisting repression, it is given more weight in the evaluation of that capacity. Specifically, if online civil society in one case is deemed, for the most part, fragmented and incohesive, its capacity would not exceed a moderate level irrespective of other aspects. More details about measurement are provided in Appendix B.

Table 2-1: Major Indicators of Online Civil Society Capacity

HIGH	MEDIUM	LOW
high penetration rate	moderate penetration rate	low penetration rate
strong political linkage	strong/medium political linkage	medium/weak political linkage
vibrant critical media	vibrant/moderate critical media	moderate/weak critical media
high cohesiveness	high/medium cohesiveness	fragmentation

According to these criteria, Thailand and Cambodia demonstrate, for different reasons, low capacity of online civil society. Although Thailand had moderate Internet penetration (26.3% in 2010), political linkage between online communities and political parties was undermined by the political discord between them. While independent online media were thriving, they were still far from prominent in information provision as compared to traditional media. More importantly, political competition between Thaksin Shinawatra and traditional elites not only dragged the country into devastating political conflict, but also divided the Thai online society into two antithetic camps (Nelson 2012). Although the Thai online civil society would rank moderate in other indicators, its fragmentation inevitably downgraded its capacity. Meanwhile, the capacity of online civil society in Cambodia is also low because the size of its online community is too small to have meaningful collective actions. Dimensions of political linkage, critical media, and cohesiveness are all affected negatively by the underdeveloped status of Cambodia's cyberspace.

By contrast, online civil society has much greater capacity in Malaysia. Malaysia is the most networked country in Southeast Asia after Singapore. Linkage between online communities and offline political organisations was firmly cultivated. The fact that five opposition members elected in the 2008 parliamentary election were blogger-cum-politicians undoubtedly demonstrated the strong political linkage. A number of prominent online media platforms, such as *Malaysiakini* and *Merdeka Review*, offered opposition forces valuable tools for political information and campaign dissemination. On the other hand, there was little evidence of major counter-movement on Malaysian cyberspace, thus raising the cohesiveness of its online civil society. Besides, the Philippines also meets several requirements of high civil society capacity. In fact, civil society in general has been influential in the Philippines since its democratic transition decades ago (Tuaño 2011).

The capacity of online civil societies in Indonesia and Singapore is somewhere between that of Thailand and Malaysia. Serious cleavages among online communities were not found in either country, but deficiencies in other indicators, such as penetration and political linkage in Indonesia and critical media in Singapore, placed their online civil society capacities at a moderate level.

The remaining question

In general, the actual outcome of Internet control practices in these countries corresponds with our expectation deduced from the theoretical framework. However, this model does not cover an important question: where do transgressive threats and the capacity of online civil society result from? Without further exploration of the sources of these variables, it is difficult to understand the divergent outcomes of Internet politics and Internet control in Southeast Asia. For instance, Malaysia and Singapore share similar conditions of single-party dominance, traditional media censorship, and other human rights abuses but the capacity of online civil society is strikingly greater in Malaysia than its southern neighbor. To address remaining similar puzzles, I will examine historical and contextual conditions through which the independent variables are shaped. Critical to this is the early Internet development during the 1990s which set the different trajectories of Internet politics in particular countries. Whether the Internet was developed in an open or restricted political context at its early stage would have significant effects in the future on institutional design and government capacity in regulating the Internet. The following section analyses these conditions in the 1990s that have had long-term impacts on current Internet politics and control.

Contextual Conditions and the Beginning of Internet Development

As discussed above, this book focuses on the evolving process of Internet control practices. It distinguishes between early conditions that shape the initial governmental policies on Internet regulation and factors that determine the level and approach of Internet control. In the early stages of Internet development, the main factor that prevents or incites elites to adopt restrictive actions on Internet usage are major changes in political and social context. These changes, or openings in political opportunity, alter the nature of political regime and/or features of political interactions within that regime. This study argues that two sets of such contextual changes — political democratisation and economic liberalisation — are of particular importance for the initial environment of Internet development.

Perhaps the greatest change that has such impacts lies in the drastic shift of the political system from autocracy to democracy, or vice-versa. The establishment or restoration of democratic rule is often marked by the abandonment of authoritarian practices and the formulation of democratic provisions, procedurally and/or constitutionally, for political rights and civil liberties (Dahl 1998). It is expected that the new government formed, based on democratic institutions and seeking international and domestic legitimation, would respect human rights and thus lower its reliance on repression. However, a sudden and complete transition to democracy may not be present everywhere. Some countries undergo a long oscillating process that contains gradual steps towards democratisation but remains far from achieving genuine democracy. Nonetheless, these steps, if significantly reshaping intra-elite or state–society relationships, could create an atmosphere of liberal and democratic discourse, enhance public perception and expectation about democracy, and thus increase the "audience costs"[6] of aggressive behaviours.

Therefore, this study looks at those political events that not only entail fundamental changes in regime type but also signal incremental improvements in democratic institutions and procedures. Since the Internet system embodied an entirely new sphere for developing countries during the 1990s, its regulation could be more easily influenced by these changes. Political leaders in the period of democratisation might be able to retain certain authoritarian institutions inherited from previous regimes (Lawson 2000; Mickey 2011), but it would be much harder for them to establish new repressive institutions amid increasing public awareness of democratic values.

This is especially the case for Internet regulation, because even before Internet technology was introduced, its democratic potential had been well perceived and discussed in civil societies of some Southeast Asian countries, such as Indonesia (Hill and Sen 2005). As a result, this study argues that steps and signs of liberalisation, preceding or accompanying the early introduction of Internet technologies, would reduce state capacity to install initial Internet controls. This contradicts some previous findings that the process of democratisation increases rather than decreases political killings and restrictions (Zanger 2000; Davenport 2004). But considering that the repressive actions during the transitional period might result from the institutional legacy of the previous regime (Gurr 1986) and that the purpose of such repression might be for political elites to recapture and reorganise the new power structure, Internet control in the early period appears to be different from other repressive actions since it requires new coercive institutions and contributes little to the post-transition elite struggles.

In addition, transformation in economic development could also affect a government's early decision on Internet control, though in a more covert way. Drastic programmes of privatisation and liberalisation, driven by the exhausted dividend of state-led economic growth, result in less state involvement in economic policies, especially in the new technology-based industries. Since Internet technologies are seen, by most developing countries, as a new catalyst for economic modernisation, the approach these governments adopt to regulate their economies becomes entangled with the way they control the new digital sphere. Moreover, the increasing reliance upon foreign direct investment would also reduce the likelihood of Internet control, as Western investors and multinational corporations tend to think highly of transparency and human rights protection. Concerning foreign investment, Zdenek Drabek and Warren Payne (2001) reported in their working paper for the World Trade Organisation that "high levels of non-transparency can greatly retard the amount of foreign investment that a country might otherwise expect". Meanwhile, a number of studies have confirmed the positive correlation between foreign direct investment and increased government respect for human rights (Richards et al. 2001; Blanton and Blanton 2007). In this sense, a hands-off manner in the Internet industry could be used as an incentive to attract more inward flows of foreign capital and technology. It also serves as an indicator of the extent to which the host government is market-friendly and liberally oriented. This factor could be particularly strong during the early stage of Internet development as economic interests easily override the potential threat of the Internet. Therefore, this study posits that a major shift in development strategy in the 1990s, favouring privatisation, external economic linkages, and a substantial dependency on foreign investment, would constitute another group of factors that prevents government from early Internet control.

Why are these contextual changes significant? The direct output of these factors is the characteristics of the political environment in which the Internet was initially developed. Contextual constraints, resulting from liberalisation and democratisation, impel elites to adopt a laissez-faire approach, with minimum political intervention and censorship, in early Internet regulation. For instance, in order to attract foreign investment in its grand strategy of knowledge-based economic transformation, the Malaysian government voluntarily proclaimed in 1996, a Bill of Guarantees that no censorship would be imposed on cyberspace. When these liberalising or democratising effects are absent, government authorities would face far fewer obstacles in deploying early Internet control strategies. For example, development and administration of Internet technologies under such circumstances would be closely supervised by government agencies instead of academic or commercial organisations, while legislation that regulates Internet usage would be enacted at the earliest stage without efficient resistance. In this sense, contextual conditions would affect the early institutional design of Internet regulation, creating a foothold for subsequent development of Internet control.

Moreover, in their long-term effects, contextual conditions would indirectly shape the form of online political contentiousness as well as the construction of online civil society. On this score, a byproduct of the 1996 Bill of Guarantees in Malaysia is the emergence of several influential online media that practice independent journalism against the state media monopoly. Meanwhile, democratisation in Thailand during the 1990s altered the traditional power network that was centred on the monarchy, further polarising Thai society both politically and ideologically. Therefore, to investigate the contextual conditions of early Internet development in the 1990s would enable us to better understand the initial government decision regarding the regulation of the Internet, as well as the political dynamics both on and off the Internet that unfolds in the subsequent decade.

Adopting this framework, we now briefly survey the contextual conditions in the Southeast Asian competitive polities. Of the six countries in this study, all of them except Singapore underwent a clear trend of liberalisation or democratisation, though composed of different combinations of pressures, during the 1990s. In Thailand, after a coup leader, Suchinda Kraprayoon, breached his promise of not seeking the premiership, massive demonstrations broke out in 1992, ending with tragic bloodshed in Bangkok, a dramatic intervention from the King, and, consequently, the weakening of military power that had dominated Thai politics for decades (Tamada 2008). Increasing calls for political reform succeeded and substantial steps toward democratisation culminated in the promulgation of the 1997 "People's Constitution" which involved expanded public participation in the drafting process and enshrined important improvements in democracy.

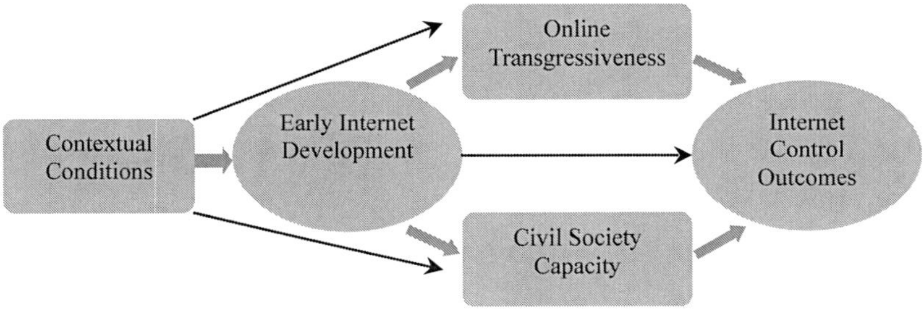

Fig. 2-2: A two-level framework for Internet control

In Indonesia, although the unprecedented financial tsunami was the last straw that brought the "New Order" to an end, certain underlying openings had antedated the crisis, including the economic structural transformation programmes that began in 1980s and the inability of President Suharto to reunite elite factions within the regime. Democratic transitions were also witnessed in the Philippines and Cambodia. While the Philippines saw successive elections being held in the post-Marcos era, which brought the country back onto its democratic track, Cambodia swept away its totalitarian shadow and Vietnamese occupation with its first democratic election in 1993, supervised by the United Nations, with only minor irregularities reported (Kingsbury 2005).

Meanwhile, Malaysia in the 1990s experienced no substantial change in democratisation, but critical openings for liberalisation could still be found such as when the National Development Policy was unveiled in 1990, that emphasised further liberalisation and transformation to a knowledge-based economy, and when a serious split in the ruling party occurred in late 1990s and resulted in a reformasi movement gaining momentum. By contrast, no major openings parallel to those discussed above was present in Singapore during the same period. On this score, Garry Rodan (1993, 79) argued that "the political pressures emerging in Indonesia and South Korea for either an opening up of the economy or a more regularised bureaucracy are not in evidence in Singapore".

Table 2-2: Signs of Liberalisation and Democratisation in Selected Countries

Country	Early Internet control	Major elements of contextual changes
Thailand	NO	Demonstrations in 1992 and 1994 People's Constitution in 1997
Indonesia	NO	Economic liberalisation since the 1980s Political transition in 1998
The Philippines	NO	Post-Marcos democratic consolidation Successive democratic elections in the 1990s
Cambodia	NO	UN-supervised democratisation in 1993
Malaysia	NO	New economic programmes in 1990 Mahathir-Anwar split in 1998
Singapore	YES	(absence)

The existence or lack of liberalising/democratising conditions is well reflected in the contrast of early Internet control policies between Singapore and the five other countries. Singapore has pioneered the practice of Internet control in the form of online surveillance and monitoring, being the first country in the world to block websites (Rodan 1998). The other five countries, constrained by different political openings, showed virtually no action to censor the Internet, despite some proposals being raised periodically, which were shelved shortly afterwards. Some may argue that such difference is shaped by the personal foresight of Singapore's leadership. But considering the fact that the Association of Southeast Asian Nations (ASEAN) Committee on Culture and Information had already discussed the issue of political control on the Internet in 1996 (Rodan 1998), it might be untenable to suggest that other Southeast Asian leaders at that time were unaware of potential Internet threats. As a result, this study argues that the presence of liberalising and democratising conditions is the major determinant in early governmental response to Internet control. The contextual conditions, together with variables at the agency-level (transgressiveness and online civil society), offer a full picture of how Internet control practices are developed institutionally and historically in Southeast Asia.

Conclusion

To understand Internet control in competitive political systems, this book explores both agency-level explanations that directly affect government strategies, and contextual conditions that have shaped early Internet development and regulation and provided the foundations for agency-level variations. At the agency level, government decisions on the level and form of Internet control hinge on the transgressiveness of online politics and the capacity of online civil society. While the former indicates the political challenge raised by online activities and thus the urgency of government response, the latter amplifies (or diminishes) the cost of control policies, preventing the government from (or prompting the government to) scaling up Internet control strategies.

In this study, transgressiveness is measured by two indices: scale and content. The former indicates the size and composition of online social movements, while the latter describes the extent to which online political claims aim at changing the fundamental dimensions of the socio-political order. Meanwhile, four indicators are used to evaluate the capacity of online civil society. Internet penetration, political linkage and critical online media demonstrate different features of online communities. More importantly, fragmentation or polarisation of online communities seriously weakens the capacity of online civil society and makes it easier for government authorities to mobilise public support of Internet control. A high level of transgressiveness and low capacity of online civil society, therefore, result in Thailand's pioneering Internet censorship policies. By contrast, in spite of medium to high levels of transgressiveness, the Malaysian government is unable to adopt systemic Internet control policies due to concerted opposition from Malaysia's strong and cohesive online civil society. While the Indonesian government, compared with Malaysia, faces slightly fewer threats from online political activities, the online civil society in Indonesia is also slightly weaker, making, on average, the implementation of Internet control in these two countries similar.

In general, these agency-level variables have helped explain the strategic choices made by Southeast Asian governments to control the Internet. But analysis of contextual conditions would enhance our understanding of where the agency-level diversity stems from and how Internet control practices are institutionalised historically. On this score, this book investigates the historical context in the 1990s which has shaped initial Internet development and regulation in Southeast Asian countries. During the 1990s, the presence of liberalising and democratising conditions created, for early Internet development, a political environment characterised by laissez-faire policies and democratic discourse. Under such circumstances, government authorities would adopt a politically friendly approach — with little regulation on Internet content and behaviour — in promoting Internet development. When these conditions are absent, as in the case of Singapore, Internet control policies would be deployed at an early stage, indicating a greater tendency to institutionalise Internet control practices. However, unlike agency-level variables, these contextual conditions are less linearly correlated to ultimate Internet control outcomes. The political dynamics in a particular country are also changing constantly, resulting in collateral changes of contextual factors. Therefore, it is necessary to employ a case-by-case approach in which trajectories of political development, as well as trajectories of Internet control policies, can be clearly captured and fully examined. By doing so, this book hopes to provide a systematic analysis — at both contextual and agent levels — on the phenomenon of Internet control in particular, and contribute to the broad understanding of political repression in general.

CHAPTER THREE

INTERNET CONTROL IN A COMPETITIVE AUTHORITARIAN REGIME: CASE STUDY OF MALAYSIA

Introduction

This chapter examines the case of Malaysia where the competitive authoritarian regime has, unexpectedly, imposed only limited restrictions upon cyberspace. Although online transgressiveness appears to be increasing, especially with the stunning outcome of the 2008 elections, a high level of online civil society capacity arguably helps to prevent the government from deploying more extensive Internet controls. Meanwhile, the sources of online transgression and civil society capacity in Malaysia can be found in contextual factors including economic liberalisation and associated political change in the 1990s.

In the political continuum, ranging from liberal democracies on one side and authoritarian and totalitarian systems on the other, Malaysia is bracketed in between since it accommodates simultaneously democratic and non-democratic traits (Case 2009). The Federal Constitution of Malaysia, promulgated in 1963 to incorporate Malaya, Sabah, Sarawak, and Singapore,[7] is by nature democratic: it enshrines the fundamental civil liberties such as freedom of expression, and it stipulates popular and regular elections as a way of choosing political leaders and legislative members at the federal as well as state levels. In fact, unlike those politically-closed regimes in which ballots have either disappeared for decades (like in Myanmar) or been strictly confined within a single party's elite circle (like in Vietnam), successive national elections in Malaysia have been held regularly in five-year cycles, and competitiveness has also persisted with the ruling coalition losing on several occasions at the state level. However, from at least the late 1960s until 2008, the UMNO-dominated government had not only maintained power in every election, but always retained a two-thirds majority in parliament (Crouch 1996b, 114). While electoral means were manipulated and biased to "maintain and legitimize those already in power, with national political leadership determined by the contest for the United Malays National Organisation leadership" (Jomo 1996, 90), lack of democratic institutions and accountability resulted in frequent suppression and violation of basic civil rights. Therefore, the political regime in Malaysia, due to its ambiguity, has variously been conceptualised as a "semi-" or "pseudo-" democracy (Diamond et al. 1989; Case 1993; Case 2001), or as "electoral" or "competitive" authoritarianism[8] (Schedler 2006; Levitsky and Way 2010). All of these terms reflect the hybrid nature of the Malaysian political system that exhibits "a repressive and a responsive character" (Crouch 1996a, 7) simultaneously.

Meanwhile, another distinction that characterises Malaysia's political regime lies in its resistance to political change. In contrast to Samuel Huntington's (1991, 137) prediction that "the halfway house does not stand", the competitive authoritarianism in Malaysia remains strongly resilient with the ruling party coalition (Barison Nasional) holding power since the country's authoritarian turn in the late 1960s. Even when it was exposed to the unprecedented financial crisis in 1997–98, Malaysia was able to maintain political order, unlike Indonesia, through perpetuating elite cohesion (Case 2002), relying on a strong party institution (Brownlee 2007), and adopting consistent financial policies (Pepinsky 2009). It was not until 2008 that the UMNO-led coalition lost, for first time since 1969, its two-thirds parliamentary supermajority together with control over four state governments, while failing to regain a fifth. Nonetheless, the incumbency remains unchanged and the 140–82 division in parliamentary seats still indicates the strength of the ruling coalition. Compared with other Southeast Asian competitive systems, Malaysia succeeds in ostensibly conforming to electoral procedures on the one hand and perpetuating authoritarian controls on the other, without inducing any overturning social instability.

However, while Malaysia has relatively less democratic credentials among our three country-cases, it implements Internet control policies only moderately, at most. There is little evidence of Internet filtering and blocking activities, either overtly (like Thailand) or covertly (like Indonesia). In fact, it was not until the 2008 election, after which the then Prime Minister Abdullah Badawi bluntly admitted that "we certainly lost the Internet war" (*New York Times* 2008), that Malaysian authorities began to seek tighter Internet regulation. Even so, the government has done this through mixed strategies with limited harassment against Internet users and active engagement with online communities. Therefore, it is of necessity to move beyond the "democraticness" lens and examine in detail what has caused the mixed, restrained response of the Malaysian government. In fact, the low-medium level of Internet control witnessed in the post-2008 era stems simultaneously from the moderate transgression of online politics as well as the entrenched status of Malaysia's online civil society. The former, with its inseparable linkages with Malaysia's electoral politics, has propelled the government to react in accordance with its electoral needs, while the latter has substantially limited the scale and forms of that reaction. Meanwhile, when new forms of transgression loomed during the 2011 state election in Sarawak, the ruling coalition resorted to new strategies in dealing with heightened threats.

Prior to that discussion, however, we should look at the historical process in which Malaysian politics, Internet development, and Internet politics have evolved over time. This will enable us to better understand the formation of online transgression and the sources of the capacity of online civil society in Malaysia. Of particular significance are two sets of contextual developments in the 1990s and early 2000s: one economic, that involved the grand plan of knowledge-based economic transformation, from which projects such as the Multimedia Super Corridor (MSC) originated; and the other political, that saw the reformasi movement prospering in Malaysian politics. The first part of this chapter analyses the impacts of these contextual developments upon the politicisation of Malaysia's Internet space. It starts with a background account on how Malaysia's competitive authoritarianism operates.

Authoritarian Paradox: Contextual Conditions and Internet Development

For decades, Malaysian elites have successfully perpetuated a competitive authoritarian system which "combined electoral competition with varying degrees of authoritarianism" (Levitsky and Way 2010, 3). While regime stability was, in general, maintained throughout the 1990s, there were some notable economic and political developments that gradually reshaped the state–society relationship as well as the dynamic of Malaysian politics in the following decade. This section highlights these contextual changes and explores the impact on Internet development.

Competitive authoritarianism in Malaysia

As previously introduced, the political regime in Malaysia has certain democratic traits. Opposition parties, professional associations as well as some civil groups are generally permitted to register and advance their respective political courses. When they contest in federal and state elections, which are regularly held with a relatively fair balloting and counting procedure, there is a chance, though limited, for them to defeat candidates of the ruling coalition (Case 1993, 186–187). In fact, political competition does exist, as the opposition parties normally garner 40% of popular votes (Levitsky and Way 2010) and elections are considered as the solely viable means to power (Jomo 1996; Case 2001). With the competitive electoral process, the Malaysian government has to routinely respond to popular demands just as governments in fuller democracies would do (Crouch 1996a).

Although these democratic traits prevent Malaysia from dropping into the more authoritarian categories, the UMNO-dominated government has, during its long period of governance, developed and consolidated a wide range of political control methods that, once institutionalised, could easily be activated when state repression is needed. Article 150 of the Constitution stipulates that a proclamation of emergency could be issued by the king on the advice of the Prime Minister, which would endow parliament with unrestricted power to make any relevant laws and ordinances. When such emergent situations occurred (as with the 1969 riots), as Harold Crouch (1996a, 78) observes, it "left the government with far-reaching and legally unchallengeable powers". While emergency powers are rarely used, powers derived from the Internal Security Act (ISA), passed in the early 1960s, initially for containing the communist underground, have been exploited by the Malaysian government extensively in purposes far beyond the communist threat. These powers enabled the Minister of Home Affairs to detain without trial; ISA justified any detention if the behaviour of the detainee was deemed to be "prejudicial to the security of Malaysia or any part thereof or to the maintenance of essential services therein or to the economic life thereof" (quoted from Crouch 1996a, 79). During the 1990s, although the political situation in Malaysia was more stable than in previous decades, detention under ISA was still periodically used for political ends. Major cases in this respect included the arrests of 14 members of the Al-Arqam movement in 1996, the November 1997 detention of ten male Muslims on the alleged grounds of practicing Shi'a Islam, and, even more sensational, the apprehension of former deputy Prime Minister Anwar Ibrahim as well as his political associates in 1998 (Amnesty International 1999).

Moreover, a series of methods have been adopted to restrict freedom of expression and discussion. The majority of traditional media — newspapers, radio, and televisions — was, and still is, essentially owned and controlled directly or indirectly by the investment branches of the major member parties of BN, especially UMNO, the Malaysian Chinese Association (MCA), and the Malaysian Indian Congress (MIC) (Zaharom Nain 2008, 157). Since prominent media groups, such as the *New Straits Times*, the *Utusan Melayu* and the *Star*, were all affiliated with the incumbent government, the news and commentaries they provided were rarely critical of, and in fact biased towards, the government (Anuar 2005; Abbott 2011a), disqualifying them as the watchdog or the "fourth estate". On the other hand, stringent laws to limit media as well as public discussion were introduced or tightened before the 1990s. For instance, the Printing Presses and Publication Act (PPPA), which replaced the Printing Presses Act in 1984, required every local regular publication to have an annually renewable license or printing permit granted by the Ministry of Home Affairs. Meanwhile, the Sedition Act and the Official Secrets Act were often employed as a pretext to restrict the opposition's scope for public criticism, as was witnessed in the 1974 government crackdown against student demonstrators (*Operasi Mayang*) and the 1987 suppression of opposition politicians (*Operasi Lallang*) (Pepinsky 2009, 67). Therefore, while opposition forces and civil organisations were permitted to participate in Malaysian politics, they were effectively prevented from acquiring larger political influence; while competitive multi-party elections were regularly held, the incumbent ruling coalition never relinquished its dominance.

Together with other manipulative methods designed to calibrate electoral competitiveness,[9] these authoritarian institutions enabled the ruling coalition in Malaysia to garner immense political control and perpetuate hegemonic rule. Meanwhile, underlying the regime's resilience were two sets of economic and political developments. The first involves the government's plan to transform Malaysia into a knowledge-based economy.

Envisioning a knowledge-based economy: The Multimedia Super Corridor and Bill of Guarantees

In the 1990s, the Malaysian economy experienced recovery. During the previous decade, the economic downturn in developed countries had sharply dragged down Malaysia's economy (which relied heavily on the export of raw materials such as tin and palm oil) from extraordinary growth into severe recession. For instance, the overall export price index between 1984–86 plunged by around 30% (Athukorala 2010, 3). Politically, economic resources became insufficient for the ruling coalition to reward its business supporters (Crouch 1996a). The direct consequence of that recession was that the government re-emphasised the necessity of macroeconomic transformation and abandoned its plan of heavy industry commitment to promote foreign direct investment (FDI) and construct a sustainable knowledge economy (Athukorala 2010). In 1991, Malaysia unveiled its National Development Policy featured by an emboldened "Vision 2020". As the then Prime Minister Mahathir Mohamad envisaged before the audience of Malaysian business and political elites, "Vision 2020 is intended to be a major step toward establishing a scientific and progressive society, a society that is innovative and forward-looking, one that is not only a consumer of technology but also a contributor to the scientific and technological civilization of the future" (Lepawsky 2005).

On the advice of a team of consultants, the IT industry was recommended and chosen as the most critical strategic tool to boost Malaysia's national development and to achieve developed country status, as proclaimed in the "Vision 2020" (ITU 2002). The major project designed under this plan is the Multimedia Super Corridor (MSC), an eight billion (Malaysian Ringgit) project on the model of Silicon Valley, which was designed not only to "leapfrog available information infrastructure" for Malaysians, but also as a "gift to the world" (Khoo Boo Teik 2003, 31–33). The MSC, located at the south of Kuala Lumpur, circles an area of 750 km^2 which is even larger than the island of Singapore (Lepawsky 2005). It comprises two new cities: Putrajaya, as the new administrative centre for the Malaysian government, and Cyberjaya, which aims to accommodate worldwide IT tycoons. By its own account, there were more than 1,200 approved MSC companies and 87 world-class status companies as of 2009, including CISCO, Dell, IBM, Microsoft and the like.[10] The government has attached great importance to the MSC project and even hoped that "by 2020, the entire country will be an MSC" (Mahathir 1997).

However, the Malaysian government had to give some incentives, or indeed make concessions, to provide the "world's best soft infrastructure" (Khoo Boo Teik 2003) and to attract MSC's corporate residents. In 1996, it declared a 10-point Bill of Guarantees which included the pledge of no-censorship on the Internet, together with other incentives such as tax reduction. In fact, on the MSC's advertising webpage, the Bill of Guarantees is highlighted at the top of a list that particularises the business advantages offered by the MSC.[11] Therefore, it was primarily the desire to attract foreign investment that prompted the Malaysian government to promise a free, uncensored Internet environment from the very beginning. This promise was further institutionalised in the Communications and Multimedia Act (CMA), promulgated in 1998, which stated explicitly that "nothing in this Act shall be construed as permitting the censorship of the Internet".[12]

Besides the rationale for investment attraction, it is also noteworthy that the early development of the Internet did not spell much political threat or challenge for the BN coalition as well as its personal leaders. The first Internet service provider in Malaysia, JARING, did not reach the public until 1995, indicating a very low level of Internet penetration in Malaysian society at that time. At the same time, the government and print media had taken the initiative to embrace the information age. In 1994, the federal government made its presence felt online when it created Civil Service Link (CSL), a database containing public service information for public access (although it was actually mainly for business access). In the following year, Malaysia's bestselling English daily, *The Star*, also launched its electronic edition, imitated shortly by *New Straits Times* (Tong Yee Siong 2004, 278–279). The content of their online version was basically a mirror of the print edition which was directly or indirectly manipulated by the ruling party. In this sense, Internet development for the Malaysian government was principally profitable rather than threatening.

If the economic contextual shift, marked by the MSC project and the Bill of Guarantees, has provided the institutional foundation for a free Internet space, the reformasi movement at the end of the century suddenly politicised this space and turned it into an online public sphere. The following discussion analyses the political change on this score.

The reformasi movement: Change and continuity in Malaysian politics

Although, in general, the BN has maintained elite cohesion through extensive patronage networks, cleavages still occurred intermittently, especially amid economic downturns.[13] The 1997–98 Asian financial crises played a role in enlarging the split between Mahathir and his deputy, Anwar Ibrahim, concerning the proper economic approach to recovery (Felker 1999; Pepinsky 2009). Anwar was subsequently sacked from his cabinet post as well as from the UMNO in September 1998, ostensibly for his moral misconduct involving adultery and sodomy charges (Abbott 2001; Khoo Boo Teik 2003). Moreover, two separate trials, with vague evidence, sentenced Anwar to jail for six and nine years respectively, alongside lavish efforts by mainstream media, police and judiciary to discredit his personality (Abbott 2001).

These efforts, however, backfired. Anwar's personal charisma, the injustice of his case, as well as the surging anti-Mahathir sentiments, converged in massive social movements with Anwar as the central icon. "Reformasi", as announced by Anwar in the "Permatang Pauh Declaration", became the flagship of these movements, which echoed Indonesia's anti-Suharto movement against "kolusi, korupsi, and nepotisme" (collusion, corruption and nepotism) (Khoo Boo Teik 2003). Continuous rallies during 1998–2000 drew tens of thousands of demonstrators, unprecedented in Malaysia for decades. More importantly, the supporters of the reformasi were spread across a broad social base: the participants included not only "elderly men, middle-aged men and women, young girls" (Khoo Boo Teik 2003, 104), but also a large number of NGOs, university students, opposition parties, workers, civil servants, and businessmen (Weiss 2006, 133–137; Nair 2007, 351). As Musa Hitam, the former deputy Prime Minister, put it, "if the reformasi movement and demonstrations could be given any significance in terms of Malaysian politics [...] it never turns racial [...] It is more issue-based than racial" (Gan 2001).

A new opposition coalition formed around the reformasi movement and brought together Keadilan (National Justice Party), PAS and DAP under the banner of Barisan Alternatif (Alternative Front, BA). However, although the BN suffered substantial decline in parliamentary votes (a drop of 10%) and seats (from 166 to 148), as well as state assembly seats in the 1999 elections (Mutalib 2000, 68–70), the BA failed to achieve its goal of winning at least one-third of the seats in parliament. Furthermore, the BN re-consolidated its power with a landslide victory in the 2004 general election. With turnout rates at reformasi rallies dwindling since 2000, it seemed that the movement had been in demise since that time (Martinez 2002; Nair 2007).

Nonetheless, there are many long-term ramifications arising from the reformasi movement. Three aspects are of particular importance to this study. Firstly, the reformasi movement offered a platform that conjoined the opposition parties and boosted ties between political parties and civil society. On this score, Meredith Weiss (2006, 160) argued that the reformasi "marked a change in Malaysian politics both at the level of organisation and strategizing and at the level of popular priorities and participation". To some extent, it sowed the seeds for greater electoral challenge when the political opportunity structure turned the scales in favour of opposition forces again, as the 2008 political tsunami later proved. On the other hand, the reformasi movement presented only a moderate form of political transgression. The icon of the movement, Anwar, was himself complicit in the very political system that he mobilised his supporters against (Nair 2007). The substance of political reforms proclaimed by the opposition coalition, as well as the idea of opposition coalition per se, was not new, as both had their predecessors in the previous decade (Khoo Boo Teik 2003). More importantly, the call for political change appeared only in abstract terms that did not touch on the cornerstone of Malaysia's divided, ethnicity-based polity (Nair 2007, 356). Therefore, the political challenge posed by the reformasi movement appeared to be less systemic. The movement persisted in the post-2008 era (see Pepinsky 2012) and would shape the form of political contentiousness in cyberspace. Last but not least, as the government extensively mobilised the mainstream media to attack Anwar, misrepresent the movement, and black out the opposition parties, the Internet space soon became politicised and the major outlet for reformasi-related information and ideas. It is argued that in the 2008 general election, the Internet played a crucial role in affecting the eventual outcome (see, for example, Case 2009; Moten 2009b; Sani 2009a). But the sources and forms of that power trace back to this period (the late 1990s). In other words, it was at this time, in the background of reformasi movements, that Malaysia's online public sphere began to take shape.

Malaysian Internet space: An online public sphere in formation

Alongside these contextual changes was the rapid development of the Internet in Malaysia. As Fig.3-1 below demonstrates, a dramatic boom in Internet development has been achieved in Malaysia since 1996, with Internet users as a percentage of the total population soaring from only 6.7% in 1998 to 55.3% in 2010. With its netizens population reaching almost 16 million as of 2010, Malaysia has undoubtedly surpassed most of its Southeast Asian neighbours in terms of Internet penetration.[14]

While government plans to informationalise the country have quantitatively enlarged the online community, it was arguably the reformasi movement that transformed Malaysia's cyberspace politically. During the reformasi movement, the government manipulated the traditional mainstream media which reported with a strong pro-government bias (Wong 2001). This government-control of information prompted dissenting voices and criticism to resort to alternative mediums of expression. As a result, pro-Anwar and reformasi-related websites mushroomed immediately after 1998, with various names indicating their pro-reformasi and anti-government stance such as *Laman Reformasi* (Reformasi Website), *Reformasi Diary*, *Anwar Online*, *freemalaysia*, *Minda Rakyat* (People's Mind), and *Konspirasi* (Conspiracy). These websites contained all sorts of critical information that was absent on mainstream media, ranging from announcements and eye-witness accounts of reformasi events, transcripts of Anwar's lawsuit proceedings, Anwar's own writings from prison, political commentaries, to satire and denunciation of ruling elites and even fabricated rumours (Holmes and Grieco 2001; Khoo Boo Teik 2003; Abbott 2004; Brown 2005; Weiss 2006). For example, the *Reformasi Diary* (www.sabrizain.org/reformasi/diary/), run by Sabri Zain, provided detailed "participatory observation" of the movement, especially the "face-off" between unarmed, ordinary demonstrators and repressive, grim police equipped with batons and water cannons. According to Khoo Boo Teik (2002), the *Reformasi Diary*'s accounts of the reformasi movement were unparalleled "for their accuracy, balance, and spirit". One study in 2004 identified at least 191 such reformasi-related websites established after 1998 (Tan 2004), which may reflect the extent of reformasi's impact on cyberspace. On this score, Graham Brown (2005, 46) argued that after Anwar was ousted, cyberspace "as a political medium and as the medium of *reformasi* became virtually synonymous".

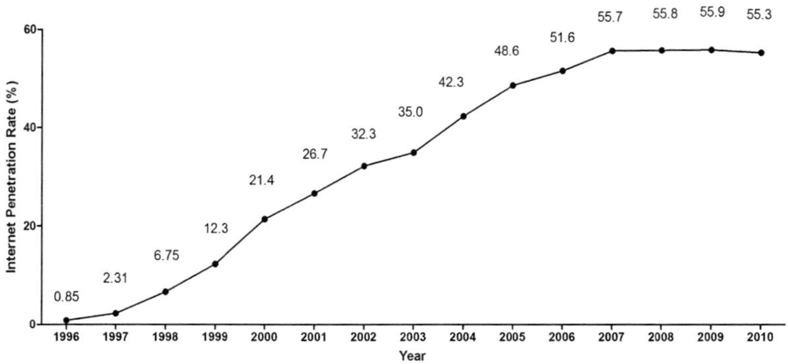

Fig. 3-1: Growth of Internet Penetration Rate in Malaysia

Although the majority of reformasi websites vanished or ceased to operate as the movement subsided (Tan 2004), alternative media and online journalism stood out, became institutionalised, and brought about even greater impacts on Malaysian politics. As previously mentioned, the traditional media landscape in Malaysia was dominated by direct or indirect censorship and ownership that made mainstream media rarely critical of the government. But as public distrust against mainstream media soared in the aftermath of Anwar's case, the increasing demand for independent news gave rise to a number of alternative media which, due to their professionalism, were different from, and more sustainable than, those reformasi sites.

One typical example of this is the *Malaysiakini* (www.malaysiakini.com). It was started by two veteran journalists, Steven Gan and Premesh Chandran, who aimed to promote freedom of press through "different thinking, different approaches, and a different atmosphere" (Steele 2009). What distinguished *Malaysiakini* from mainstream media, in fact, were the stories it covered, the stories that traditional media "carelessly" or deliberately overlooked or even concealed. For example, during its early days, *Malaysiakini* broke a story about how mainstream newspapers, in both English and Malay, refused to accept paid advertisements by the opposition party coalition, the Barisan Alternatif (BA), thus uncovering the discrimination and prejudice of traditional media toward the opposition bloc. Moreover, it also exposed the unusually close friendship between Chief Justice Eusoff Chin and prominent lawyer V. K. Lingam, which may have compromised the impartiality of the courts towards Lingam (Chin 2003).

The political significance of *Malaysiakini* was tested and enhanced in the 1999 general election. During the electoral period, many opposition leaders began using the Internet as their major medium for transmitting their views to the public, especially when they frequently suffered a "blackout" in mainstream media. According to one observer, it was not uncommon for the opposition party to print hard copies of *Malaysiakini*'s news and articles and to distribute them in political gatherings (ceramahs) before voting day (Chin 2003, 133). And on the night when polling results were out, *Malaysiakini* was the first to report that Terengganu state had fallen into the hands of the PAS, UMNO's arch-nemesis, while government-controlled media kept silent on the Terengganu failure until after the BN has secured a two-thirds majority in parliament (Tong Yee Siong 2004, 282). Therefore, independent news websites like *Malaysiakini* not only promoted objective journalism in Malaysia, but also facilitated freedom of information flow and public discussion. As James Chin (2003, 134) put it, "by giving space to stories that would otherwise be 'spiked' by the mainstream media, MK.Com (Malaysiakini.com) succeeded in creating a bigger political space for the opposition in Malaysia". Other prominent news websites in this regard include the *Harakah* online edition (though partisan and less independent since being operated by PAS), the *Aliran* and the *Merdeka Review*. Due to their independence and impartiality, online news portals like *Malaysiakini* have obtained much popularity, especially among young people, and somehow weakened and discredited the state-controlled media space.

On the other hand, blogging has become a significant tool for the public to participate in political discussion and some outstanding bloggers have emerged as a new stream of political actors. While the online news websites offered the public independent journalism and professionalism based on groups of outspoken yet marginalised journalists, the advent of web-blogs — easily edited websites with the most recent articles at the top — has deepened and enlarged the scope in which the general public, particularly individuals, could participate in Malaysian politics. According to a survey conducted by Universal McCann, Asia was found to be driving the adoption of social media, with China, South Korea, and Malaysia taking the lead in online content generation and socialising (Ooi 2007). Another report in 2007, meanwhile, indicated that more than 10,000 Malaysia-based blogs were operating in cyberspace (cited from George 2007, 900). Among the most prominent bloggers are many opposition leaders such as Parti Keadilan Nasional (now Parti Keadilan Rakyat), leading member Raja Petra Kamarudin who also owned the *Malaysia Today* website (www.malaysia-today.net) and DAP leader Lim Kit Siang who ran three blogs (such as blog.limkitsiang.com) with multiple posts published every day.

Furthermore, there are even more bloggers who made their names entirely through blogging. Reputedly the most influential blogger was Jeff Ooi, a former advertising copywriter, who became well known for his political blog *Screenshots* (www.jeffooi.com). Incredibly, he also won a seat in Jelutong, in the northern Penang state in the 2008 general election (Sani 2009a, 157). Compared with professionalised journalists who covered general issues, the bloggers, due to their diversified offline occupations and experience, were capable of producing in-depth analyses on specific subjects. For instance, when a dispute broke out between former Prime Minister Mahathir and then International Trade and Industry Minister Rafidah Aziz on the distribution of Approved Permit (AP) scheme in the automobile industry, the mainstream media eagerly reported this public quarrel. But it was online activist Raja Petra who pushed deeper and revealed the AP holders' links to government ministers, such as one of the most powerful AP holders being the cousin of Abdullah Badawi's son-in-law (George 2007, 901).

Meanwhile, the government has, in general, kept its promise of no censorship on the Internet. Even in the heyday of the reformasi movement, despite the government's tightening of traditional media control and physical repression against protesters (Khoo Boo Teik 2003), there was no evidence of Internet censorship. From the reformasi movement to the 2008 election, there have been only two incidents that involved infringement upon Internet freedom: in 2003, the police raided *Malaysiakini*'s office, seized its 15 computers and 4 servers, and summoned 5 editors who were charged for publishing a report on the website which was reckoned as "seditious" (Tong Yee Siong 2004, 307); and in 2007, lawsuits were filed by government-controlled NST Press against two bloggers Ahirudin Attan and Jeff Ooi for their online criticism of the poor quality of the newspaper, the *New Strait Times* (Sani 2009a, 160). However, in both cases, the government refrained from imposing further, serious punitive measures.

To some extent, the lack of extensive and systemic Internet control has made Malaysia's cyberspace a virtual public sphere with, in general, free communication and expression. As Tong (2004, 289) observed, the Internet technology "which was intended for economic gains, was geared towards political expression which in turn challenged the ruling coalition's stranglehold on state power". Such a challenge reached its climax in 2008 when balancing economic gains and political losses from an open Internet appeared to be unfeasible for the Barison Nasional and its leaders.

Critical Juncture: The 2008 General Election and the Trend of Internet Repression

With a 70% voter turnout, the 12th general election of Malaysia was held on March 8, 2008, after a short campaign period of 13 days (Singh 2009). It is politically significant not only for its unexpected result, but also for the increasingly critical role of Malaysia's cyberspace. The change of political dynamics on the Internet has been further illustrated by the 2011 state election in Sarawak, in which opposition parties attempted to replicate the 2008 political storm. This section starts with a brief review of the historic election, discusses the political transgression and online civil society formed in cyberspace, and explains Barison Nasional's moderate response in dealing with the cyber challenge.

Political tsunami on March 8

The 2008 general election has been viewed by many observers as a historic event in Malaysia that marks the commencement of political transition from competitive authoritarianism toward liberal democracy (Abdul Rashid Moten 2009a; Case 2009; 2010; Johan Saravanamuttu 2009). Preceding the general election were a series of unusual demonstrations, thick and fast in the second half of 2007, that may have foretold the BN's political disaster. In September 2007, around 800 lawyers marched in Putrajaya, where the Malaysian government resided, and demanded judiciary reform (Reuters 2007). Less than two months later, tens of thousands of protesters launched the “Bersih” (“clean”) rally[15] in Kuala Lumpur, calling for clean and fair elections (Yacob 2007). A 30,000-attended HINDRAF (Hindu Rights Action Force) rally followed suit at the end of November, protesting the racial discriminatory policies. These massive rallies, unprecedented to some extent, are regarded as the prologue to the larger political change (Zaharom Nain, interview by author, April 11, 2011). Facing surging public discontent, the Prime Minister Abdullah Badawi dissolved parliament and state assemblies[16] in February 2008 and called for an early election, more than one year in advance of his tenure ending.

Meanwhile, the incumbent Barison Nasional attempted to maneuver the electoral process to retain its rule. Many undemocratic devices, recorded in the “menu of manipulation” (Schedler 2002) and other works delineating semi-authoritarianism (see, for example, Case 2006), still remained in the 2008 election. For instance, the ruling parties still monopolised state resources and patronage, and had the Election Commission under their control (Case 2010, 109–110). Opposition parties were unfairly disadvantaged in advertising their campaign materials since “almost the entire print media, as well as radio stations and television channels, devoted much of their news programs and election coverage to promoting the government’s achievements” (Moten 2009b, 27). In addition, to keep the influential opposition leader, Anwar Ibrahim, out of the electoral contest, BN deliberately fixed the polling day one month before he was eligible to take part (Perez 2009). Therefore, from the perspective of the ruling parties, not much changed in the 2008 election.

Although before the election few expected that BN would obtain a victory tantamount to 2004 in which BN won 62% of the total votes and 90% of parliamentary seats, no one could have anticipated the opposition’s triumph in depriving the BN coalition of its two-thirds majority and five state governments. The outcome of the 2008 election, reported on March 8, was stunning. The Barison Nasional’s share in the poll fell from the previous range of 55–62% to only 50.14% and they secured 140 out of the 222 seats in parliament (Moten 2009b; Case 2010), eight seats less than the two-thirds required. The performance of BN was indeed abysmal when compared with that of the 2004 election. As Table 3-1 shows, the ratio of parliamentary seats between BN and opposition parties narrowed considerably from less than 90:10 to 63:37 within four years. If we break down the result geographically, the gap is even closer among peninsula states, where BN secured 51.8% of seats with merely 49.8% of popular votes (Brown 2008). BN also performed poorly at the state level. Four state governments in Selangor, Penang, Perak and Kedah were lost while Kelantan remained firmly in the opposition's hands. By contrast, in its worst performances before 2008, the BN had only failed to capture two states (Saravanamuttu 2009).

Table 3-1: Seat distribution in 2004 and 2008 parliamentary elections

	% votes	Peninsula seats	%	Borneo seats	%	Total seats	%
2004 election*							
Barison Nasional	63.9	148	89.2	51	98.1	199	90.87
Opposition parties	36.1	18	10.8	1	1.9	19	8.68
2008 election							
Barison Nasional	50.14	86	51.8	54	96.4	140	63.06
Opposition parties	46.4	80	48.2	2	3.6	82	36.94

Source: compiled from Case 2010; Moten 2009a; Moten 2009b.
* One seat in this election was won by an independent candidate in Sabah.

Moreover, the BN now has to contend with a more integrated opposition coalition in the form of Pakatan Rakyat (People's Pact) which, centred on the Parti Keadilan Rakyat (People's Justice Party), had "a unified platform of multi-racialism, social justice, democracy and more equitable development" (Moten 2009a, 191). Such strong performance from a united opposition front has even led some to observe that a de facto two-party system was forming (Saravanamuttu 2009). In addition, analysts also highlight the vote swing of all major ethnic groups away from the ruling parties, indicating a more fundamental transformation in Malaysian politics (Ong 2008). In view of these surprising facts, the mainstream media worldwide, such as *The Economist* (2008) and *Newsweek* (Holland 2008), independently adopted the phrase "political tsunami" to describe this election.

Transgression in the Malaysian cyberspace

The historic 2008 election has prompted curiosity in explaining the unprecedented setback for the ruling coalition. Some attribute the electoral outcome to the dissatisfaction of Abdullah Badawi's unfulfilled promises among voters and the consequent protest votes (Moten 2009b; Case 2009;

Chin and Wong 2009; Singh 2009). Others point to the legitimacy crisis of Barison Nasional due to public doubts over government policies and institutional functioning (Case 2010; Maznah 2008). Still others underline the importance of Malaysian civil society for "strategizing opposition collaboration, standing as candidates, informing debates, and expanding media options" (Weiss 2009, 741). Most analysts, nonetheless, acknowledge the role the Internet has played during and preceding the election. As Tang Hang Wu (2009, 17) argues, "while the presence of Internet activism *per* se does not guarantee political success, the confluence of all the factors […] *together* with the presence of credible Internet news portals and a remarkable proliferation of social political blogs and websites proved to be detrimental to *Barisan Nasional*". In fact, as the following discussion reveals, though not decisive, the Internet is not dispensable either in interpreting the 2008 election. The first part of this section briefly analyses the Internet factor in the 2008 election, and then evaluates the moderate transgression it represents and the strong, cohesive civil society formed on cyberspace.

(1) The Internet factor in the election

Immediately after the election, Badawi admitted that the government had lost the online war. As he acknowledged, "we didn't think it was important. It was a serious misjudgment. We thought that the newspapers, the print media, the television were important, but young people were looking at text messages and blogs" (*New Straits Times* 2008). The Internet's impact on the 2008 elections can be analysed by considering the following three aspects: the Internet-facilitated movements prior to the election, the empowerment of opposition parties and politicians, and the negative effects on the ruling parties.

First of all, regarded as the prelude to the 2008 tsunami, the major demonstrations in 2007 were all associated with the use of Internet technologies. The video clip that allegedly showed the prominent lawyer, V. K. Lingam, brokering top judicial appointments, was released on Anwar Ibrahim's website, which further triggered a royal commission of inquiry and an unusual "walk of justice" by Malaysian lawyers (Sani and Zengeni 2010). Meanwhile, the Bersih and HINDRAF rallies were also, according to Andreas Ufen (2009, 616), "to a large extent organized via and amplified by new media such as YouTube, Malaysiakini; blogs, such as those by Jeff Ooi, Ronnie Liu, and Ahirudin Attan; and the independent news portal 'Malaysia today', run by Raja Petra Kamaruddin". Most importantly, the success of these movements in galvanising support from the opposition base indicates that the Internet has served as a critical tool in unifying and integrating long-fragmented opposition groups (Khoo 2010; Welsh 2007). Cyberspace, in this sense, becomes an informal tie among disparate dissidents and opposition parties that coalesce into a powerful electoral force. On that score, Brown (2004, 88) has vividly described, in 2004, that "a PAS supporter in Kelantan may have little inclination or opportunity to engage with the West Coast, Chinese-based DAP. One click, however, can bring him from the PAS Web site to the DAP's. Arguably, this represents the greatest counter-hegemonic potential of the Internet for the opposition". In 2008, such potential was largely fulfilled. During the electoral period, the Internet facilitated communication between opposition forces, and more importantly, the communication between opposition parties and their electorate.

Instead of suffering a blackout in traditional media, which was a common phenomenon in previous elections, information and political appeals of opposition parties were disseminated and amplified through independent online media. *Malaysiakini*, which was established initially for the 1999 general election, became the most dominant source of information, rather than the discredited government-controlled media. There were so many visitors on *Malaysiakini* during election period that on polling day the site overloaded and crashed. At its peak, according to Mohd Azizuddin Mohd Sani (2009a, 154), the site attracted some 500,000 visitors an hour.

Public attention, deviating from mainstream media, once one of the "3-M" pillars (machinery, money and media) for BN's victory, was redirected toward alternative new media, including news websites like *Malaysiakini*, *Aliran*, *Agendadaily* and the party websites as well as personal blogs from the opposition front. Through these new channels, opposition politicians were able to, in urban areas at least, circumvent the discrimination of print media by airing freely in cyberspace their own political discourse that would have otherwise been blocked. As previously discussed, *Malaysiakini* has revealed the bias of mainstream media in publishing political advertisements. But online media, free from government control, harboured the opposition forces in its more popular form. As DAP leader Lim Kit Siang said, who himself ran three personal blogs with frequent updates, "We cannot neutralize the state-controlled media [...] But Internet pick-up rates will keep getting higher. We will not be blacked out forever" (*Agence France-Presse* 2008).

Furthermore, the blogger-turned-politicians, such as Jeff Ooi and Tony Pua, demonstrated strong popular support in the election, implicating the dramatic political power embedded in cyberspace. In all, five bloggers have successfully transferred their online popularity into a polling majority and parliamentary seats. While government backers doubted whether bloggers could make their presence felt, Tony Pua, the blogger-turned-DAP candidate with no mass grassroots, won the Petaling Jaya Utara seat, beating his MCA rival Chew Mei Fun by almost 20,000 votes (Lee 2008). It is interesting to note that in contrast to the daily updates and abundant video clips of ceramah (political meetings) on Pua's website, the site that Chew maintained only had two event items, highlighting the launch of the site and a public meeting respectively. As Tony Pua admitted, the Internet was politically important for him to express opinions and find followers (Tony Pua, interview by author, April 19, 2011). Meanwhile, Jeff Ooi was even appointed by DAP to organise the party's "e-campaign" (Sani and Zengeni 2010). Besides online popularity, another factor for the electoral triumph of these bloggers lies in the Internet's function of soliciting funding for election campaigns. The DAP candidate Tony Pua, for instance, managed to collect more than RM 10,000 via credit card and online transfers through his website (Sani 2009a, 151). In this sense, the Internet has become a rather significant channel to garner electoral funding.

With a political alliance built up, an electoral campaign facilitated, and resources buttressed, opposition candidates faced fewer disadvantages than they did previously and thus performed much better. A quantitative study (Gong 2009) on political blogs during the last general election supports this argument. It finds that in the 2008 election, politicians with blogs were five times more likely to win an election compared with those without blogs, ceteris paribus. Also, if a political candidate ran against a blogger, his/her odds of winning were reduced by 26% relative to competing with a non-blogger (Gong 2009). Moreover, it concludes that "all else being equal, opposition bloggers are almost eight times as likely to win an election as opposition non-bloggers", while no significant difference is observed between ruling party bloggers and non-bloggers (Gong 2009). Although this insight may question the significance of the Internet in impacting the overall electoral outcome, it demonstrates the role that the Internet has played in elevating the opposition front into a strong and cohesive political power.

Thirdly, new media not only provided a platform for interaction and communication between opposition parties and the electorate, but also spoiled the ruling coalition's image by revealing the sex, sleaze and corruption scandals of the top elites. For instance, Chua Soi Lek, the Health Minister, resigned in January 2008 after a secretly filmed sex video was leaked on YouTube which identified him and a female friend. The negative effects endured. While he successfully defeated the incumbent MCA president, Ong Tee Keat, in the 2010 internal party contest, a Merdeka Centre survey found that merely 9% of respondents considered Chua a capable leader, and their reservations were mainly caused by this sex scandal (Choong 2010). In this sense, the usual tactic of the ruling coalition, in close cooperation with traditional media, of promoting its own political ideology while defaming the opposition has been overturned in cyberspace.

In addition, compared with the opposition's active employment of information technologies, the BN's embrace of new technologies was far less impressive. Barisan Nasional's campaign site, http://bn2008.org.my, was unveiled only two weeks prior to the election, and its content mainly highlighted its past achievement while trying to counter the opposition's allegations (Moten 2009b, 27). Despite the fact that UMNO Youth has maintained its "cyber troopers" to counter online "misinformation" and rumours (Weiss 2009, 754), their own campaign efforts still relied on mainstream media which was outdated by the rising tide of online media, especially among the urban youth. Even as the election date approached and cyberspace filled with the opposition's discourse, the Minister of Information still stated that the government was not afraid of blogs or the Internet at all (Syed Akbar Ali, interview by author, April 5, 2011). Such disdain was soon proved ignorant in the aftermath of the election.

(2) Moderate level of transgression online

As the discussion in the previous chapter suggests, we measure the level of online transgressiveness by its scale and content. With regard to the first indicator, political use of the Internet sparked massive social movements with clear political demands. As mentioned above, preceding the 2008 elections were a series of large-scale demonstrations characterised by cyber mobilisation. Most typical of these are the Bersih (clean) movements that successively organised three waves of massive — and, to some extent, violent — rallies in 2007, 2011, and 2012 respectively. The turnout of these rallies rose steadily from 10,000–30,000 in the first wave to almost 80,000 in the latest one (*The Economist* 2012). With extensive use of the Internet platform, the Bersih movements were even able to build a global network which organised simultaneous rallies in 83 cities in different countries and shared live information via that network.

Also relevant to the scale of online transgression is the extent to which the Internet space has brought new political actors into Malaysian politics.

On this score, alternative media and blogs became increasingly important as sources of information and in shaping public discourse. The blogger community created a new political force due to its increasing political influence and more direct political participation (see previous section).

Meanwhile, despite the fact that Internet penetration rate is, as would be expected, lower in Malaysian rural areas where the BN's monopoly over traditional media still bears heavily on electoral outcomes, in the 2008 election the opposition forces and new media also found their way into the countryside through various means. In rural constituencies with little Internet access, members of opposition parties, or simply young dissidents, downloaded popular online materials, printed them out, and shared them with village voters. The distribution of online information was also witnessed in some mosques where Muslims gathered in large numbers (Zaharom Nain, interview). Sometimes, the young population working periodically in the urban area served as the conveyors of information when they returned home with democratic and liberal ideas (Khoo Kay Peng, interview by author, April 12, 2011). Noting this new pattern of political communication, the *New Straits Times* (2008) comments that "the reality is that kampong folk and those in rural areas now have kith and kin who have moved to the towns and cities [...] unflattering information, true or false, travels even faster with cyberworld denizens, who then spread the word outside it". In the state election of Sarawak three years later, such a strategy (or phenomenon) of information penetrating into rural constituencies occurred again.

However, with regard to the content indicator, core political claims raised by online contentious groups mainly target certain features (especially the electoral process) of the Malaysian political regime while leaving the fundamental socio-political order basically untouched. This downgrades online transgression in Malaysia to a moderate level. Major social movements with extensive online and offline presence mostly appealed for reforming particular parts of the political system rather than dismantling or replacing that system. For instance, political demands of the Bersih movements, unprecedented in Malaysia for their number of participants and persistence, included (1) cleaning up the electoral roll, (2) reforming postal ballot, (3) applying indelible ink, (4) extending campaign period, (5) allowing free and fair access to mass media for all parties (6) strengthening public institutions, (7) combating corruption, and (8) ending dirty politics.[17] To a large degree, these demands are piecemeal and pragmatic, indicating gradual, partial changes to the political order instead of a radical overturn. By contrast, political claims made by transgressive movements in Thailand directly undermined the fundamental aspects, especially the monarchy, of the Thai political system, although movements in Malaysia and Thailand shared great similarity and both were largely identified as movements for democratisation.

To better understand the nature of transgressive content on Malaysian cyberspace, this study has briefly reviewed one of Lim Kit Siang's personal blogs (blog.limkitsiang.com), one of the most influential in Malaysia's blogosphere, from February 2007 to March 2012. The top ten topics of his blog content, as indicated in the category section on that site, include "Najib" (with 1,009 blog posts), election/elections (738), nation building (689), parliament (656), UMNO (655), corruption (570), police (477), DAP (382), "1Malaysia" (338), and "bersih (referring to the Bersih Movements)" (337).[18] These categories represent the major purposes of Lim Kit Siang's blog: to question the policies of the incumbent government as well as political leaders, and to garner larger electoral support.

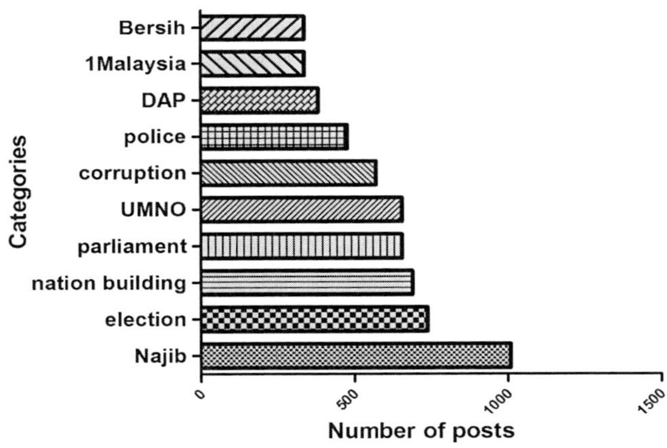

Fig. 3-2: Top Ten Topics on Lim Kit Siang's Blog

Nonetheless, online contentiousness like this seldom challenges the essential principles and institutions that sustain the established political order. For example, political systems in both Malaysia and Thailand are characterised by a constitutional monarchy system. But unlike Thailand where the monarchy faces mounting threats from cyberspace and even the idea of constitutional monarchy is seriously questioned, Malaysia sees few incidents of such fundamental challenge. Another core dimension of Malaysian politics lies in the ethnic cleavages (see Gomez ed. 2004), which are also untouched in the content of online transgression. In this regard, Thomas Pepinsky (2011, 10–13) argues that even with the new technologies and platforms, "the fundamental terms of political debate — which reflect, in turn, the essential logic of Malaysian politics and the ethnicity and class cleavages that animate it — have not changed" and "the existing cleavage structure means that the opposition's ideas only resonate with a fraction of the constituency that the opposition needs to defeat the BN". In this sense, the opposition's use of the Internet is primarily election-based rather than system-targeted. This nature has, to some extent, shaped the government's response strategy, also election-focused, which will be discussed later.

(3) High level of online civil society capacity

Malaysia performs well in all four indicators relating to online civil society capacity. It is the second most networked country in Southeast Asia, after Singapore, with an Internet penetration rate between 55% and 65%, according to different estimations.[19] Moreover, interactions within the online community are strengthened by the increasing use of social networking tools. The population with Facebook accounts, for example, expands sharply from over one million in 2009 to more than ten million two years later, accounting for 45.2% of the total population (Abbott 2011b, 13).

Secondly, Malaysia's online civil society has strong, coordinated relationships with offline political organisations. As previously mentioned, online politics and offline reformasi movements became synonymous in the aftermath of Anwar's dismissal (Brown 2005). During the 2008 elections, the connection between online communities and offline politics became even more entrenched, with alternative media serving as the major outlet for the opposition's political discourse and for bloggers assuming greater political roles in the electoral process. Perhaps the best example of such cooperation between online communities and offline politics was the Bersih (the 2011 and 2012 updated movements, the Bersih 2.0 and 3.0 respectively) movements that called for clean and fair elections. These were strongly supported by the three opposition parties, the PKR, the PAS, and the DAP. Prior to the Bersih 2.0 rally, PAS president Abdul Hadi Awang and deputy Mohamad Sabu publicly galvanised PAS members to join the demonstration (Yow 2011), while PKR and DAP also pledged their backing (Chi 2011). Among its endorsees listed on its website are many civil society organisations active both online and offline, such as Aliran, Centre for Independent Journalism, Southeast Asian Centre for e-Media and so on.[20] The movements per se have strong online presence: as of March 13, 2012, the number of supporters of the Bersih 2.0 on

Facebook reached 208,127,[21] at least four times the number of attendants of the Bersih 2.0 rally on July 9, 2011.[22]

The third element of online civil society capacity involves critical online media. On this score, alternative media such as *Malaysiakini* have proved their prominence and influence during the past decade. Statistics show that 82% of Malaysian Internet users turn to online media for news information on a weekly basis (Abbott 2011b, 14). In fact, online media in Malaysia, being independent from and critical of the government, enjoy much higher credibility than traditional mainstream media do. In a survey conducted during 2007–08, researchers found that among interviewed blog readers, 38% distrusted local mainstream media (Tan and Zawawi 2008). By contrast, only 18% regarded alternative media as unreliable, 20% disbelieved blog content, and 26% were sceptical about foreign mainstream media. Meanwhile, a larger proportion of respondents showed greater trust towards alternative media (34%) and blogs (31%) than the traditional media (26%) (Tan and Zawawi 2008, 61–63). The mistrust of Malaysia's mainstream media is also indicated in a regional comparison. According to the 2012 Edelman Trust Barometer (2012), Malaysian interviewees' trust in media (47%) was not only lower than the global average (52%), but also the lowest among its regional counterparts included in the survey (see Fig.3-3).

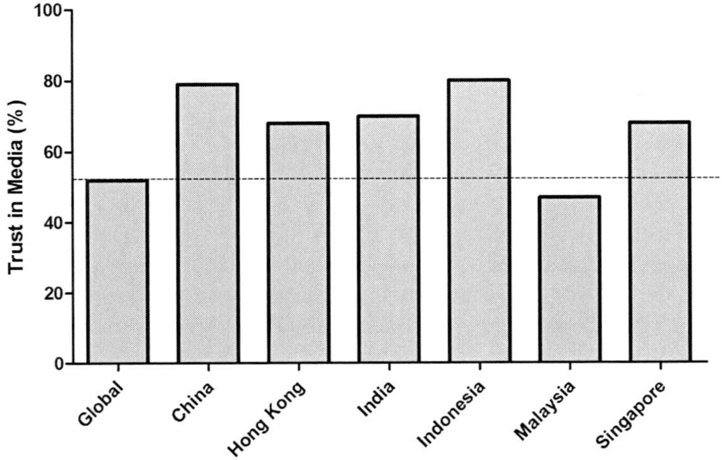

Fig. 3-3: Popular Trust in Media
Source: Edelman Trust Barometer 2012

Last but not least, the capacity of online civil society in Malaysia is boosted by the fact that there is little evidence of major counter-movement on cyberspace, indicating a great cohesiveness between online communities. Meanwhile, public awareness of the importance of Internet freedom appears to be cohesive and unambiguous. According to the World Values Survey, when asked to determine the first choice for their own country, 11.3% of Malaysian respondents underscored the need for greater public expression and participation, which was higher than most regional counterparts such as China (8.1%), Taiwan (4.9%), Thailand (8.3%), Indonesia (7.9%), and Vietnam (9.4%) (Abbott 2011a, 20). With traditional media distrusted, cyberspace thus embodies an invaluable channel for public participation and deliberation. Therefore, it could be expected that any governmental move to upgrade Internet control practice would meet strong resistance from the coordinated online communities. Evidence on this score will be offered in the next section that further explains Malaysia's Internet control outcome.

Explaining Malaysia's Internet control outcome

As discussed above, Malaysia's online political contention is centred on discrete features, rather than fundamental dimensions, of the political system, thus posing less systemic threats to the government. Online transgression mainly targets the electoral process which has, for long time, discriminated in favour of the ruling coalition. The government, in response, adopts a dual strategy which actively engages, and garners support from, the online communities and selectively penalises some key political actors without using full-fledged censorship measures. Its approach in dealing with the blogger community, a new political player in Malaysian politics, is a good exemplification of such moderate, but complex responses.

Since political blogs proved pivotal in the 2008 political election, the foremost task of the Malaysian government is to engage and co-opt, if possible, the blogger community before the electoral tsunami strikes again. Right after the election, the Information Minister, Ahmad Shabery Cheek invited bloggers to go on television in a 20-minute programme on Sunday evening, beginning from April 20, 2008, to discuss social, political, and economic affairs. By the same token, other politicians in the ruling coalition parties organised small meetings with well-known bloggers, or invited them to attend events as a way of creating a means of communication. A recent example has seen a prominent blogger from Blogger House Malaysia invited by the government to follow Prime Minister Najib Razak at a Turkish conference where this blogger broadcast the Prime Minister's speech and other live events via his blog site (Syed Akbar Ali, interview).

Parties and politicians in the ruling coalition even hire bloggers and other netizens as "cyber troopers" to disseminate pro-government information, counter online criticism, and publish articles that attack opposition leaders. These pro-government bloggers are often paid covertly through political parties' allowances or indirectly through government-related media companies. Since 2008, their online presence has been increasingly felt in the blogosphere in general and on prominent opposition websites in particular (Syed Akbar Ali, interview; Tony Pua, interview; Hishamuddin Rais, interview by author, April 8, 2011). This strategy indicates the government's increasing focus on the crucial blogosphere and its new attempts to engage and interact with bloggers and netizens, instead of simply ignoring their voice. However, the engagement involves mostly pro-government bloggers or those the government deems to be moderate, while the most critical and outspoken netizens are generally excluded (Khoo Kay Peng, interview).

When co-optation fails, the government turns to harassment. On May 6, 2008, within less than two months since the general election, blogger and owner of *Malaysia Today* (www.malaysia-today.net), Raja Petra, and former banker Syed Akbar Ali became the first and second Malaysian netizens to be charged under the Sedition Act. Raja Petra was accused of implying in an online post that the then deputy Prime Minister Najib Razak and his wife were involved in the October 2006 murder of model Altantuya Shaariibuu (Reporters Without Borders 2008a), while Syed Akbar Ali was charged with posting a seditious comment about Malays and Islam on the *Malaysia Today* website. Three months later, Raja Petra was ordered by a Kuala Lumpur high court to expose the identity of people who posted comments on his *Malaysia Today* website, and to remove the three articles that prompted a defamation suit against him (Reporters Without Borders 2008b).

However, these were not the only cases of harassment against netizens: in 2010 Khairul Nizam Abd Ghani, another Malaysian blogger, was arrested for allegedly insulting the late Sultan of Johor, Sultan Iskandar ibni Almarhum Sultan Ismail (Chandranayagam 2010); Irwan Abdul Rahman, executive editor of the *Malay Mail* daily, was prosecuted for publishing falsehoods as he satirised the nation's biggest power producer Tenaga Nasional Berhad in his "clearly tongue-in-cheek Internet posting" (Kuppusamy 2010); a blogger called Namewee was arrested because his posts questioned the decades-old special privileges given to the native Malays and the Bumiputra. Sometimes the government also takes action when anti-government information flows into the offline world. For instance, a well-known cartoonist under the pseudonym of Zunar, whose political cartoons are popular on *Malaysiakini* and among online communities, was arrested in 2010 when he compiled his drawings, once kept online, into a collection for publication. On the day before the book was to be published, Malaysian police raided the printing house and seized all the copies (Zunar, interview by author, April 7, 2011). Due to these repressive incidents to deter and contain Internet threats, Malaysia's ranking on Press Freedom Index plummeted from 131 in 2009 to 141 in 2010 (Reporters Without Borders 2010), even lower than Singapore, its peninsula neighborhood with a harder form of electoral authoritarianism.

The dual strategy of simultaneously engaging and containing the online community has been, to some extent, confirmed by the ruling elites. At the 1st Malaysia-ASEAN Regional Blogger Conference held in 2011, in which Najib officiated, the Prime Minister urged the blogging community to be ethically responsible, but reiterated the government's commitment to no censorship. On the latter score, he stated that "Tun (Mahathir) made the promise to the world that Malaysia would never censor the Internet. My Government is fully committed to that. We intend to keep his word" (Najib 2011).

Besides the mixed strategy in dealing with bloggers, the government's electoral concern vis-à-vis the Internet challenge is further reflected by the divergent attitudes towards information freedom among ruling coalition parties, especially between the urban, Chinese-based MCA and the rural, Malay-based UMNO. For instance, in a survey of elected MP's attitudes toward a Freedom Of Information Act (FOI Act), all nine MCA MPs and three out of the four Malaysian Indian Congress (MIC) MPs who responded expressed support for such a law in the interest of transparency and accountability (Loh and Surin 2011, 72–73). As one MCA parliamentary member in Pahang said, "It is obvious that flow of information is unstoppable, so we must learn to embrace this fact instead of fearing it" (Loh and Surin 2011, 286). Nonetheless, while MPs in MCA and MIC unanimously support such action, for UMNO MPs, the attitudes toward information freedom are more ambivalent. Out of the 22 MPs replying to this issue, eight were supportive of enacting the FOI; three flatly rejected such proposal; and the rest blurred their stance in one way or another (Loh and Surin 2011, 72–73).

Map 3-1: Distribution of urban, Chinese, and online population in peninsula states

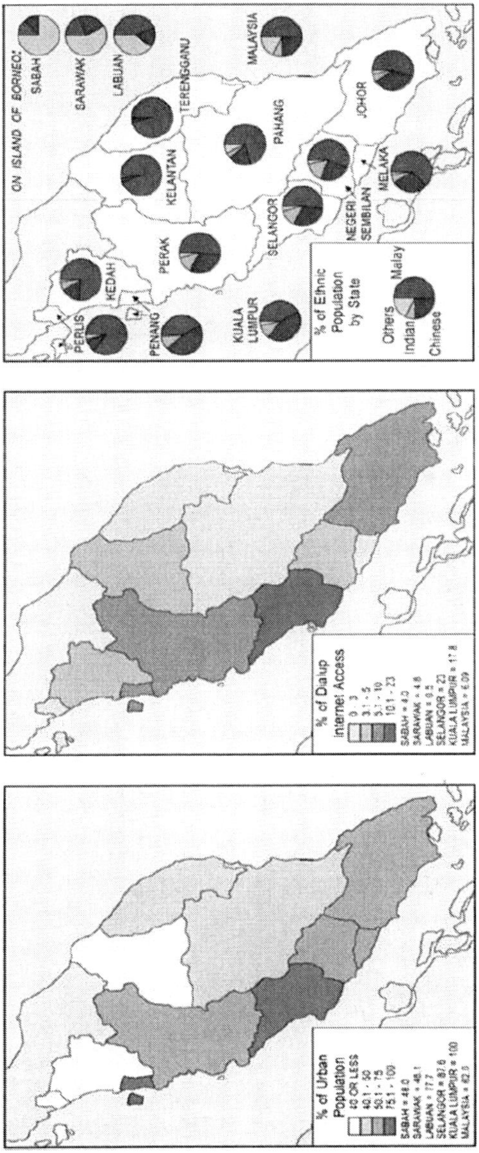

Source: Lepawsky 2005, 16

Therefore, the attitudes of UMNO MPs towards information freedom — highly associated with media and Internet freedoms — are in stark contrast to the attitudes of MCA MPs. The major factor underlying this difference points to the electoral demands of UMNO's and MCA's respective strongholds. As Map 3-1 illustrates, Malaysia's urban, Chinese and Internet population, to a large extent, coalesce in those peninsula states such as Penang, Perak, Selangor, Johor, and the Federal Territory of Kuala Lumpur (Lepawsky 2005). Since the MCA relies heavily on electoral support from urban, Chinese-based constituencies (Lim 2002), this means that the party has to placate voters in areas where the access rates, and thus the impacts of the Internet, are considerable. To advocate greater media and Internet freedom, as a result, would cater to the interests of the potential electorate of the MCA. By contrast, rural and Bumibutra constituencies account for a large share in UMNO's electoral base (Lim 2002), making the party elites — at least those from rural constituencies — less pressured to pursue such policies. In this sense, the incentives and disincentives for Internet control spring mostly from the electoral needs of ruling elites.

Moreover, the strong, cohesive online civil society in Malaysia has resisted government plans to escalate Internet control measures. In the aftermath of the 2008 elections, the Malaysian government launched a series of initiatives, usually behind the scenes, to regulate cyberspace, including the deployment of an Internet filtering system modelled on China's "Green Dam" programme and the real-name registration of bloggers (Chandranayagam 2009; Heacock 2009; Freedom House 2011). However, such reported moves drew fierce criticism from both civil rights groups and opposition parties which accused the government of breaching its 1996 guarantees on Internet freedom. For instance, on August 7, 2009, just hours after the Minister of Information, Communications, and Culture, Rais Yatim, disclosed the government's intention to establish an Internet filtering system, Prime Minister Najib publicly denied such a proposal. As he admitted, the government could not implement the filtering practices "firstly because it is not effective" and secondly because "it may cause dissatisfaction among the people because in this ICT and borderless age, information moves around freely" (*The Malaysian Insider* 2009). Since the technical feasibility of Internet filtering has been widely acknowledged by a number of studies and empirically confirmed in many Asian countries,[23] it is reasonable to argue that the latter factor (strong public outcry) is one of the major concerns of the Malaysian government.

Another major factor is the repercussion on foreign investment. After the Internet filtering plan, as cited above, was revealed, a company official from a US Internet portal operating in Malaysia warned that if government authorities "block foreign Internet websites, search engines and social media like Facebook, revenues are going to fall and people will start switching out" (*Reuters* 2009). When such plans resurfaced a year later, the DAP MP Tony Pua also cited the danger that it might shake investors' confidence (Yow 2010).

Meanwhile, the Internet control practices even enhanced the solidarity of online communities. For instance, the lawsuits against Jeff Ooi and Ahirudin Atten by the New Strait Times Press triggered a "Bloggers United" movement to protest against the case and collectively boycott and criticice the *New Strait Times* (Tan and Zawawi 2008, 23–24). The movement later evolved into a formally registered organisation named the National Alliance of Bloggers (All-Blogs) whose executive council members included celebrities and politicians such as Patrick Teoh and Elizabeth Wong (Tan and Zawawi 2008, 25). By comparison, such organisational strength is much weaker in both Thailand and Indonesia.

To sum up, Malaysia in the post-2008 era has seen an increase in the use, as well as rhetoric, of Internet control practices. However, despite occasional harassment against bloggers and the employment of pro-government "cyber troopers", none of these actions have been systemic or pervasive. To date, the proposed plans to upgrade the Internet control system have been shelved in anticipation of strong public resistance. While the election-based online transgression shapes the government's response in a way that also underscores electoral needs, the collective force of the online civil society raises the cost for further Internet control strategies. Meanwhile, the reaction of ruling elites towards Internet threats would be readjusted if new forms of online transgressiveness emerge. The Sarawak state election in 2011 demonstrated this.

Sarawak Report vs. *Sarawak Reports*: New transgression on cyberspace

The largest state by size in Malaysia, Sarawak, is traditionally considered a stronghold for the incumbent ruling coalition Barison Nasional. The BN coalition parties in Sarawak, such as the Malay/Melanau Parti Pesaka Bumiputera Sarawak (PBB) and the Sarawak United People's Party (SUPP), have always retained an overwhelming advantage "through manipulation of the electoral system, politicization of ethnicity, control over state resources, media bias and outright vote buying" (Welsh 2006, 5). As a result, although a trend for broader representation has been observed (Pandian 2010; Welsh 2006), the 2006 state election in Sarawak still witnessed a landslide victory for BN parties which captured 62 (87%) of the 71 seats. Even amid the 2008 political tsunami, BN in Sarawak remained strong and won all parliamentary seats except one, which, some have argued, was like a "blue wave" for the Barison Nasional (Mersat 2009). In fact, as previously mentioned, BN had actually lost its popular votes in West Malaysia. In that sense, Sarawak, the vote bank of BN, is essential for the maintenance of BN's rule in the whole country.

However, with another state election in Sarawak looming, opposition forces began to plan a replication of their 2008 victory. What spurred their hope was the gradual transformation of the mindset among urban voters. Already, in 2008, these urban voters changed their major focus to issues such as human rights, integrity, transparency, and accountability (Mersat 2009). The Internet thus provided a useful platform for opposition parties to inform people about and mobilise them around such issues, given traditional media were tightly in the government's hands. A website called *Sarawak Report* (www.sarawakreport.org) established by Clare Brown, the sister-in-law of former British Prime Minister Gordon Brown, became highly popular ahead of the election. It revealed the tremendous assets and properties that BN party cronies, particularly the billionaire Chief Minister, Abdul Taib Mahmud, had grabbed through exploitation of local natural resources.[24]

While such information became widespread and put urban communities in Sarawak as well as the whole country in a rage, there was even an effort to disseminate the information of Taib's corruption scandal to the larger population. For instance, a Radio Free Sarawak was established to broadcast interviews, news and analyses that people would "never get to hear on any of the other government-controlled radio stations in Sarawak".[25]

In a similar vein, the electoral campaign of opposition parties also centred on Taib's corruption and called for a change in chief minister. Just as in 2008, opposition politicians printed online stories and articles and distributed them among rural voters who had little access to the Internet (Khoo Kay Peng, interview; Tony Pua, interview). Other online media also contributed to information dissemination by sending their own journalists to Sarawak (Steven Gan, interview by author, April 7, 2011). Certain news stories that would have otherwise been blocked were thus able to circulate in the cyberspace. For example, while the mainstream media reported Najib's visit to Sarawak in April exclusively in favour of the BN, the embarrassment of Najib being reproached by a passerby for electoral funding was totally ignored and only covered by independent journalists and bloggers (Hishamuddin Rais, interview). With the concerted effort of the opposition front and civil groups, it seemed that the political tsunami would sweep across the East Malaysian state. In this sense, Internet usage during the Sarawak election posed new transgression as it was prying open the traditional vote base of the BN.

Facing a strong opposition force in Sarawak, the Malaysian government played its old tricks of Internet control. It ordered the Malaysian Communication and Multimedia Committee (MCMC) to investigate Radio Free Sarawak, accusing the latter of defamation (Khoo Kay Peng, interview). But more importantly, the government adopted another covert and more indirect strategy.

Firstly, a website under the name of *Sarawak Reports* (www.sarawakreports.org) was created, plausibly confusing the Internet users due to its strong resemblance to the original site. The content it covered mainly complimented the BN parties' achievements in developing Sarawak, a stance that countered the anti-government *Sarawak Report*. Secondly, Distributed Denial of Service (DDoS) attacks were used several times ahead of the polling day. It was reported that the websites of *Sarawak Report* and *Malaysiakini* were bombarded by the unremitting influx of data requests several days before the election was to be held. *Sarawak Report* was totally brought down and forced to switch its address (*The Malaysian Insider* 2011). However, none of these actions were directly associated with government agencies, despite pervasive speculation that the hackers and the imitative website were paid by ruling parties (Khoo Kay Peng, interview). In fact, this new style of government-sponsored, privately-executed Internet control has been widely witnessed in countries like Russia and Iran (Klimburg 2011; Morozov 2011).

In addition, the government also hired bloggers to travel to Sarawak and report the election favouring the ruling coalition. In one post, for instance, "Rocky's Bru" (one of the famous pro-government bloggers) criticised Clare Brown, saying she should "go after her own brother-in-law for failing the Britons with his environmentally unfriendly policies when he was PM".[26] With a greater cautiousness toward cyberspace, although BN could not prevent a poorer performance, slipping seven more seats into opposition hands, the political tsunami tantamount to 2008 did not occur. The Barison Nasional has realised the political significance of the Internet in the time of elections and shifted its strategy of Internet control, as previous attempts of overt repression were largely ineffective. The "*Sarawak Report* vs. *Sarawak Reports*" story, symbolising this changed strategy, would be likely to recur when the next general election is approaching.

Conclusion

In general, Internet control in Malaysia is maintained at a low-to-moderate level, though it evidently increased after the stunning election of 2008. A number of bloggers faced prosecution by the government and its associated corporations. Proposals such as constructing a filtering system, registering bloggers, and licensing alternative online media have been repeatedly discussed. But they mostly failed to be implemented due to the government's fear that such plans would further alienate the electorate and impair foreign investment. The outcome of Malaysia's Internet control practices is shaped collectively by the moderate online transgressiveness and the strong online civil society capacity. While the former impels the government to counter the Internet threat in a manner that accords with its electoral needs, and divides the ruling elites on their perceptions of Internet freedom, the latter serves as a constraint to more systemic Internet control policies. In contrast, as the next chapter will discuss, online transgressiveness in Thailand is much greater, posing fundamental challenges to the political order, and the online communities are largely polarised. As a result, while authorities in Thailand extensively block websites and prosecute critical online dissidents in order to re-shape state-promoted ideology and obstruct mobilisation and communication, the Malaysian government is more focused on how to win back the online sphere before the next election takes place.

This chapter also explores the contextual conditions that affect the formation of online transgression and online civil society in Malaysia. The government's plan in the early 1990s to construct a knowledge-based economy gave birth to the Multimedia Super Corridor (MSC) project and the official promise of no-censorship of cyberspace, which created a free environment for the development of the online public sphere. Meanwhile, the reformasi movement directly triggered by the Anwar–Mahathir split further politicised cyberspace, setting precedent for online politics during the 2008 election and its aftermath.

The uniqueness of the Malaysian case is that these important events, the 1996 Bill of Guarantees and the 1998–99 reformasi movements, shaped a trajectory in which the government deliberately left the Internet uncensored, and, consequently, this decision backfired, weakening the ruling coalition's hegemonic position. A more expected trajectory for such a semi-authoritarian regime would have seen repressive policies applied at an earlier stage and a culture of self-censorship embedded in cyberspace, a scenario more resembling that in Singapore. But in the end, it is still the agency-level factors — the intensity of transgressiveness and the capacity of online civil society — that directly determine the strategy and extent of Internet control. As the online communities remain highly coordinated and a national election looms, the Najib government is unlikely to pursue any greater Internet censorship. But some covert strategies, such as anonymous attack on critical websites, may probably recur as they did in the 2011 Sarawak election. In this sense, the "menu of manipulation" (Schedler 2002) would be expanded in the new information era.

CHAPTER FOUR

CONTROLLING THE INTERNET IN AN UNSTABLE DEMOCRACY: CASE STUDY OF THAILAND

Introduction

The case of Thailand sees a puzzling relationship between an electoral, yet unstable, democracy and intensive Internet controls. This chapter argues that Internet control outcome in Thailand results from high level of online transgressiveness and low capacity of online civil society. It is noteworthy that fragmentation of the latter has enabled the government to garner greater public support in controlling cyberspace — a scenario that has implications for other parts of the world.

At the turn of the twenty-first century, there was at least moderate optimism about Thailand's political development. With the political power of the military plausibly weakened (Tamada 2008), the "People's Constitution" promulgated, and a popularly elected leader, Thaksin Shinawatra, assuming the reins of government, Thailand by the early 2000s had indeed seen its democratisation process taking off. In accordance with this development, Freedom House changed Thailand's status from being "partly free" to "free" between 1998–2005, making it one of the only two "free" countries in Southeast Asia at that time,[27] while the Polity IV project gave Thailand a remarkably high score of 9 out of 10 continuously, from 1992–2005, on its democracy index.[28] Perceiving these positive signs, some political analysts enthusiastically hailed "a level of stability in Thai politics new to most observers" (Mutebi 2004, 86). However, both stability and democracy suddenly declined, contrary to international and intellectual expectations, as Thaksin was ousted in 2006 by a military coup and a protracted political crisis set in.

Meanwhile, even more astonishing was the harsh censorship imposed on cyberspace following the deposition of the Thaksin administration. Internet control practices become institutionalised after the hurried passing of the Computer Crime Act (CCA) in 2007 and culminated in the 2010 political crisis when hundred thousands of websites were blocked and a number of netizens arrested. Such methods have, in fact, made Thailand a pioneer of Internet control among Southeast Asian competitive regimes. Categorising the Thai Internet as being "under surveillance", Reporters Without Borders (2010) warned that Thailand risked "getting transferred into the next 'Enemies of the Internet' list". For students of Internet politics and Southeast Asian studies, then, it is necessary to explain why Internet freedom in Thailand has deteriorated so rapidly and extensively.

On this score, some observers (see, for example, Pavin Chachavalpongpun 2010) readily lay the blame on the return of authoritarian politics reflected in the unconstitutional military coup in 2006 and the electoral manipulation that brought the Democratic Party into power in 2008. Indeed, the controversial Computer Crime Act was passed by a national assembly selected by the military, with the immediate aim of curbing public criticism against the military's political intervention. It was during the Abhisit government (2008–11), which represented the traditional political establishment, that the Thai Internet control apparatus operated in full swing. However, several important points may prompt us to rethink the fundamental causes of Internet control in Thailand.

Firstly, there is evidence that Internet control practices had started in the second term of the Thaksin administration, which was popularly and democratically elected. Secondly, although the CCA was a new project undertaken by the military-appointed government, the lèse-majesté law that provides the major rationale for Internet censorship has long been institutionalised and practiced. Last but not least, after the pro-Thaksin Pheu Thai Party won the national election in July 2011, the new government, headed by Thaksin's sister Yingluck Shinawatra, announced that Internet censorship policies would be preserved, if not increased (Crispin 2011). Moreover, simply ascribing Internet control to authoritarianism cannot sufficiently explain why countries with harder forms of semi-authoritarian regimes, such as Malaysia and Cambodia, practice Internet censorship much less than Thailand does. In this sense, while political change serves as the important background of political struggles on the Internet, strategic choices made by the Thai government to control the Internet may stem from other factors.

This study argues that the intensive Internet control practices in Thailand result directly from the high level of transgressiveness of online politics and from the weak, polarised status of its online civil society. On the one hand, the Red Shirt movement and the surging anti-monarchy discourse in cyberspace have made the Internet a political space that greatly threatens the traditional political system maintained by the Thai establishment. On the other hand, as Thai online communities are polarised between pro-Thaksin and royalist forces, collective resistance against Internet censorship appears weak and ineffective. Under such circumstance, the government authorities can even effectively garner substantial public support in their campaign against "illegal" online activities.

Furthermore, this chapter traces the historical evolution of Internet regulation in Thailand, providing a full picture of how the Internet control policies have developed over time. It analyses the conditions that have shaped the political context in which Internet technologies, Internet politics, as well as Internet regulations, came into their current form. It starts by outlining the political context in the 1990s, when the Internet was first introduced to Thailand, right up to the period under Thaksin's premiership, when Internet control policies were introduced. The third part analyses how agency-level factors — level of transgressiveness and the capacity of online civil society — determine Internet control outcomes.

Contextual Conditions in the 1990s: The Internet's Introduction in a Time of Democratisation

Thai politics during the 1990s, especially during the first half, was permeated with conflicts and debates for democratising the political system that was characterised by "bureaucratic polity" (Riggs 1966) and money politics. Any political or social institution in Thailand, including the policy regime concerning Internet development and administration, would inevitably be affected by the events and discourse of the Thai political transition. Prior to discussing the political development in this period, however, it is important to briefly consider the early history from which the political context in Thailand was formed.

Political and social contexts in Thailand

Despite the 1932 "democratic revolution", which greatly reduced the absolute power of the king, the resulting constitutional monarchy system did not immediately bring democratisation to the Thai people. In fact, the security concerns of the Thai state, firstly during the Second World War and later for the need to suppress communist threats, have made the Thai military, who have always come to power through coercive or violent means, perhaps the most powerful group on the stage of Thai politics. Therefore, throughout the remainder of the twentieth century, Thai politics frequently saw one military government overturning another through military coups (Tamada 2008, 69).

The direct consequence of this continuous military influence was that the democratisation process in Thailand was manipulated, hindered, and often reversed, and political rights, such as freedom of expression, were limited and repressed (albeit with some periodical exceptions). Before 1991, Thailand had fifteen general elections, but only four of them generated a change of government, while only one election saw a change from one popularly elected government to another. Therefore, to a great extent, "elections performed merely the symbolic function of ensuring the legitimacy of purportedly democratically chosen military governments" (Suchit 1996, 184). Under such circumstances, the media in Thailand, which was assumed to function as watchdog against the government, has been frequently used by the government as a political tool, and its development was featured by "its interplay with authoritarian control, and its manipulation by competing elites" (Woodier 2008, 188). Even as 1980s Thailand witnessed relative political stability (Fig.4-1),[29] its politics, mainly under the Prem administration, were dominated by the conservative pact binding the military sector, bureaucrats, and the royal family (McCargo 2005) that left limited space for liberal and civil groups to make their voice heard.

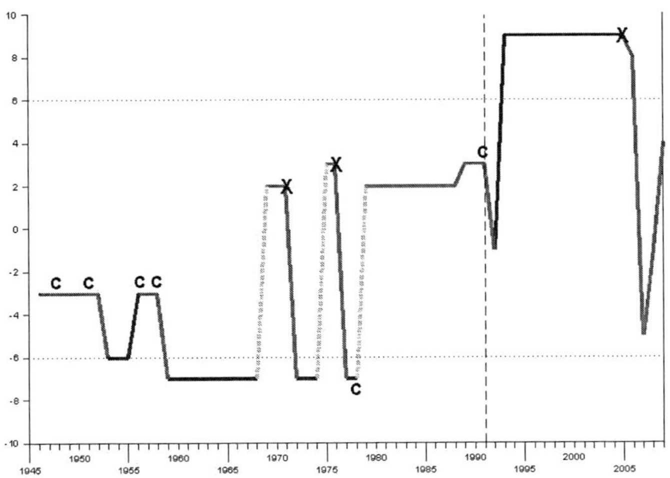

Fig. 4-1: Democratisation in Thailand, 1946–2008
Source: Polity IV Country Reports

Another distinctive element in Thai politics involves the increasing powers of the monarchy. The resurgence of the royal role began during the 1950s, when Field Marshal Sarit Thanarat seized power through a military coup and encouraged monarchical revival. Since then, the King, Bhumibol Adulyadej, has been actively engaged in promoting national, especially rural, development (Baker and Pasuk 2009). His political prominence ascended steadily with his intervention and mediation into political crises in the mid-1970s, and more significantly, in 1992 when nation-wide television broadcast him summoning rival leaders and then resolving the political deadlock. As a result, the notion of "democracy with the king as head of state" has prevailed as a national ideology and been boosted by the National Identity Office (Baker and Pasuk 2009, 233–235). The royal family is, therefore, seen as not only a symbol of constitutional monarchy, but also a guarantee for national unity and stability and a fundamental pillar of political order. This ideology has further curbed public space for dissent in Thailand, which has an even more crucial impact in the new information era.

Liberalisation during the 1990s

While a conservative ideology still predominated, as Fig.4-1 above shows, a dramatic trend towards democratisation occurred during the 1990s and a form of highly democratised government was set up that endured for over a decade. Marking this great change and a general "third wave" of democratisation, a number of theoretical explanations have been offered to identify the key determinants that drove Thailand into a democracy, such as the rise of middle class (Huntington 1991), importance of business associations (Anek 1992), retreat of military from politics (Tamada 2008), economic globalisation (Englehart 2003) and so on. To decide which factor was most significant for Thai democracy — which probably developed as the collective result of the elements mentioned above — is not the principal task here. However, there is a series of events that reflect the political development towards a generally democratic and liberal atmosphere in Thailand.

In May 1992, large-scale protest rallies broke out in Bangkok, demanding the resignation of Army Commander-in-Chief Suchinda Khraprayun from the Premiership.He was the leader of 1991 coup and reneged on his promise of not being Prime Minister. This crisis ended with disastrous bloodshed and an intervention from the king, leading to a weakening of military power and increasing calls for political reform. The reforming of Thai politics in the mid-1990s was comparatively smooth and rapid. After a hunger strike by activist Chalat Worachat in May 1994, the Committee on Developing Democracy (CDD) was established in June, the Constitution Drafting Assembly (CDA) created in late 1996, and the "People's Constitution" promulgated and enforced a year later. The major and foremost objective of the political reform in this period, according to Bowonsak (1998, 52) (who was the leading figure in drafting the 1997 Constitution), was "to take politics out of the hands of politicians and turn it into citizens' politics by expanding citizens' rights and freedoms and transforming a representative democracy into a citizens' participatory democracy". As a result, politics in Thailand during the 1990s was quite different from previous eras, in that the political discourse and institutional design were integrated, if not overwhelmingly, into an atmosphere of liberalism. The power was distributed to a group of people — or "liberal regime framers" as Michael Connors (2009, 357) labelled it — that advocated for "the ideals of limited government, separation of powers, rule of law, and contingent freedoms and liberties". It is at this time that Internet technologies were introduced in Thailand.

How was Thailand networked?

Just like many of its Southeast Asian counterparts, Thailand got initial access to the Internet system through the efforts and collaboration of a small number of academics. As early as 1986, Kanchana Kanchanasut, a professor at the Asian Institute of Technology (AIT), together with her colleague Tomonori Kimura, decided to develop a basic computer network in Thailand in order to connect other colleagues and friends through email communications (Sirin et al. 1999, 9). The first email network in Thailand, called the Thai Computer Science Network (TCSNet), was established in 1988 with Australian assistance (from the International Development Plan), which connected two servers in Prince of Songkhla University and AIT to the University of Melbourne. However, this early system used Unix to Unix Copy Protocol (UUCP), rather than TCP/IP protocols, to enable its email exchanges. UUCP made it possible for users to communicate without full connection with international networks based on the TCP/IP, which was more technologically advanced and internationally standardised. Therefore, it is not until the end of 1992 that the Internet in its real sense was born in Thailand — at that time Chulalongkorn University in Bangkok acquired a new leased line that enabled local network members to gradually upgrade their dial-up connections to TCP/IP (Sirin et al. 1999, 14).

In addition to academic involvement, the private sector, primarily Bangkok-based international computer vendors, also greatly contributed to the early development of the Thai network. Companies such as IBM, Digital Equipment Corporation (DEC), and Hewlett Packard (HP) were all reported as donating equipment to help expand the Thai Internet (Thaweesak 1997). The collaboration between universities, and between academic and private sectors, boosted the popularisation and commercialisation of the Internet. In 1995, Internet Thailand Service Centre, later known as Internet Thailand, became the first commercial Internet Service Provider (ISP) in Thailand, followed soon by the KSC Comnet. However, the Thai Internet in its early years was mostly confined in scope to university researchers and in usage to email communication. Although Internet users increased sharply from a mere 200 in 1992 to over 5,000 in May 1994, this figure was still trivial when compared with the large population in Thailand (over 60 million). It is not difficult to see that "ordinary" users, at that time, were extremely rare if academics and technicians were not counted. Envisioning the great significance the Internet may present in future development, the Thai government under the Banharn administratio approved, in 1996, the first National Information Technology Policy, namely IT2000. This plan, with its 4.2 billion Thai Baht budget, was aiming towards "developing a national IT infrastructure, human resources, and enhancing government service using the computer networks" (Sirin et al. 1999, 24). Under IT2000, a substantial growth in Internet users emerged during the second half of the 1990s, despite the fact that the 2.3 million users recorded in 2000 still only accounted for 3.8% of the Thai population.

Early institutions for regulating the Net

This brief account of the Internet's formation in Thailand has shown that its development was primarily pushed forward by inter-university cooperation, which implies a relatively liberalised environment surrounding the early Internet system. This somewhat decentralised environment stemmed both from the democratisation discourse and process during the 1990s that made power centralisation and regulation of the Internet difficult and from frequent government reshuffles that impeded consistency in policy implementation and institutional design. Therefore, while the National Information Technology Committee (NITC) was formed in 1992, chaired by the Prime Minister and composed of ministers, permanent secretaries as well as senior public- and private-sector leaders, its proposals were focused on utilising information technologies for social and economic development and coordinating relevant IT-related development activities (United Nations 2005, 8), thus leaving the Internet out of government control. The IT policy framework IT2010, succeeding IT2000, continued such focus by emphasising the utilisation of information technologies that "would lead to sustainable development of a knowledge-based economy and society" (Winley et al. 2007, 2).

But this is not to say that the Internet industry was entirely free during this period. In fact, while the general atmosphere during the 1990s embodied positive discourse and transition towards a democratic regime, extensive reforms of the bureaucratic system, patronage relations, and the powerful executive branch had to wait longer to harvest its transformative effects. Furthermore, the strong ties between government and businesses established in early decades have not seen notable change. Therefore, the almost exclusive regulator of Internet industry in the 1990s, at least before the ratification of the 1997 Constitution, was the state enterprise Communications Authority of Thailand (CAT) and the overall telecommunication industry was in the hands of two state-owned companies.[30]

The monopoly of CAT over the Internet system was evident in its regulation of Internet Service Providers (ISPs): it stipulated that all ISPs must be a joint venture with CAT, with the CAT holding 35% of the total equity for free; ISPs had to purchase leased circuits to the Internet only through or from CAT; CAT reserved the right to veto the decisions made by an ISP's board of directors; the ownership of all equipment for networking would be transferred from ISPs to CAT after the ISP is created (Sirin et al. 1999, 27). These provisions ensured CAT's monopoly in the Thai Internet system. The major negative effect of this monopoly exists much less in the political sphere than in commercial sphere. Since CAT represented both an operator and a regulator, the real market mechanism in the Internet industry had not been established and the development of the Internet in Thailand was, to some extent, retarded due to relatively high costs and lack of competition.

Political consequences of early interaction

The socio-political context of Thailand during the 1990s highlighted a trend of liberalisation and democratisation, which provided uncensored and apolitical surroundings for Internet development. However, some features of the Thai political system also produced obstacles to this development, such as the bureaucratic system and the state-monopolised telecommunication industry. Of course, early usage of the Internet posed little political challenge to Thai authorities. Before the commercialisation of Internet in 1995, the Thai government reserved Internet facilities for state educational institutions and governmental agencies. As a result, in the early years, the major users of Internet communications existed either within university campuses, or inside government buildings. Although Pirongrong Ramasoota Rananand (2003, 299–300) noted that a networked news group "soc.cul.thai" was useful in information sharing and communication during the 1992 political crisis, given the small size of the user group at that time (around 200 in 1992), its political influence should not be overstated.

The first phase of interaction between the Thai political regime and Internet system, on the whole, did not create much tension or disharmony. However, its impact would soon grow stronger. With limited state control, the commercialisation of the Internet was facilitated after 1996. This brought enormous profits and opportunities to several private enterprises, including Thaksin's Shin Corporation. Civil society groups, as well as the opposition political force, could now exploit the potential of the Internet in a more contentious way. The discontent over CAT's monopoly, meanwhile, gave rise to further institutional changes, including the establishment of the Ministry of Information and Communication Technology, which may have provided a new dynamic for controlling the network.

Internet Development under the Opportunist (Populist) Rule

While the political power and economic resources, as well as the state apparatus in Thailand, have been historically dominated by shifting alliances of a conservative pact among bureaucrats, the military, and, increasingly since the 1950s, the palace, the country has witnessed a move towards "a form of parliamentary rule and greater capitalist control" (Connors 2008, 480). This trend reached its zenith when Thai Rak Thai won a landslide victory in the 2001 general election and Thaksin Shinawatra was sworn in as Prime Minister. As a businessman who made his fortune mainly through the telecommunications industry, Thaksin inevitably had veiled interests in regulating telecommunications, including the Internet, in a way that emphasised the commercial profits of the digital space. Before analysing Thaksin's influence, we will first examine the 1997 Constitution that was the direct catalyst for Thaksin's rise.

"People's Constitution" and the rise of a populist government

Resulting from public deliberation over political reform in the early 1990s, the 1997 Constitution was expected to bring fully democratised politics to Thailand. The fact that the constitution drafting process was led mostly by prominent academics, such as Bowonsak Uwanno of Chulalongkorn University, and that public meetings and hearings on the constitution draft were conducted around the country, meant this expectation was met to some extent. With its goals for weakening the patron–client relationship in rural areas, increasing accountability of government officials and elected politicians, strengthening the executive branch as well as political parties, the labelled "People's Constitution" brought some significant changes to the Thai political system (Table 4-1).

Table 4-1: Constitutional reforms

	1978/1991 Constitutions	1997 Constitution
House of Representatives	*Multi-seat constituencies (1-3 seats) *Bloc vote	*Mixed-member system *400 single-seat constituencies *100 national party list seats
Senate	*Appointed	*Elected using SNTV, nonpartisan
Party switching	*Allowed	*90-day membership requirement
Party restrictions	*Full team *25-50% of constituencies	*5% threshold for list tier
Superintendent institutions	*None	*Several
Decentralisation	*Limited	*Mandated

Source: Allen Hicken 2006, 384

In the electoral system, the House of Representatives was elected with a mixed-member voting system comprising of 400 seats from single-seat constituencies and 100 seats from nation-wide party lists. It replaced the multi-seat constituency system with each constituency containing one to three seats. Under the new voting system, every voter had two separate votes, one for an individual single-seat constituency and one for a preferred political party. Meanwhile, even greater change occurred in the Senate formation process. Historically, senators in Thailand were selected and appointed by the Prime Minister and thus included mostly bureaucrats, military generals, and businessmen affiliated with the ruling party. However, the new constitution prescribed that all senators should be elected by popular votes in provincial constituencies and that they were prohibited from belonging to political parties or campaigning for votes. Furthermore, all candidates for parliament were required to obtain a bachelor's degree or equivalent (Hicken 2006). Together with many other policies, such as the creation of several autonomous institutions including the Electoral Commission and the Constitutional Court, these political reforms were intended to strengthen political parties' identities and increase the power of the Prime Minister.

An important consequence of these reforms was the rise of Thai Rak Thai, a cohesive party with an appealing populist campaign, and Thaksin, a CEO-type premier who was believed to be capable of pulling the Thai economy out of the 1997 financial catastrophe. Concerning the linkage between constitutional reform and the success of Thaksin, Allen Hicken (2006, 397) argued that "the new institutional environment, with its increased incentives and rewards for party-centered campaigns and programmatic appeals" should be considered as the primary factor behind Thaksin's rise. How, then, did this political change, from previously conservative-dominated politics to a CEO-style populist ruler, affect the broad area of the telecommunication industry? This is the question to which we now turn.

The "Thaksinization" of Thai telecommunications

As mentioned earlier, the main portion of Thaksin's wealth stemmed from the success of the telecommunication industry. Shinawatra Corporation, or Shin Corp, was the product of Thaksin's business prowess and one of the big four telecom companies in Thailand — the other three were Telecom Asia (TA), Thai Telephone and Telecommunication (TT&T), and United Communication (UCOM), all of which relied heavily on loose political alliances and concessions from the government. While the other three ended up with enormous debts as a result of the economic crisis in 1997, Shin Corp managed to narrowly escape the crisis' worst impacts. Crucially, this economic disaster greatly altered the structure of competition among the big four telecoms, and consequentially "all the rules were reconfigured and other telecommunications groups were eventually forced to enter into an alliance with Shin Corp" (McCargo and

Pathmanand 2005, 36). Furthermore, Thaksin transferred this economic victory into a political opportunity by establishing the Thai Rak Thai (TRT) party one year after the outbreak of the 1997 Asian financial tsunami. According to Duncan McCargo and Ukrist Pathmanand (2005, 36), the major motives behind the foundation of TRT, were “firstly to protect his business and secondly to help fellow domestic telecommunications groups and other large-scale businesses”. It indicates that Thaksin participated in Thai politics principally for commercial interests, which may result in different policy stances from that of either the conservative pact or previously prevailing liberal regime framers.

Even before assuming the post of Prime Minister, Thaksin began to expand Shin Corp in a dramatic way, using TRT as an important platform to make extensive allies. In 2000, Shin Corp bought 39% of the stock in iTV, an independent television station (while all other TV stations in Thailand were under government control), and further increased its shares to 77.5% in 2001. During this period, Shin Satellite also launched its first Thai broadband Internet portal site and Shin Corp established a terminal for its new satellite iPSTAR covering major countries in the Asia-Pacific region. Meanwhile, AIS[31] purchased an over 90% share in Digital Phone Company which made the Shin Corp the first company in Thailand to manage two mobile phone networks (McCargo and Pathmanand 2005, 44–45). These strategic moves reflected that Shin Corp’s expansion was not to diversify its business, but instead to merge all kinds of telecommunications, including print media, Internet, television, radio, and so forth, into a gigantic conglomerate.

However, the convergence of Thai telecommunication meant anything but the liberalisation of the industry and the protection of civil liberties. Since the 1997 Constitution greatly strengthened the power of premiership, and the political reforms ensured the gradual transfer of telecommunication administration from TOT and CAT to a newly created entity, the National Telecommunications Commission, Thaksin, after taking the office of Prime Minister, was able to have a tight grip of the telecommunication industry. In fact, the acquisition of iTV enabled Thaksin to dismiss the most critical and outspoken reporters in that television station ahead of general elections.

After Thaksin gained political power, a series of coercive actions against the freedom of the press was seen and reported. The first type of these actions was the termination or restriction of critical programmes on state-owned media. As Barnes (2003) noted, political debate was replaced by game shows or other entertainment programmes on the government controlled channels while Thaksin called for “more positive news”.

Second, law suits were filed and various investigations undertaken against many media outlets which remained unfriendly toward the Thaksin administration. For instance, the Thai-language paper *Naew Na* faced nine libel lawsuits because of its criticism of the government. Also, after the newspaper owner refused to sack one of his critical journalists, several firms close to the government cancelled advertisements in the paper (Reporters Without Borders 2003). In addition, Thaksin and his allies also interfered with supposedly independent agencies, such as the Election Committee and the Constitutional Court, thus leaving the media unprotected. In summarising Thaksin's impact on telecommunication, Jonathan Woodier (2008, 205) pointed out that "from his early days in power, Thaksin had embarked on a communication strategy that succeeded in making Thailand slip more than 50 places toward the bottom half of the world rankings on media freedom". Therefore, the "Thaksinization", a term coined by McCargo and Pathmanand (2005), of Thai telecommunications was characterised by commercial convergence and political centralisation.

Online challengers and selective control methods

The relatively harsh stance towards the media by Thaksin's government inevitably spilled over into cyberspace, which had already shown its political potential by that time. Some of the famous Thai print media, such as the English newspapers *Bangkok Post* and *The Nation*, started their online experiment as early as 1995. Various forms of online forums, such as the popular www.pantip.com, and later on weblogs, enabled users to express discontent and antagonism that might directly target the government. On some occasions, this might target the political system of Thailand, and even the highest symbol of that system, the king. Thailand is among the few remaining countries in the world to prosecute crimes of lèse-majesté, where individuals can be sentenced to three to fifteen years in prison for insulting, defaming, or threatening the Thai royal family in any public arena, which naturally encompasses the Internet. Moreover, the employment of the Internet by some separatist groups in Thailand posed another challenge. For example, the Pattani United Liberation Organisation (PULO), one of the most active separatist movements calling for a free and independent region in Thailand's Muslim south, has set up a website (www.pulo.org) to disseminate its information and mobilise Muslim dissidents.[32] These political threats, together with the ubiquitous problems of online pornography and gambling, constituted the major concerns of government regulation during this period.

According to a report released by Privacy International (2003a), the Thai National Information Technology Committee (NITC), as a subordinate body of the Ministry of Information and Communications Technology (MICT) established under the 1997 Constitution, announced, in July 2001, its intention to crack down on "inappropriate" content of websites. It proclaimed that it intended to implement new measures that required ISPs "to keep subscriber's log files and caller ID for at least three months, to include a customer responsibility clause in their terms of service, and to react immediately and block access when informed of inappropriate content on web sites" (Privacy International 2003a). While the implementation of first two tasks remained unclear, the government indeed deployed an indirect strategy to wipe out the Internet content that it deemed to be illegal or harmful.

During the Thaksin administration, at least three different organisations were involved in blocking Internet content: the Royal Thai Police, the Ministry of ICT and the Communications Authority of Thailand. Firstly, the Royal Thai Police was tasked with analysing websites, establishing an email hotline, and monitoring all Internet cafés. With regard to the second task, in 2002, the police department designed a form on which netizens could report websites they considered obscene, defamatory or unlawful. In its first year, 7,700 websites were reported, among which almost 70% were for pornography, 5% for child pornography and, significantly, 7% for posing a threat to national security (Privacy International 2003b). An interview with one of the police officers in charge of regulating Internet content has provided the criteria by which the police would take actions accordingly. The three most important items filtered by the Thai police were named as "lèse-majesté", "narcotics" and "separatism and guerrilla warfare" (Pirongrong 2003, 299).

Secondly, the Ministry of ICT (MICT) circulated its daily blocklist, a list containing the URLs of inappropriate webpages, to Thailand's 54 commercial ISPs to enforce. In a blocklist released in 2004, there were reportedly 1,247 blocked URLs, most of which were pornographic sites, along with several sites devoted to online gaming and one site belonging to the separatist movement (ONI 2007). However, that list was the last one MICT has made public, and according to an analysis conducted by the Freedom Against Censorship Thailand (FACT 2006), the websites being blocked not only included those related to separatists movements, but also those with content about the Thai monarchy, and interestingly, some sites linked to anonymous proxy servers that could be used to circumvent the censorship. This demonstrated a trend that broadened the scope and increased the intensity of Internet censorship under Thaksin's rule. This trend coincides with his reported grandiose plans in 2005 of blocking "800,000" websites (*Agence France-Presse* 2005).

The third organisation involved in blocking internet content is the Communications Authority of Thailand (CAT), which sporadically ordered ISPs to block groups of websites but on a scale that was much lower than the Royal Thai Police and the MICT.

The blocking process was ostensibly indirect: the responsible departments compiled the list of websites to block and passed it on to privatised ISPs who had the actual authority to implementing the blocking. However, MICT made it clear that the ISPs' licenses could be at risk if the block was not properly implemented (Privacy International 2003b). Besides "indirect" control, a series of information technology laws, as part of the reform embedded in the 1997 Constitution, was enacted or drafted before and during the Thaksin government, including the Electronic Transactions Act, E-Commerce Act, Privacy Data Protection Law, Universal Access Law, and, most importantly, the Computer Crime Act which did not come into force until 2007. These laws helped to build the legal framework for more effective and legitimate Internet control in Thailand.

Nonetheless, the overall control of the Internet in Thaksin's era should not be overstated. Compared to his strong interference in traditional media, Thaksin did not manage to tame the online world to the same extent. The blocking of websites primarily focused on immoral content such as pornography, or gambling, while arrests in the name of unlawful online behaviour were rare. Several reasons underlie such selective control. Firstly, Thaksin and his Thai Rak Thai party won landslide victories in both the 2001 and 2005 general elections, which indicated his popularity with not only the rural and urban poor, but also the urban middle class as well (albeit to a less extent after 2005). His major opponents mainly stemmed from traditional political elites and were occasionally business competitors, who had considerable political power that initially stemmed not from cyberspace, but the "real world". This explains why Internet control was tightened after 2005, since more middle class citizens turned against him and thus made the Internet a more dangerous tool against his government.

Secondly, given that Shin Corp had tremendous commercial interests in information technologies and the online industry, the governmental policies on Internet regulation, which were supposed to serve Thaksin's business profits, should be moderate in order to maintain an attractive and lucrative Internet system. Evidence could be found in the fact that when the draft of the Computer Crime Act was submitted in 2002, which would grant state officers widespread powers of search and seizure, Thaksin expressed concern that it may infringe on human rights and, consequently, the draft was postponed (Privacy International 2003a).

Thirdly, Thailand missed the chance to develop a sophisticated censorship method, which required high technological capacity and investment, during the relatively liberalised period of the 1990s when Internet usage started to spread. Therefore, the Thaksin government, especially in his first term, did not have adequate power to deploy a system as effective as China's "Great Firewall". However, it is significant that several governmental organisations, including MICT, were set up to regulate the Internet, and a series of relevant laws were either promulgated or under review at that time. All these provided new opportunities for the government to control the Internet in a more effective and extensive way, which was proved feasible when massive political crisis broke out in the last months of Thaksin's rule.

Transgressiveness, Online Civil Society and Thailand's Internet Control

"This was not a classic antigovernment protest, but a civil war between competing elements of the Thai state". — Duncan McCargo (2009, 13)

Following the 2005 general election in which TRT won an even larger margin, a series of incidents marked the long-lasting political crisis in Thailand. Four elections, together with a military coup, the first in more than a decade, reflected the unstable nature of the Thai political regime, which was also polarised between rural and urban poor (as red shirts) and urban elites (as yellow shirts).[33] This section starts with a brief discussion on the context of the political crisis, and analyses how the high level of transgressiveness and the weak capacity of online civil society resulted in draconian Internet control policies.

The 2006 coup and protracted political turbulence

Since Thaksin Shinawatra was ousted in the 2006 military coup, a large number of studies have provided detailed narratives on the post-coup political crisis (see, for example, Connors 2008; Kengkij and Hewison 2009; Kitti 2009; Pasuk and Baker 2009; Ferrara 2010; Kitti 2010; Dalpino 2011). It is thus unnecessary to recount the whole story here. However, Jim Glassman's (2011) insightful analysis, which outlines two layers of conflict, could be a useful and concise way in summarising the

Thai political crisis. According to him, the first layer of conflict lies in "an inter-elite struggle between groups characterized as royalists and groups characterized as supporters of deposed Prime Minister Thaksin Shinawatra" (Glassman 2011, 37). The Thaksin premiership from 2001 to 2006 produced some aggressive policies against the traditional political establishment, such as reshuffling and promoting Thaksin's favourites in the military and the police, reorganising bureaucracy, redistributing governmental business patronage and concessions, and restructuring social welfare to maintain his electoral popularity (McCargo 2005; McCargo and Ukrist 2005; Pasuk and Baker 2009). These policies rewrote the traditional social contract and greatly disturbed the interests of conservative elite groups. The term "network monarchy" (McCargo 2005) is used to denote the palace–military–bureaucracy alliance. Since the 1997 Constitution largely contributed to the rise of Thaksin and TRT (Hicken 2006), the most effective way for the traditional elites to fight back was, thus, through unconstitutional means. In this sense, the military coup in 2006, as Kevin Hewison (2010, 128) pointed out, "was about opposing the changes Thaksin wanted and preserving the status quo that involved the dominance of the old oligarchy".

Political conflict between the two camps escalated after the coup. The military-appointed interim government hastily promulgated a new constitution in 2007 in order to block Thaksin's (and his proxies') access to power (Dressel 2009). When these reforms failed to prevent the People's Power Party (the successor of dissolved Thai Rak Thai) from winning the ballot, judicial institutions, including the Supreme Court and Constitutional Court, were politicised (Dressel 2010) to firstly disqualify the premiership of Samak Sundaravej and later disband the People's Power Party. The succeeding government, led by royalist-backed Democrat Abhisit Vejjajiva, also lacked legitimacy since it was not popularly elected and was under criticism of being a puppet government of the elite. Electoral democracy seems to have returned after the 2011 election in which the pro-Thaksin Pheu Thai Party won a landslide victory, but the conflict between royalists and pro-Thaksin forces still appears to be protracted.

The second layer of conflict occurs at the societal level. Political change during and after the Thaksin era not only fuelled the struggle between royalists and populists, but also stirred up social confrontations between thoese siding with the respective camps. On one side, the People's Alliance for Democracy (PAD), under the leadership of media mogul Sondhi Limthongkul and former Major-General Chamlong Srimuang, who played an important role in the 1992 uprising, accused

Thaksin of an abuse of power, insulting the royal family, infringing human rights, and corruption and nepotism that eroded governmental accountability (Kasian Tejapira 2006). While supporters of the PAD, dressed in yellow shirts,[34] are commonly depicted as those mainly from the urban middle-class and civil servants, some argue that the actual composition is far more complex (McCargo 2009). However, these PAD supporters strongly attach their identities to the subject of the monarchy and view Thaksin as a traitor to the constitutional monarchy. According to an ABAC poll[35] conducted in 2008, around 60% of PAD supporters believed that it was more important to protect the monarchy than their own lives.[36]

When the pro-Thaksin government re-organised its power in 2008, the yellow shirt protesters subsequently organised massive rallies in a manner more devastating than the 2005–2006 ones: Prime Minister Samak Sundaravej suffered from government paralysis and even had no access to his own office as the PAD laid siege to Government House, the Prime Minister's Office compound, National Broadcasting Television, as well as the airports in Phuket and Krabi. His successor, Somchai Wongsawat, found himself in a similar embarrassing situation when protesters surrounded the parliament and took over the major international airports (Suvanaphumi and Don Muang) in Bangkok (Kitti 2009, 179–181).

On the other side of the social confrontations are the pro-Thaksin social forces, especially the United Front of Democracy against Dictatorship (UDD), the red shirts. As a recent study shows (Naruemon and McCargo 2011), the red shirts are composed mainly of "urbanized villagers" who straddle both rural and urban areas and make a living by shifting among farming, small businesses, and labouring works. Most of them are beneficiaries of the Thaksin-government's economic, social and political policies, and thus have a strong feeling of injustice and illegitimacy towards the military coup and traditional elites that overthrew Thaksin's rule. As with the PAD, the UDD leadership covers people from various backgrounds, such as professional politicians, academics, and social activists (Naruemon and McCargo 2011, 995–997). The Red Shirt movement attracted worldwide media concern when protesters stormed into a hotel in Pattaya and forced a series of ASEAN scheduled summits to be aborted in 2009 (Kitti 2010). Since then, the Democratic Party-led government faced continuous opposition from the UDD demonstrations. The movement reached a climax in 2010, when a court ruling resulted in the seizure of Thaksin's assets, which ended up with bloody clashes between red shirt protesters and security forces, causing scores of civilian deaths and hundreds of injuries (Chambers 2010).

The alternate, and sometimes simultaneous, political uprisings of the PAD and the UDD respectively have made Thai politics turbulent, severely dividing Thai society. As Duncan McCargo observed (2009, 18), "families, marriages, and lifelong friendships were undermined by the ongoing conflict; some people divided their social circles into two distinct groups, carefully avoiding situations in which the different viewpoints might mix and clash". Efforts to reconcile the conflicts at both layers turned out to be difficult. Royalists refuse to accept "the verdict of the electoral majority" (Thompson 2008, 387) that disturbs the established political structure. The trinity of "nation, religion, and the king" and the notion of "democracy with the king as head of state" are held by traditionalists to be indispensable to the Thai state (Ferrara 2011). However, for opposition forces, Thaksin was mandated democratically by the Thai electorate to rule the country and was overthrown unconstitutionally. As some believe that the monarchy has acquiesced, and even orchestrated, the military coup and the ousting of Thaksin, the palace, together with the monarchical system, has suffered from increasing criticism. As a result, according to Michael Connors (2009, 369–370), "competing modes of legitimation, forms of leadership and the exercise of power have not settled into any enduring pattern of dominance" in the Thai politics.

Due to the enduring political crisis, political rights in Thailand have greatly deteriorated. While the military coup temporarily suspended electoral politics and dissolved a number of political institutions, the politicisation of the judiciary further undermined the Thai democracy. As post-coup Thai politics embodies an uncompromising dilemma in which non-elected political actors — the alliance of palace, military and bureaucracy — frequently use veto power to oppose the rule of a popularly elected government, the Thai political regime could be regarded as a "tutelary democracy" (Chambers 2010) which is transitional and unstable. However, it is noticeable that electoral politics has seemingly returned to normalcy with a generally free and fair election in 2011.

Meanwhile, the decline in civil liberties was only slight.[37] Although the 2007 Constitution, passed by the military appointed National Assembly, has further dispersed executive and parliamentary power to unelected agencies, such as the judicial branch, the section on civil liberties is basically unchanged from the 1997 Constitution. As Bjorn Dressel (2009, 312) comments on the new constitution, "public participation is encouraged by lowering the threshold for a public petition to table legislation to 10,000 signatures and for starting impeachment procedures against officeholders to 20,000 signatures (both were previously 50,000)".

Such features in the Thai political system, together with political cleavages in Thai society, have opened up enormous political opportunities for transgressive political actions. In order to overwhelm their rivals, both sides in the political conflict resort to extra-constitutional means and methods, thus paralysing the electoral procedure. The Internet and related information technologies thus become a significant platform to sustain and express their transgressive behaviours. The next section measures the level of transgressiveness of online politics and the capacity of Thai online civil society.

Transgression in Thai cyberspace

Over the past decade, Thailand has experienced a rapid development of the Internet. As Table 4-2 demonstrates, while Internet users accounted for merely 12.6% of the overall population in 2007, three years later, the penetration rate had promptly climbed to 26.3%. The offline political crisis has thus been well exhibited in this flourishing new space. This section begins by a brief discussion of the role the Internet plays in the Thai political conflict, and then analyses the characteristics of the transgressiveness and Thai online civil society.

Table 4-2: Internet development in Thailand

Year	Netizens	Population	Penetration
2000	2,300,000	61,528,000	3.7%
2007	8,465,800	67,249,456	12.6%
2009	16,100,000	65,998,436	24.4%
2010	17,486,400	66,404,688	26.3%

Source: Internet World Stats, available at http://www.internetworldstats.com/asia/th.htm

(1) Cyberspace in the political conflict

One of the central features of Thailand's political imbroglio from 2005 to present is "worsening schisms" (Ganesan 2010), best represented by the two antagonistic social movements — the red shirts versus the yellow shirts. The Internet and other information technologies have empowered these movements by changing the mobilising structures.[38]

The red shirts are organised under the United Front for Democracy against Dictatorship (UDD). Despite self-imposed exile, Thaksin Shinawatra, the de facto master of the movement, was able to communicate with his supporters through the Internet. Establishing his "Thaksinlive" account in 2009, Thaksin has used Twitter (a microblog website) to "attack his political rivals, mobilise his supporters, console and encourage his three children, defend himself against any allegations and publicise his charitable activities" (*Bangkok Post* 2010). As of 2011, this account has gained nearly 180,000 followers. His official website, www.thaksinlive.com, carries his biography and uploads his statements, past speeches and videos. He also holds a video and radio broadcast account at the Ustream website in which his images and speeches can be projected to supporters during political rallies and meetings. On this score, Jon Russell (2010b) dubs Thaksin as the "master of social media", which "gives Thaksin a free platform to air his opinions and views whilst allowing him to maintain contact with those who can longer see him in person".

Moreover, apart from Thaksin, other leaders in UDD also understand the significance of Internet technology. The "Ratchaprasong News" Facebook group that disseminates news and information about the Red Shirt movement was created in early 2010. It has garnered more than 4,300 followers and become the third largest Facebook group in Thailand (Sean Boonpracong, interview by author, March 25, 2011). In fact, as early as 2007, a pro-Thaksin website (www.hi-thaksin.net) appealed to voters to vote for the People's Power Party for the sake of Thaksin (*Bangkok Post* 2007).

On the other hand, the People's Alliance for Democracy (PAD), which organises the yellow shirts, uses the Internet to attack Thaksin and his supporters. Since 2005, Sondhi Limthongkul, the founder of PAD, has been using his media outlets and websites to criticise Thaksin. When the red shirts were branded as anti-monarchist in the 2010 demonstrations, a "Social Sanction" group was established on Facebook, encouraging social punishment against UDD supporters. It soon gained thousands of followers and began to hunt down red shirt members. Personal information of targeted people would be published online, while some people showing support for UDD were even sued by social sanction members or expelled from public institutions (Pinpaka Ngamsom, interview by author, March 28, 2011).

In this sense, the Internet has offered both social movements a new channel to connect their political leaders with their mobilised supporters, as well as a new platform to express and disseminate their political claims. It is true that other communication outlets — such as television (for example, the ASTV for the yellow shirts and the PTV for the red shirts) and community radio (perhaps more important for organising movements in the rural areas) — have also played an important role in mobilising and sustaining these movements. This study does not intend to make a comparison of the exact impacts of each communication mode. In fact, the different media spaces are often inter-connected as some online information is re-broadcast in radio or TV programmes and vice versa. But the Internet space is arguably more interactive in nature and rich in the volume of information, thus providing a more effective way of social mobilisation. For instance, using the Skype software, Thaksin Shinawatra was able to deliver a speech, which assured compensation for the victims in the 2010 bloodshed, to a crowd of around 50,000 red shirt supporters during their rally at Bonanza Khao Yai in Nakhon Ratchasima in February 2012 (*Bangkok Post* 2012). Such an instant connection between the exiled political leader and his supporters would be impossible without the help of new information technologies.

(2) High transgressiveness of online politics

The political usage of the Internet, especially the usage by the pro-Thaksin camp, has created a high level of transgressiveness, thus posing an intense political threat to the traditional political establishment. In terms of scale, the Internet facilitated massive social movements that persisted for much of the post-Thaksin period. These movements easily mobilised tens of thousands of supporters who, as discussed above, occupied government agencies, blockaded roads, airports, and even an international summit, and confronted each other in a prolonged (and sometimes violent) manner. The most severe of these occurred in March–May 2010, when a massive red shirt protest (about a hundred thousand people participated in it, as estimated) turned violent and resulted in enormous casualties (more than 90 people died in this event) as well as a government decision to declare a state of emergency (Dalpino 2011).

Moreover, a major proportion of participants in these movements, especially the red shirts, are constituted by new political groups. As a recent study suggests, although most of them are not really poor farmers as the Thai public tends to view them, the red shirt supporters represent a new class of people who travel between rural and sub-urban areas, engaged in both farming and non-farming activities, and participate actively in the market-economy (Naruemon and McCargo 2011). They benefit economically from Thaksin-era policies, such as the small and medium enterprise fund, and politically from the decentralisation process initiated in the 1990s. On the later score, Naruemon and McCargo (2011, 1000–1) find that many red shirt protesters serve locally as "community organisers" and "vote canvassers" who connect upper level political domains (at provincial or national levels) with local constituencies.

When their supreme patron, Thaksin Shinawatra, was toppled, the Internet space enabled them to express their political frustrations. With the help of new information technologies, they could circumvent the media monopoly imposed by traditional elites and, as Prapart Pintoptang (2010) argues, become active citizens who advance their own political initiatives. As one political activist put it, "in the past, only a small group was exposed to different ideas [...] but now the Internet has multiplied the effects of information dissemination, with more radical political ideas spreading ..."; therefore, "political communities have been expanded and reshaped" (Arthit Suriyawongkul, interview by author, March 27, 2011).

Meanwhile, by using Internet technologies, these political actors are engaged in new strategies. As discussed above, the long-distance communication and mobilisation between exiled political leaders (Thaksin and several other deposed politicians) and domestic supporters would be barely imaginable without the effective use of Internet technologies. In addition, many protestors use various Internet platforms, such as social networking sites, online forums, and weblogs, to mount criticism against the government, most of the time anonymously. The interactive nature of Web 2.0 applications appears so challenging that the government, ironically under Thaksin's younger sister Yingluck Shinawatra, stipulated in November 2011 that any Facebook users — even foreigners abroad — who simply "share" or "like" online content deemed to be insulting the Thai monarchy could be prosecuted (*The Washington Times* 2011).

With regard to content, online political contentiousness in Thailand targets the fundamental dimensions — especially the institution of monarchy — that sustain the socio-political order. Online transgressiveness is thus intensified by these system-level political claims. Even after the 1932 revolution that brought the absolute monarchy to an end, Thailand's traditional political structure embodies a hierarchical system with the palace sitting at the apex of political power (McCargo 2005; Handley 2006; Chambers 2010; Ferrara 2011). "Networked" around the palace are a range of conservative elites and political institutions that have collectively "impinged upon democratic development" (Chambers

2010, 838). Fig.4-2 provides a schematic overview of the traditional power structure.

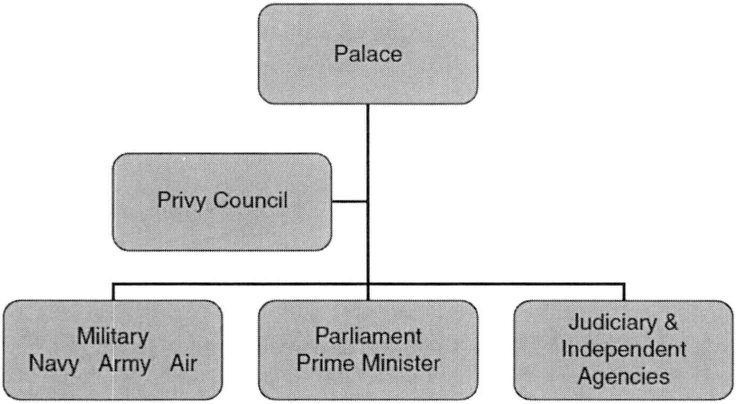

Fig. 4-2: Model of Thai political structure
Source: Chambers 2010

However, due to its alleged involvement in the 2006 military coup (see Giles Ji Ungpakorn 2007; Thongchai 2008), the Thai monarchy has suffered from increasing public criticism, especially from pro-Thaksin forces. Statistics showed that in 2010 there were 36 prosecutions in lèse-majesté cases (cases that involve an anti-monarchy offence), rising sharply from only 18 cases in 2005 and none in 2000 (*The Washington Post* 2011). It should be noted that the majority of red shirt protesters seldom, at least not overtly, label themselves as anti-monarchists. However, it is also true that many prominent leaders in the movement — such as Jakrapob Penkair, Kokaew Phikulthong, and Surachai Sae Dan — have been accused and charged of making anti-monarchy comments publicly (Pavin 2011). In addition, as a loosely connected network, the Red Shirt movement also contains radical elements (such as the Red Siam and the Seh Daeng faction) that make strong political claims wishing to transform the overall political system (Naruemon and McCargo 2011).

When such fundamental criticism finds no outlet in the traditional media, it flocks to cyberspace. In fact, many of the high-profile lèse-majesté cases are related to Internet usage. For instance, the blogger, Nat Sattayapornpisut, who ran a blog entitled *Stop Lese Majeste* (http://www.stoplesemajeste.blogspot.com/?zx=b9d258483696f2f4) was charged under the CCA as the blog contained many articles, video clips, and even surveys that were offensive to the royal family. Chiranuch

Premchaiporn, the webmaster of *Prachathai* news websites, faced 20 years in jail since she failed to promptly delete the anti-monarchy comments that appeared in the discussion board by anonymous netizens. And a professor in Chulalongkorn University, Giles Ji Ungpakorn, had to flee to the United Kingdom after publishing his book that accused the palace of orchestrating the 2006 coup (Pavin 2011, 1029–30). The book was banned from publication in Thailand, but copies were freely accessible on the Internet, as were his other critical writings.

It is difficult to accurately calculate the total amount of anti-monarchy content (in terms of either the number of posts/articles or that of offensive users) in cyberspace. But some official figures indicate a skyrocketing rise. In the second half of 2008, six court orders were issued to block a total of 1,928 URLs that contained lèse-majesté information, while these numbers rose sharply to seventeen court orders and 27,312 URLs in the first half of 2010 (iLaw 2010). Under the traditional political system, the monarchy is completely inviolable and thus any criticism of the monarchy is, indeed, to fundamentally overturn the political order.

In addition, some activists have made system-level political claims in an even more explicit way, perhaps best reflected in the Red Siam Manifesto which was authored by Giles Ji Ungpakorn and circulated on the Internet.[39] Among its other claims, such as those regarding welfare and equality, the Manifesto noticeably states that:

> The enemies of democracy […] are united around an absurd and un-scientific ideology: the ideology of the Monarchy. This ideology seeks to make Thais into grovelling serfs […] So long as we crawl before the ideology of the Monarchy, we shall remain no better than animals […] the best way to solve this problem is to build a Republic where all public positions are elected and accountable.

In this way, the political contentiousness on Thai cyberspace embodies a struggle between two different notions of democracy, each with its own political structure. The traditional establishment enshrines a "democracy with the king as head of state" (Baker and Pasuk 2009), while the transgressive political claims call for a democracy that emphasises civilian rights and people sovereignty (Nelson 2012). Efforts to develop the latter type of democracy are fundamentally incompatible with the traditional system. As Siriporn Nogsuan Sawasdee, a political scientist at the Chulalongkorn University, said in an interview, "If we want to pursue real democracy, there is no place for the higher institution to be involved" (*The Jakarta Post* 2010).

Based on our discussion above, the Internet has enabled Thai netizens to express otherwise "unsayable" political ideas and to organise otherwise less coordinated massive social movements. It, therefore, constitutes a high level of transgressiveness towards the traditional political system. On this score, political scientist Chaiwat Satha-Anand (interview by author, March 24, 2011) regards the Internet as "both constructive and destructive".

(3) Polarised online civil society

While transgressiveness remains high, the capacity of Thailand's online civil society is weakened by the polarisation of its online communities, which reduces the cost of Internet control. As our theoretical framework suggests, the capacity of online civil society is measured by four indicators: penetration, political linkage, critical media, and cohesiveness. As shown in the beginning of this section, the Internet in Thailand has experienced a rapid growth over the past decade. That said, the proportion of the Thai population that has Internet access is still moderate. The 27.4% Internet penetration rate recorded in 2011 only narrowly outnumbers that of the Asian average (26.2%).[40]

With regard to political linkage, Thailand's online political contentiousness also falls short of a level equivalent to that of Malaysia. On the one hand, the Internet-facilitated movements from both sides have close associations with offline political organisations. While the Red Shirt movement is tied to the pro-Thaksin parties, especially the Pheu Thai Party, the Yellow Shirt movement firstly gained support from the Democratic Party and, in 2009, created its own party organisation, the New Politics Party (or Karn Muang Mai, KMM).[41] Offline political leaders such as Thaksin and Abhisit, in addition, are enthusiastic Internet users who also communicate with their supporters in cyberspace.

However, the differing political stances of movement organisations and political parties, especially between the red shirts and the Pheu Thai Party, have, to some extent, undermined their linkage. While some radical elements in the Red Shirt movement express anti-monarchy views on the Internet as well as on the stages of massive rallies, the Pheu Thai Party, with Thaksin included, has tried to distance itself from an anti-monarchy image and rhetoric (Pavin 2011). To boost its legitimacy, moreover, it has to take an intransigent attitude against the anti-monarchy activities, most of which exist only in cyberspace. Therefore, once coming into power after the 2011 election, the Yingluck-led Pheu Thai government immediately expressed loyalty to the palace by promising to crackdown on anti-monarchy sentiments. Subsequently, a "war room" at police headquarters and a 22-member committee headed by deputy Prime Minister Chalerm Yubamrung was established to "scour and purge the web" for lèse-majesté content (Crispin 2011). In this sense, despite both being pro-Thaksin groups, the Pheu Thai Party and the grassroots Red Shirt movement do not share a common interest in protecting Internet freedom. This has undermined the collective power of online civil society to resist Internet control practices.

The fast growth of the Internet in Thailand has indeed given rise to a boom in the new media industry. The critical role of these online media in providing alternative information and facilitating public discussion can be seen in a number of cases. For example, the anti-Thaksin campaign, led by the media tycoon Sondhi Limthongkul, adopted a multimedia strategy with the online newspaper, Manager.co.th, being its flagship. Manager.co.th soon became an important online source for political news in Thailand (Isriya 2012). Nonetheless, the influence of online media on independent and critical information provision should not be overestimated. On this score, Pichai Chuensuksawadi, the chief editor of *Bangkok Post*, remarks that "despite the rapid and increasing growth of the Internet in Thailand over the past 10 years, news websites are ranked very low when compared to more popular websites" (*People's Daily* 2010). This negative view is substantiated by the fact that, unlike Malaysia where news websites (such as *Malaysiakini*) rank high in terms of pageviews, the most popular (local) websites in Thailand are portal or teen entertainment sites such as Sanook.com and Pantip.com.[42] News and information provided by these portal and forum sites, as well as political blogs and social media, often lack reliability and professionalism. According to the 2009 Sripatum Poll, Thai respondents prefer television (68%) and newspaper (13.6%) to the Internet (12.1%) as their major source of news.[43]

While online civil society appears to be moderate in terms of penetration, political linkage, and critical media, the fragmentation of online communities seriously undermines its capacity. Splits between opposite online groups are explicit and fundamental. While anti-monarchists find the Internet space useful in expressing their populist ideas, royalists regard the Internet as an accomplice in lèse-majesté offence. Some online groups and netizens, due to their deep-rooted reverence for the monarchy, become Internet hunters who search for "unlawful" content and behaviour. One typical example is the "Social Sanction" group on Facebook which encourages fellow netizens to identify anti-monarchy Internet-users, expose their personal information, and scold, threaten, and humiliate them in various ways (Poowin 2010). In a well-known case, a teenage girl was accused by "witch-hunters" of posting "problematic" remarks on her Facebook page. Her personal details were then widely publicised by the "Social Sanction" group, which finally resulted in the denial of her entry into a prestigious university (Pirongrong Ramasoota, interview by author, April 1, 2011).

Although some independent organisations, such as the Thai Netizen Network (TNN), are advocating for Internet freedom, their claims often refer to the abolishment of lèse-majesté provisions (Article 112). They thus become identical to the anti-monarchists of the Red Shirt movement. In fact, at a red shirts' conference in April 2011 that the author attended, held at the Law School of Thammasat University, many participants were from Internet-freedom advocacy groups such as the TNN and the Freedom against Censorship Thailand (FACT). As a result, Thailand's online communities are highly polarised between different political ideologies. As a political activist put it, "in Thailand, when you make a pronouncement in favour of some political attitude or belief, the other side feels you must be their enemy" (*Bangkok Post* 2010). The polarised status of online civil society has empowered the government to adopt repressive actions against Internet usage, as an element of the society per se is engaged in practicing Internet censorship, which will be further explained in the following section.

All in all, Thailand's Internet space has a high level of transgressiveness and a weak, polarised online civil society. The following part discusses how these factors lead to harsh Internet control policies almost unseen among the region's other competitive regimes.

Explaining Thailand's Internet control outcome

The severity of Internet control in Thailand has drawn international attention. Freedom House's (2011) report sorted the country into the "not free" category in terms of Internet freedom. This section first briefly reviews the Internet control practice, including its institutions and methods, in Thailand after the 2006 coup. The second part elaborates how such practice results from the factors discussed above.

(1) Institutions and approaches of Internet control

Perhaps the most important legislation of Internet control in the post-coup era is the Computer Crime Act (CCA). It was hastily promulgated in 2007 by the interim government of General Surayud Chulanont after several attempts to tighten the country's media space.[44] It became the first law considered by the military-appointed National Legislative Assembly (NLA) and the first law promulgated by the cabinet of Surayud within a short period for public scrutiny. The law brought great controversy in Thai society since it empowered the authorities to block online content and mete out prison terms over disputed online information, based on provisions (especially sections 14 and 15) that were ambiguous and thus subject to government interpretation. For instance, while Section 14 of the CCA listed a number of behaviours (all ambiguously defined) that were deemed offensive to the law, Section 15 further stipulated that "any service provider intentionally supporting or consenting to an offence under Section 14 within a computer system under their control shall be subject to the same penalty as that imposed upon a person committing an offence under Section 14".[45] This clause, in fact, compelled intermediary actors, such as ISPs and webmasters, to share the responsibility of Internet control with the government. Even officers in the relevant department of the MICT admitted that there were no clear criteria used when defining which "inappropriate" websites to block, in terms of political content (Araya Sawasdichai, interview by author, March 29, 2011). However, such ambiguity has largely enhanced the government's power to suppress public criticism, and this law has become the major mechanism to control the Internet, especially during massive political crises.

Meanwhile, other agencies have been set up to bolster the government's institutional power in controlling the Internet. In 2010, the Abhisit government launched a "cyber scout" project, to recruit and train volunteers to closely monitor websites that might infringe on national security and harm the royal institution. The project, jointly conducted by the ICT, Justice, and Education ministries, aimed to initially employ 200 "scouts" of ordinary netizens, including "students, teachers, government officials and the private sector, who have computers and Internet literacy" (*The Nation* 2010). Upon the announcement of this project, some observers drew historical parallels to the "Village Scouts" in the 1970s, established to battle communist threats (Farrelly 2010). In the same vein, as mentioned previously, the Pheu Thai government also created a "war room" at police headquarters and a 22-member committee headed by deputy Prime Minister Chalerm Yubamrung (Crispin 2011). The "war room", officially named the Office of Prevention and Suppression of Information Technology Crimes, had a much smaller team of around ten computer specialists, yet with specialised computer programmes to trawl online information (*The New York Times* 2011).

Once illegal online content is detected by these formal and informal agencies, it does most likely result in the blocking of the host website.

After the military coup, websites that were clearly opposed or presented a challenge to the military government were immediately clamped down upon, such as the anti-coup website, www.19sep.org, and the official site of the Thai Rak Thai Party (www.thairakthai.or.th) (*The Nation* 2006). Since 2007, however, the number of blocked websites has increased rapidly. With regard to the overall scale of online censorship, different sources of information have provided a rough yet reliable figure. Based on statistics obtained from the court, the report by the iLaw project (2010) suggested that nearly 75,000 URLs had been blocked in the three years after 2007. Meanwhile, the cyber inspector who led the "war room" team admitted that around 70,000 websites were banned within four years (*The New York Times* 2011). The climax of Internet blocking, however, came as the Red Shirt movement escalated in 2010. According to the Global Voices Advocacy (2010), during and after the draconian actions the Abhisit government took against red shirt demonstrators in 2010, a shocking number of 113,000 websites were blocked. This figure vastly outnumbers the accumulated amount recorded from judicial court orders during the same period. It indicates that many blocking practices were taken in an extra-judicial way as the result of the status of emergency enforced during the crisis.

Furthermore, in a number of cases, the government not only censored the sensitive content, but also harassed Internet users. During the 2010 political crisis, the Ministry of ICT announced a blacklist of 200 persons banned from posting on the Internet, including the former minister of the Prime Minister's Office and Thaksin's confidante Jakrapob Penkair, and Professor Giles Ji Ungpakorn from Chulalongkorn University (Pavin 2010). According to Reporters Without Borders (2010a), at that time, there were at least a dozen Internet users being prosecuted for lèse-majesté offences. The arrest list includes Jonathan Head, a BBC correspondent in Southeast Asia; Professor Giles Ji Ungpakorn; two prominent bloggers, Nat Sattayapornpisut and Praya Pichai; and *Prachathai* webmaster Chiranuch Premchaipoen. The actual number of "criminals" is probably much higher, since "other netizens have been briefly arrested or interrogated, but it is difficult to quantify their exact number, because many cases are not being publicized for fear of reprisals" (Reporters Without Borders 2010a). In one case, a 61-year-old man was sentenced to 20 years in prison due to four SMS messages he sent.[46]

Apart from blocking practices and the harassment of Internet users, the Thai government also demonstrates its power of Internet control at the infrastructural level. According to some participants in the Red Shirt movement, in 2010, several days before the military crackdown on protesters, the government, with cooperation from domestic service providers, totally cut off mobile and Wi-Fi signals in the Rajprasong area where hundreds of thousands of red shirt protesters were assembled. People had to travel by motorcycles to other unblocked places, with short video recordings, in order to disseminate live information about the Red Shirt movement (Arthit Suriyawongkul, interview). Although the specific procedure of such a blackout remains unclear, this move was designed to obstruct further mobilisation and disrupt communication within the movement.

The massive content blocking and strict law enforcement on the basis of lèse-majesté definitely affects how Internet users perceive the threats and costs of being critical online. Although the precise effects on users' psychological status defy measurement, the proliferation of prosecutions against prominent figures inevitably "intimidate other Internet users inclined to criticise the king and induce them to rely on self-censorship" (Reporters Without Borders 2010a). According to Professor Pirongrong Ramasoota (interview), the "chilling effects" of such repressive actions have prompted some major online forums to require real-life ID registration for every netizen. The popular forum, Pantip.com, even filters politically sensitive key words such as "king", "queen", or the "royal family". Furthermore, Internet control has, to some extent, weakened the role of the Internet in political communication. For instance, staff of the Prachatai website acknowledges that after the blocking of the original URL, the number of Prachatai visitors has decreased by 50%, despite the fact that they have changed the website address to circumvent the blocking (Pinpaka Ngamsom and Mutita Chuachang, interview).

To sum up, Thailand's Internet control practice involves draconian laws, vigilant governmental and citizen agencies, massive blocking activities, as well as some unconventional means such as the "switch off" of Internet communications. These methods have made Thailand the most repressive country in cyberspace among Southeast Asian (semi-) democracies.

(2) Why do transgressiveness and civil society capacity matter?

Repressive Internet controls are a direct response to the transgressive use of the Internet. Evidence can be found both statistically and rhetorically. As the iLaw report (2010) indicates, out of the 75,000 URLs blocked during 2007–10, 57,330 (76.4%) were due to lèse-majesté content. By contrast, far fewer URLs were blocked for other reasons: 16,740 (22.3%) related to pornographic materials, 357 (0.48%) to abortion, and 246 (0.33%) to gambling. The account given by Surachai Nilsang, the head technician of the "war room", pointed to an even higher ratio: he claimed that about 60,000 of the 70,000 banned websites resulted from insults to the monarchy (*The New York Times* 2011). Moreover, the frequency and scale of government Internet control practices increased simultaneously with the escalation of Thailand's political crisis. Table 4-3 shows that while the court ordered a blocking of less than 2,000 webpage addresses (URLs) containing lèse-majesté content in the second half of 2008, the number increased rapidly to more than 5,000 in the first half of 2009, and exceeded 10,000 in the following period, with court orders being issued more frequently. The intervention into cyberspace culminated in the first quarter of 2010, when the court issued a total of 12 orders to block 20,522 URLs. It is noteworthy that in March alone, six orders were issued and 9,672 URLs blocked (iLaw 2010), the month in which large-scale red shirt protests began to converge around the Phan Fah Bridge in Bangkok (Dalpino 2011). These statistics demonstrate that Internet control actions are mainly triggered by the transgressive use of the Internet — online content and behaviours that directly challenge Thailand's political establishment.

Table 4-3: Court order for blocking lèse-majesté content

Timing	**Jul.-Sep. 2008**	**Oct.-Dec. 2008**	**Jan.-Mar. 2009**	**Apr.-Jun. 2009**	**Jul.-Sep. 2009**	**Oct.-Dec. 2009**	**Jan.-Mar. 2010**	**Apr.-Jun. 2010**
Court Order	3	3	11	8	5	6	12	5
Blocked URLs	1,037	891	2,973	2,370	3,297	7,885	20,522	6,790

Source: Compiled from iLaw Project, 2010

The urgency to protect the current Thai political system is also indicated in the words of those in charge of Internet control actions. Governments under both Abhisit and Yingluck have publicly expressed their concern over increasing anti-monarchy discourse. Amid strong calls for reforming the lèse-majesté laws (Section 112 of the Criminal Code), Yingluck and Chalerm reiterated firmly that the institution of the monarchy should be protected (*Bangkok Post* 2012). For people implementing Internet control policies, the need to defend the royal family is the major motive. As the cyber inspector says in an interview, "the thing that drives us to do our duty (of Internet control) is that we love and worship the monarchy" (*The New York Times* 2011). By the same token, people recruited for the "cyber scouts" expressed a similar sentiment. According to an AFP report, one recruited scout explains that "my inspiration to be a cyber scout is the king. There are many ways to protect the institute, and this is one of them".[47] In this sense, as online transgressiveness heightens, it frustrates those who intend to defend the traditional political order.

Secondly, low capacity of online civil society further stimulates greater repression on cyberspace. To a large extent, the government's Internet control schemes rely on public participation. A brief description of how website blocking is usually practiced could be indicative: in the content control department in the Ministry of ICT, officers look through a great number of reports filed by ordinary citizens (a central email and a hotline are set up to garner public reports on illegal content) and browse the target websites to confirm the illegal behaviour. They would then apply for a court order to block the URL of that site (Araya Sawasdichai, interview). Likewise, the "war room" established under the Yingluck government also obtains information from public reporting, receiving around 20 to 100 daily email complaints against improper Internet usage (*The New York Times* 2011). More importantly, public support for Internet control is seen in the formation of "cyber scouts" who are netizen volunteers with a strong sense of duty in defending the royal institution. Without active public participation, the government capacity to crack down upon illegal websites, especially those with lèse-majesté content, would be considerably weakened, given the massive volume of information flows in cyberspace. The rationale for their participation, meanwhile, springs from the polarised social confrontation between different political ideologies. In an extreme case, to defend the monarchy, a woman from northern Thailand launched a campaign, strikingly collecting 130,000 signatures, that called for dismantling current democratic institutions and replacing it with a king-supervised "good and moral" government.[48] With active public participation, the Thai government faces less resistance when it attempts to control the Internet than other countries with a united online civil society.

On this score, Thai citizens' attitude on media freedom could be indicative. According to a 2008 public survey conducted by the World Public Opinion (2008), while 48% of Thai respondents thought the media should have freedom of publication and expression without government control, another 37% believed that the government should have the right to censor media content that would cause political instability. By contrast, this ratio (48% to 37%) is, in general, below the average level (57% to

35%) (which covers 20 nations around the world), and in particular, well below the more advanced democratic regions such as Hong Kong (76% to 18%) and South Korea (72% to 26%). The relatively small discrepancy between the number of those who advocate for media freedom and those who support government control is indeed a reflection of Thailand's polarised society.

Conclusion

To date, Thailand has constructed perhaps the most repressive Internet control apparatus among Southeast Asia's democratic and soft authoritarian regimes. Under the ambiguously defined clauses of the Computer Crime Act and the lèse-majesté laws, the government authorities have blocked a massive number of offensive websites and prosecuted dozens of online dissidents. The private sector, including ISPs and content providers, are often compelled to follow the government's instructions on Internet control or to practice self-censorship. However, simply attributing Thailand's Internet control practice to the democratic retrogression after the 2006 coup would be misleading. As discussed in the previous section, after the Pheu Thai Party took back its political power from the conservative forces in the 2011 elections, Internet control policies were not ameliorated, but intensified. This chapter shows how high transgressiveness of online contention and weak capacity of online civil society determine Thailand's Internet control outcomes. While the trangressiveness implies a significant political threat that the Thai government has to respond to, the polarisation of online civil society reduces the political cost of Internet control and, in fact, paves the way for those schemes that rely on social participation.

Moreover, the conflict in Thailand's cyberspace reflects the deeper split in Thai politics and society. As Pirongrong (2012, 109) puts it, it is the struggle between "the old norm of preserving the sanctity of a revered institution that unites the nation and the new norm of free speech that could disrupt national order". Similar struggles have recurred periodically in Thailand's history ever since the 1932 revolution but this latest political conflict is set in an age of new information technologies. The new channels and platforms offered by the Internet have enabled much larger social involvement and, indeed, arguably fomented greater splits in Thai society. As a result, political conflict in Thailand has evolved from the previous model of government vs. people to a "clash among citizens with different political orientations" (Kitti Prasirtsuk 2009, 178). Therefore, the Internet control embodies not an isolated problem, but a symptom of the underlying problems ailing Thai politics. In this sense, while governments from both sides hastily reframe their respective notions of freedom and democracy, it is perhaps more urgent to find a way to reconcile, rather than further enlarge, the existing social and political divide.

CHAPTER FIVE

INTERNET CONTROL IN THE ELECTORAL DEMOCRACY: CASE STUDY OF INDONESIA

Introduction

This chapter examines the formation of online transgression and the development of online civil society in Indonesia. It begins with a brief overview of the interaction between the development of the Internet and Indonesian politics under Suharto's "New Order". Indonesian governments in the post-transition era face moderate levels of online transgressiveness and a modest online civil society. This chapter explains how these factors result in moderate Internet controls in Indonesia.

Indonesia has, arguably but unexpectedly, undergone the most successful democratic transition in Southeast Asia. Little more than a decade ago, President Suharto seemed capable of perpetuating his authoritarian "New Order" with political elites co-opted yet fractured, civil liberties suppressed, and general elections — though held regularly — manipulated and even predetermined. In fact, the political regime in Indonesia was marked by the resilience of its semi-authoritarianism that had endured three decades, notwithstanding continuous rapid economic growth (Ottaway 2003). Even after Suharto was forced to resign amid economic crises and nation-wide demonstrations in 1998, "Indonesia looked like an unlikely candidate for democratic success" (Aspinall 2010, 20). Military generals, secessionists, and Islamists were among the potential spoilers who might have promoted their respective political agendas and reversed any democratic gains. The post-Suharto period has, however, produced some democratic procedures that had long been absent in Indonesia.

Elections for the People's Representative Council (DPR) and the local parliaments in June 1999 were remarkably free and fair, followed by the indirect presidential election of Abdurrahman Wahid. The successive power transitions from firstly Wahid to Megawati in 2001, and secondly

Megawati to Susilo Bambang Yudhoyono through the first direct presidential election in 2004, as well as the re-election of Yudhoyono in 2009, were all regarded as peaceful and unproblematic (Barton 2010). The General Election Commission (KPU), replacing the government-appointed General Election Board (LPU), has shown independence, despite its slightly declining competence (Sukma 2009), and has thus been able to, in general, administer the electoral process with unbiased orientation. These observations have qualified Indonesia as a democracy according to the minimalist definition presented by Schumpeter (1976), with the top leadership determined "through a competitive struggle for the people's vote".

Nonetheless, a series of political defects are preventing Indonesia from achieving a fully liberalised democratic regime. It is notable that the military remains unaccountable to civilian politicians and politicians are accused of pursuing personal instead of universalistic ends (Carson and Turner 2009, 382). The electoral system is described by many as elite-engineered, with resourceful and powerful candidates playing old games of money politics, vote buying, and other manipulations (Choi 2009). The latest national election in 2009 even witnessed a dramatic decline in the quality of electoral management (Schmidt 2010). Within the new democratic structure emerged radical groups, especially Islamists, who used the newly opened opportunities to promote militant and sectarian ideas (Elson 2010), while decentralisation after the "New Order" was also linked with widespread corruption and rent-seeking at the local level (Buehler 2010). However, despite these democratic flaws, political change in the late 1990s has transformed Indonesia from an authoritarian regime into an electoral democracy.

Accompanying democratic consolidation in Indonesia is the rapid, yet not extensive, development of Internet technologies. While Freedom House's annual assessments have since 2006 classified Indonesia as "free",[49] making it the only Southeast Asian country in that class, cyberspace in the post-Suharto era faces substantial control and limitations. The Indonesian government, especially under Susilo Bambang Yudhoyono, has undertaken a series of measures to monitor online communications and censor pornographic, religious, and, to a lesser extent, certain political content. These measures put Internet control in Indonesia at a level similar to, or even higher than, that in Malaysia, but much lower than Thailand and Singapore. The medium level of control witnessed in this case results from the moderate level of online transgressiveness together with the moderate capacity of online civil society. While the first factor gives some impetus to the Indonesian elites to tighten up Internet regulation, the latter further reduces the cost of Internet control practices. The dynamic interactions between online transgression, civil society, and the Internet control outcome will be investigated in the second half of this chapter.

Meanwhile, the first part of this chapter discusses the contextual conditions, Internet development, and their interplay under the "New Order" regime. Much of the literature explaining Indonesia's democratic transition gives credit to information technologies, particularly the Internet and mobile phones, which bypassed the information monopoly of the government and facilitate social mobilisation. A brief evaluation of the Internet's impacts upon political change will be made, followed by an analysis of the Suharto government's attitude and approach in dealing with emerging transgression on cyberspace.

The Internet and the "New Order"

After gaining independence in 1945, Indonesia featured "an unconsolidated democracy during the 1950s, an unstable form of semi-authoritarianism during the early 1960s," an attempted military coup in 1965 that led to Suharto's rise to power and an anti-communist purge, and subsequently an authoritarian rule behind a democratic façade persisting until the late 1990s (Case 2002, 29). Neither the liberal democratic system nor Sukarno's "Guided Democracy" were able to address various economic, social and political problems left by colonial legacies. The "New Order", therefore, reflected the resurrection of state-qua-state (Anderson 1983) which centralises the state power, balances elite factions, and enforces social quiescence. The following section will analyse the characteristics of the "New Order" and depict its political development in the 1990s when the Internet began to blossom.

Understanding the "New Order"

Suharto's "New Order" was built upon the failure of "Guided Democracy", in which his predecessor, Sukarno, attempted to maintain power by manipulating the competition and confrontation between the military and the Indonesian Communist Party (PKI). The construction of the "New Order" amid the political turmoil and economic decay in the mid-1960s was initially welcomed by Western governments and international investors, as Suharto swept into power by eliminating (through mass killings) those elements of radical and reactionary populism that agitated market capitalists (Robinson and Hardiz 2004, 40). To some extent, the new political order under Suharto even encompassed a pseudo-democratic guise labelled as Pancasila Democracy.[50] It institutionalised general parliamentary elections which were ostensibly democratic and were held six times during the "New Order". By contrast, there was only one parliamentary election in the representative democracy period in the 1950s and none during President Sukarno's "Guided Democracy" (Liddle 1996).

Despite the presence of democratic institutions, the foremost feature of the "New Order" was the enormous personal authority of Suharto. Under the reinstituted 1945 Constitution, the president was granted the power to make all key political appointments, including posts in the cabinet, senior ranks of the military as well as top levels of the judiciary (Rosser 2002). Meanwhile, he even had ultimate authority in the decision-making process (Mackie and MacIntyre 1994, 19), thus centralising executive power into personal hands. With regard to the electoral system, some observers have pointed out that "the party system, the electoral process, and the DPR and MPR [People's Representative Council and People's Consultative Assembly respectively] are so rigged, structured and managed from above, that they allow little genuine representation from below" (Liddle 1996, 44).

Aside from institutional support, Suharto sustained his pseudo-democratic rule with his family's considerable business wealth. In some measure, the fourfold increase in world petroleum prices in the mid-1970s consolidated Suharto's power base by multiplying national revenue and thus the resources that Suharto could exploit to manage internal power struggles, reward political allies, and co-opt political opponents (Case 2002, 35–36). Therefore the "New Order" was characterised by a patron–client relationship between Suharto and his supporting groups, primarily the military, the bureaucracy, and the conglomerates. For the armed forces, Suharto distributed patronage and imposed punishment not only through promotion, reshuffle and retirement, but also by promoting the military's dual function (*dwi fungsi*), recruiting the generals into bureaucratic and state business institutions. For instance, the military was able to use its effective control over state enterprises such as Pertamina (State Oil and Natural Gas Mining Company) and Bulog (Bureau of Logistics) to extract extra-budgetary revenue (Crouch 2007).

On the other hand, Suharto cultivated factional rivalries within the armed forces based on different locations, occupations, seniority as well as other factors (Case 2002, 39). Similar strategies were used in retaining a grip on the bureaucratic branches as well. For example, Case (2002, 40) argued that "throughout his tenure, Suharto shifted favour between two major factions in the cabinet, the economically nationalist technologues (best represented by B.J. Habibie as minister of research and technology) and the liberalising technocrats (found mostly in the finance ministry, the central bank, and Bappenas)". In the business sector, Suharto displayed his cronyism and nepotism by empowering and enriching a small group of Chinese business tycoons and relatives and friends of himself and other high-ranking elites. The development of the Indonesian economy soon turned on "business groups with strong political connections, including Liem (Liem Sioe Liong), Bob Hasan, and the Suhartos' Bumantara group" (Robinson 1988, 65).

Moreover, the Suharto regime was successful in de-activating social and political opposition. The social forces under the "New Order" were contained by "corporatist organisations, legitimating mentalities, substantive performance, and populist redistributions", and, when insufficient, by coercion and repression (Case 2002, 46). A vast system of hierarchical, mandatory and state-organised front groups were established under which social forces were brought under strict surveillance. For example, in 1971, the government announced the creation of Korpri (Civil Servants Professional Association) to cater for all government employees, while the wives of civil servants were organised under the Dharma Wanita (Civil Servants' Wives Association).

The party system was also calibrated to prevent meaningful political contention. In general, the elections allowed only three parties to compete: Golkar, which represented the government; the Indonesian Democracy Party (PDI) that accommodated elements of old secular nationalist and state socialist groups; and the United Development Party (PPP) that contained organisations of traditional and modernist Islam. The leadership of the two nominally oppositional parties was approved and even hand-picked by state authorities, while their major economic resources — almost all of the PDI's income and a large proportion of the PPP's — came directly from the government (Liddle 1996, 45). For the two political parties other than the state-dominated Golkar, the term "opposition" was even prohibited. Instead, they could only be referred to as "electoral participant organisations," and their primary role was to decorate the "New Order" with a democratic façade.

In a similar way, the mass media under the "New Order" was controlled and harmonised. Any newspaper publisher had to work closely with the government's line in order to obtain the Permit to Publish from the Department of Information and the Permit to Print from the military security authority. Disobedience often led to permanent removal of unyielding publications from streets. Moreover, as David Hill (2006, 47) noticed, "a government minister's pique may lead to certain papers being 'blacklisted', their journalists excluded from government press conferences and other official sources of information". Under such circumstances, political contention and social movements in the "New Order" were segmented and atomised, with dissent becoming "elliptical and stylized, expressed by small-scale demonstrations, local associations and independent intellectuals" (Boudreau 2004, 104).

In short, the "New Order" under Suharto embodied, to different degrees and at different times, elements of personal dictatorship, military government, as well as a pseudo-democratic regime. The regime stability and elite unity was maintained through a patronage network and economic and political benefits. However, when high economic growth rates disappeared and resources for patronage diminished, especially amid the sudden economic downturn, it was difficult to safeguard the conditions for rule, thus risking the regime unravelling. The following section will discuss the main context under which the Suharto regime began to collapse, which served as the background to the early development of the Internet in Indonesia. The development of the Internet, in turn, also accelerated this collapse.

Economic liberalisation, elite disunity and the collapse of the "New Order"

During the last decade of the "New Order", the iron wall of authoritarianism began to dissolve due to the transformation of Indonesia's economic, social and political contexts. Economically, partly owing to the plunge in international oil prices in the early to mid-1980s, the Indonesian government undertook a dramatic process of liberalisation and privatisation, which was further pushed by external pressures for reform, especially from the International Monetary Fund (IMF), when an economic crisis struck Asia. With interest rates liberalised, credit limits abolished, restrictions on foreign investment loosened, and state enterprises privatised, the Indonesian economy in the 1990s had been undergoing less government intervention and regulation (Rosser 2002). The developmentalist approach dominant in previous decades, emphasising a state-controlled economy and nationalist policies, was being transformed. In the telecommunications industry, liberalisation prompted the government to open up, for instance, the cellular market and value-added services (such as the Internet) to private operators in 1995 (Rasyid 2005). But more importantly, the process of liberalisation inevitably reduced the economic patronage of the Indonesian government for its political allies, resulting in frictions among top elites and cracks in the regime.

Firstly, the sudden economic crisis split up political coalitions with different economic interests around Suharto, yielding incoherent adjustment policies and furthering regime instability (Pepinsky 2009). But perhaps the most conspicuous disharmony within the "New Order" existed between the military and the civilian executive branch. According to David Hill (2006, 43), some key factions in the military had been fostering the public media's willingness to criticise the civilian cabinet members. It has been argued that the military grew disgruntled over Suharto progressively excluding it as he came to favour civilian ministers such as Habibie and Harmoko. Frictions also emerged within the military itself. Some interpretations suggested that the riots of May 1998, which served as the direct cause of Suharto's fall, were calculated and orchestrated by Lieutenant General Prabowo Subianto, Suharto's ambitious son-in-law, to embarrass and discredit his main rival within the military, armed forces commander and Minister of Defence General Wiranto (Forrester 1998). When the usually heavy-handed court determined that it would issue only light fines for arrested protesters amid the chaos and turmoil, it also indicated that the judiciary was aligning more with the emerging civil society and less with the executive and hard-liners in the military (Hill 2006, 46). After all, even Suharto's former cronies abandoned him, exemplified by Harmoko's (the then People's Representative Council speaker and Golkar Party chairman) announcement at the parliament that a special session would be arranged to remove Suharto from office (Rosser 2002, 182). With elite unity disrupted, civil society in Indonesia received larger opportunities to advance its political course.

Meanwhile, the corporatist strategies became less and less effective as relative inequalities worsened and social mobility increased. Indicators of Suharto losing political control included the increasing class and ethnic resentments, the resurgence of Islamic organisations, and the incremental popularity of "opposition" parties, especially the Indonesian Democracy Party (PDI) led by Sukarno's daughter, Megawati (Case 2002, 49–52). More importantly, traditional controls over the media were also weakened. As Hill and Sen (2005, 21) observed, "By 1994, the media had grown into a viable industry, with a workforce that was willing and able to organize itself outside the patronage of the state". A typical example came in 1994, when the government cracked down on three prominent mass media companies, including *Tempo*, *Editor* and *Detik*, due to their critical coverage of some political issues. Under these circumstances, political opportunities emerged from the factions within the "New Order" regime, contributing to the advent of a free Internet space under the authoritarian rule.

Early development and political use of the Internet

By the late 1980s, many Indonesian students who studied abroad with government-endorsed scholarships had realised the importance of Internet technology and attempted to develop it in Indonesia. Their efforts resulted in the first mailing list involving primarily Indonesian participants in 1989 and the first webpage about Indonesian affairs in 1992, both established by overseas students in North America (Hill and Sen 2005, 35). In their homeland, Internet development had taken place at roughly the same time. In the late 1980s, technicians and students at the Bandung Institute of Technology (ITB) computerised the transmission of data communication over radio, and later expanded such radio technology to connect the computers at the Ministry of Research and Technology with several universities in Jakarta, Bandung, and Bogor. In 1993, a Micro-IPTEKnet prototype was formed that involved six government instrumentalities and several major universities and research institutions around Jakarta and the island of Java. After the first commercial Internet Service Provider, RADNET, started its operation in July 1994, the speed and efficiency of the technology was improved exponentially. For instance, the connection speed from Indonesia increased tenfold from merely 64 Kbps in 1994 to 640 Kbps in 1995, while dramatically exceeding 7 Mbps a year later (Hill and Sen 2005, 37). According to Table 5-1, the Internet user population has expanded greatly since 1996. By 1998, the year that marked the collapse of the "New Order", there were around 512,000 Internet users, concentrated mainly in urban areas and universities in Jakarta, Bandung, Yogyakarta, and Surabaya.

The development of Internet connectivity has empowered political dissent and activism in Indonesia by enabling communication among NGOs and activists and the exchange of information that was previously monopolised by the central government. The Legal Aid Institute (LBH), Indonesia's leading human rights advocacy group, was probably the "best connected" NGO in Indonesia, which obtained a server in San Francisco and circulated information among its members on its network (elawjakarta@igc.apc.org). In 1995, commercial ISPs became available to the public and "cyberspace was finally recognized as a real battleground between the pro-democracy activists and the supporters of the Suharto rule" (Tedjabayu 1999). The *apakabar* email list, originally created in early 1990s for overseas Indonesian students, grew into one of the most significant sources of information for scholars and students both inside and outside Indonesia. It had become a site for extremely open and democratic debates on Indonesia, with a readership that involved more and more Indonesians in their homeland. After the banning of three leading magazines, *Tempo*, *Editor* and *Detik* in 1994, ex-*Tempo* and *Detik* staffers turned to the Internet and established their online versions of *Tempo Interaktif* and detik.com respectively (Hill and Sen 2005, 30). The information and news disseminated by these email groups was politically crucial since they strengthened public opinion that it was time for Suharto's "New Order" to end. For example, a list of assets of the Suharto and Habibie families and their cronies (which had been downloaded and circulated in photocopied forms among the public while Suharto was still in power) was compiled and leaked on the Internet (Tedjabayu 1999). Such scandals, though "ignored" by traditional media, inevitably aggravated the political resentment from the urban middle class and student groups, and thus eroded any legitimacy that the "New Order" had reserved.

Table 5-1: Indonesian Internet growth

Year	Subscribers	Users
1996	31,000	110,000
1997	75,000	384,000
1998	134,000	512,000
1999	256,000	1,000,000
2000	400,000	1,900,000
2001	581,000	4,200,000
2002	667,002	4,500,000
2003	865,706	8,080,534
2004	1,300,000	12,000,000

Source: Hill and Sen 2005, 57

Meanwhile, opposition parties also discovered the power of the Internet. On this score, a number of studies have recorded how the Democratic People's Party (PRD) — a largely student-based and unregistered political party — effectively embraced Internet technology to maintain international linkages and equip its anti-Suharto struggles (Lim 2002; Hill and Sen 2005; Lim 2006). Established in the early 1990s, the PRD was always considered by Indonesian authority as being connected with communism, Marxism, and the forbidden PKI party. After the political tragedy in July 1996, in which Megawati's Democratic Party of Struggle (PDI-P) was violently attacked, many of PRD's leading activists were sent to trial and held in continuing detention, and the movement was almost strangled. Following this incident, the PRD activists decided to move their struggles into cyberspace. With the help of information technology, it became active and efficient in communicating and coordinating at the national level, "linking its members all across the country by *warnet* connections, and also building networks with international pro-democracy institutions" (Lim 2006, 11). In a similar way, the Information Centre and Action Network for Reform (PIJAR), one of the major pro-democracy NGOs in Indonesia at that time, also survived authoritarian repression by changing its underground bulletin called "News from Pijar" (KdP) into an Internet version (Lim 2006).

Therefore, by the time the political situation grew inflamed during 1997–98, the Internet had already proved its significance by promoting political discussion and democratic transition. However, the political impact of Internet was even more apparent during the crisis. As previously mentioned, PRD, PDI-P and other pro-democracy organisations used "dark letters", "can letters" and "underground pamphlets" to disseminate alternative forms of information to the ones provided by mainstream media, particularly about the corrupt practices of Suharto's family members and his allies (Lim 2006, 13). Certain websites which published such type of information, such as *Indonesia Baru*, instructed and encouraged their website readers to print out the online content and disseminate it among their offline social networks (Lim 2002). There were indeed considerable methods to spread anti-government information from cyberspace to the offline world. For example, during the political crisis, many mysterious faxes sent by unknown fax numbers arrived at private and public office fax machines in major cities in Indonesia. Information photocopied from the Internet also appeared on announcement boards of various places, including *warnets* (Internet cafes) and campuses in Jakarta, Bandung, and Yogyakarta. Even newspaper sellers and street-vendors sold those photocopied pamphlets at traffic lights and kiosks (Lim 2003).

A closer look at the hit-rates and operation of prominent news websites may also reflect the impact of the Internet during the democratic transition. To just name one example: the Joyo News Service (Joyo) was founded in the summer of 1996, initially as an individual effort to keep abreast of what was happening in the country. The service carefully selected articles based on their unique content or perspective and circulated them within a small group of contacts. As Table 5-2 shows, the number of direct recipients of Joyo News Service grew exponentially between 1996 and 1998.

Table 5-2 Number of direct recipients of Joyo News Service

1996	6
1997	300
1998	4000
1999	2000

Source: Winters 2002

Those on the primary recipient list involved almost all the important pro-democracy movement figures: major Indonesian and international NGOs, student senates and activists, international as well as domestic editors and journalists, financial institutions such as the IMF and the World Bank, major embassies in Jakarta, hundreds of active and retired Indonesian officials, as well as active and retired Indonesian military personnel and intelligence officers (Winters 2002). However, such numbers still understate the real readership of Joyo, since many recipients forwarded the information on Joyo to others on their mailing lists. In the months leading up to the fall of Suharto in May 1998, Joyo became one of the major sources of timely and accurate information about the political situation. As one contact in Joyo put it:

> It seemed to be the major source of news for Indonesian activists for what was going on in the country and how people were reacting to it. The students took over the Indonesian Parliament, and many of the walls were plastered with Joyo articles, and they were being constantly updated. In Bandung, Surabaya, and Jakarta, the Joyo news articles were being copied and circulated. (Winters 2002, 117)

In this sense, the Internet has provided a valuable space in which anti-Suharto forces could circumvent government suppression against the movement. Political instability also prompted the use of the Internet by political dissidents. As the *Bangkok Post* (1998) commented shortly before

Suharto's resignation, "With anti-government street protests rocking Indonesia, opposition parties, students, journalists, and non-governmental groups have been busy posting news and spreading their views on the most important Indonesia-related list, INDONESIA-L (*apakabar*)". Some observers even raised further assertions that Indonesia's political crisis was "Net-driven" (Marcus 1998).

However, while acknowledging the political impact the Internet has exerted upon political communications and mobilisation during this tumultuous period, we should not exaggerate the significance of that role. When a similar reformasi movement broke out in Malaysia in 1998–99, with the similar context of an economic crisis and elite disunity, and with similar Internet effects that transcended the government's information monopoly and empowered dissidents, political instability did occur but did not induce regime change in Malaysia (see Chapter 3). In addition, Malaysia's Internet penetration rate at the onset of the reformasi movement had reached somewhere between 6.7% and 12.3%, while in Indonesia during the political crisis, it only accounted for 0.25% of the country's population.[51] As a result, it would be unreasonable to argue that the Internet was more important in terminating Suharto's "New Order" than in challenging Mahathir and the BN's hegemony. In this sense, the Internet in Indonesia served, at most, as a minor precipitant to the end of the "New Order" which was already crumbling at that time.

The different fates of Suharto's and Mahathir's regimes can be better explained by other factors, such as the effective (or ineffective) responses to the economic crisis (Pepinsky 2009), the nature of civil and political societies (Weiss 2006), and the role of the military (Honna 2003). In this sense, the political transgression generated by the Internet use in Indonesia during that time remained at a relatively medium-to-low level, compared with other immediate economic and political problems that shook the political system and forced Suharto to react. Demystifying the Internet's influence on the political change in Indonesia would help us understand the Suharto government's response toward the newly politicised cyberspace.

Governmental responses toward cyberspace

Even if the Internet threat was dwarfed by other immediate crises, Suharto and his associates had already perceived the political challenge posed by the Internet. In a speech in 1997, Suharto, in an implicit reference to the Internet and other information technologies, warned that "the free flow of global information [...] enables people to receive foreign values that can erode their sense of nationalism" (*Chicago Tribune* 1997). In fact, certain measures had been deployed to contain the online activism. It was reported that Internet Service Providers (ISPs) were frequently visited by military officials who demanded names and information of certain Internet users (Hill and Sen 2005, 50). The Indonesian armed forces even established a special Internet unit in 1995 whose major duty was to correct inaccuracies of online information about Indonesia and disseminate the government's stance through several prominent email lists. However, all these methods turned out to be ineffective in practice. As Hill and Sen (2005, 50) argued, "the Indonesian Department of Information never had the legal or technological means to enforce direct monitoring of Internet usage, or official restricting of particular sites". Shortly before Suharto's fall, the then Information Minister, Alwi Dahlan, stated plainly that "I do not see how you could regulate the Internet" (*Strait Times* 1998).

If political transgression on the Internet fell short of being one of the most urgent issues that the Suharto government prioritised, there were several additional factors that diminished the effectiveness of Internet control during the "New Order". As mentioned above, the legitimacy of Suharto's regime was weakened during the 1990s. The resurgence of Islamic organisations and the increasing discontent of students and the working class had seen the government's controlling capacity dwindle. Also important was Suharto's advancing age, which diminished his ability to identify and solve these newly emerging threats (Crouch 2000; Liddle 1999). Furthermore, the schism within the Indonesian bureaucracy made consistent efforts to regulate the Internet quite difficult. On the one hand, the Ministry of Information was in charge of monitoring the content of the Internet and was always vigilant about digital threats. However, the Minister of Research and Technology, Habibie, was far more powerful and influential. As a determined technophile, he passionately promoted the development of information technologies in the belief that these could rapidly transform Indonesia into a modernised economy (Hill and Sen 2005, 34). The ambiguous responsibility over the Internet inevitably weakened each department's capacity to control cyberspace.

Moreover, the ownership structure as well as diversity of the ISPs also complicated the implementation of regulatory policies. As previously discussed, the Indonesian government in the 1990s undertook various programmes of economic liberalisation that loosened government control over investment. This also affected the telecommunication industry. According to the editor of detik.com, Budiono Darsono, "The Suharto government at that time expedited the licenses for Internet Service Providers. The government granted licenses to smaller companies run by young businessmen; big corporations were not allowed to operate an ISP" (Winters 2002, 114). By May 1997, the Indonesian government had issued permits to 41 ISPs, of which 32 were actually operational (Hill and Sen 2005, 57). Given that these ISPs were privately owned entities, they were less likely to be monitored and controlled by the government. As public grievances increased during the last days of Suharto regime, the corporate sector began to distance itself from the state, which further frustrated any attempt to obtain cooperation from ISPs.

In all, the Suharto regime was unable and, perhaps more importantly, unprepared to adopt any efficient means to control the Internet, thus accelerating its own demise. The fall of Suharto initiated substantial change in Indonesian politics and the Internet began to penetrate more deeply into society and politics.

The Internet and Democratic Consolidation

The sudden breakdown of Suharto's "New Order" was immediately followed by a decline in state authority, a smooth transition to democracy, and the institutionalisation of democratic practices. Nonetheless, the quality of democracy in Indonesia remained underdeveloped. High-level politics was still monopolised by groups of elites active since the "New Order", while gradual dissatisfaction of voters toward the electoral system indicated the insulation of electoral politics from genuine public needs. Under such circumstances, the civil society used new information technologies to further strengthen its position vis-à-vis the state. However, online political contentiousness produced little systemic threat for the electoral democratic regime since they seldom touched the fundamental aspects of the political order. Instead, online social movements were organised to challenge particular political institution or processes that they deemed undemocratic. Capacity of online civil society, at the same time, also remained moderate due to deficiencies in penetration and political linkage. As a result, Internet controls in Indonesia were implemented at a medium level. This section starts with an analysis of the post-Suharto democratic regime in Indonesia, then discusses the moderate level of online transgression as well as online civil society capacity, and explains Indonesia's Internet control outcome.

Electoral democracy in Indonesia: "The irony of success"?

In his well-known formula of democratisation, Huntington (1991) has predicted that bottom-up "replacement", in which a dictator is overthrown by "people power", is the mode of transition least likely to consolidate. It argues that peaceful and consensual transitions, associated more with negotiated "transplacement" than sudden and violent "replacement", provide larger support for democratic consolidation (Huntington 1991, 276). However, apart from the mob violence against Chinese communities in 1998, the democratic transition in Indonesia has been, in general, peaceful and stable. In the aftermath of Suharto's fall, the first free legislative election since 1955 was held in 1999 in which the Indonesian Democratic Party of Struggle (PDI-P) attained the largest share of seats. The presidency became directly elected in 2004 and Susilo Bambang Yudhoyono replaced Megawati Sukarnoputri as the president, and was re-elected in the 2009 election. Although the credibility of elections seemed to have declined in 2009, due to serious administrative and logistical problems and post-election disputes (Sukma 2009; Mietzner 2010), few violent incidents were found in these elections and the majority of voters still considered the 2009 election to be free and fair (*The Jakarta Post* 2009).

With political participation encouraged, a vibrant media environment formed, and civil society organisations growing significantly, Indonesia has, since 2006, been given a "free" status in Freedom House's annual assessments,[52] the only country in Southeast Asia under that category. By the same token, both Economist Intelligence Unit and Polity IV Project rank Indonesia at the top of Southeast Asian countries in terms of democraticness.

Nonetheless, political stability and democratic durability in Indonesia are achieved at the cost of democratic quality (Aspinall 2010). The competence and neutrality of the Elections Commission (Komisi Pemilihan Umum, KPU) was increasingly questioned after the 2009 elections (Sukma 2009). Corruption is so endemic that Indonesia scored poorly in the Transparency International's Corruption Perceptions Index (2010), with a score of 2.8, much worse than Singapore (9.3), Malaysia (4.4), and Thailand (3.5) and only slightly better than Cambodia (2.1) and the Philippines (2.4). In addition, human rights abuses are evident in religious intolerance, as well as violence and torture against minority groups often committed by security forces (Freedom House 2011a). Meanwhile, the regime equilibrium is built upon the trade-offs between incumbent governments and a wide range of socio-political actors such as the military, regional elites, and militant Islamists.

For the military, the collapse of the "New Order" has undoubtedly shaken its previous domination, enshrined in the *dwi fungsi* (dual function) doctrine, in Indonesian politics. Substantial steps of reform have been taken to reduce the military's influence and intervention, including phasing out the military's reserved parliamentary seats (Sukma 2010). However, civilian control over the military remains incomplete and some core prerogatives are left almost untouched. For example, the human rights violations perpetrated by military staff, such as the massacre of protestors in Tanjung Priok in 1984 and the violence related to the 1999 East Timor independence referendum, were plainly ignored or not seriously examined by Indonesia's judiciary. Even when there were initial convictions, most cases were either suspended or overturned (Aspinall 2010). The military's prerogatives in terms of institutional structures were also preserved to a large extent. For instance, the Indonesian government was unable to dissolve or reform the territorial command system (*koter*), which "enabled the military to continue, indeed to intensify, its pressuring of regional administrators, while collaborating with, or extorting from, local business people" (Case 2002, 73).

With regard to the centre–periphery relationship, the Indonesian government placated regional and local elites by decentralising political and budgetary power down to local governments. However, this posed the potential risk of predatory behaviour among regional elites (Hadiz 2007; Choi 2009; Choi 2011). On this score, Choi Nankyung's (2009) research on local elections illustrates the vulnerability of democratic institutions vis-à-vis patrimonial manipulations. In most localities, entrenched regional elites would easily defeat new democratic challengers and sustain their patronage networks. Meanwhile, in places where secessionists are active, most notably in Aceh, patronage is distributed in exchange for peace deals (Aspinall 2009).

Moreover, in order to absorb Islamic political forces into democratic institutions and procedures, pluralism is sacrificed such that a Muslim democracy has been portrayed as a national symbol, different from the Christian democracy dominant in the West (Aspinall 2010). It was even reported that Amien Rais, leader of the National Mandate Party (PAN) and head of People's Consultative Council, appealed for a holy war against the Christians in Maluku (Case 2002, 78).

In fact, the electoral politics in the post-Suharto era mainly saw the re-organisation of the power of the traditional elites. On this score, Dan Slater (2004, 72) detailed how the traditional elites had virtually escaped vertical and horizontal accountability and "made their personal positions effectively impenetrable atop Indonesia's steep political pyramid". The oligarchic elites who dominated the "New Order" have survived in the democratic transition and continued their economic and political interests through unchanged rent-seeking games, though this time in a new democratic format. Money politics, in this way, still prevailed in the new political environment. While Wahid, the first elected president in the post-Suharto period, was revealed as possibly having been involved in financial scandals and attempts to protect a number of "New Order" tycoons, his successor with high reformist credentials, Megawati, was also embroiled in controversy over the use of Presidential Aid funds as well as the alleged business irregularities of her husband (Robison and Hadiz 2004). Due to the "absence of balance and transparency in the funding of political commercials during campaigns" (Mujani and Liddle 2010, 95), elites with abundant economic resources have been far more likely to win the ballot. As a result, it is not surprising that the only two new parties that passed the 2.5% threshold in the 2009 election, Gerindra and Hanura, are both the personal vehicles of wealthy, well-networked former army officers, Prabowo Subianto and Wiranto respectively.

Moreover, statistical analyses of voting behaviour (Mujani and Liddle 2007; 2010) have revealed the increasing importance of personalistic leadership in defining voters' preferences and the weakening of voters' identification with specific political parties. Based on their findings, Mujani and Liddle (2010, 97) characterised the Indonesian party system as being too fragmented and too volatile, having few democratic elements within parties, and being unresponsive toward the electorate. Even more negative was, perhaps, Thomas Carothers (2006, 175), who asserted that:

> Indonesia's main political parties remain almost archetypical embodiments of the standard lament about parties — they are intensely leader-centric organisations dominated by a small circle of elite politicians who hold onto their positions atop parties seemingly indefinitely, are immersed in patronage politics, and who are far more devoted to political intrigues in the capital than the prosaic work of trying to listen to and represent a base of constituents.

These comments indicate the worsening split between top-level elite struggles and bottom-up public participation. Therefore, although civil society in Indonesia has been greatly empowered and genuinely vibrant in the new democratic regime, it is still fragmented, preventing it from gaining greater political power.[53] This argument has been supported by many NGO activists during my field trip there (Rapin, interview by author, June 10, 2011). In summary, democratic consolidation in Indonesia has been marred by its quality–stability trade-offs. The dominant pact of the Indonesian regime in the post-Suharto period has involved retention of military privileges, the empowering of local patrimonial elites, and the resurrecting of Islamic norms. Despite its democratic format, the electoral system favoured a small group of elites with both old and new interests. The electorate was, to some extent, isolated from greater political participation. These defects have constrained Indonesia's further transformation from an electoral democracy towards a fully democratic regime. In this context, the political effects of new information technologies upon democratic consolidation, and the political transgression of online activities, are only moderate. Online civil society capacity is also moderate due to its deficiencies in several aspects.

Transgression in Indonesian cyberspace

With the largest population in Southeast Asia (estimated at 248 million in 2012),[54] Indonesia has seen Internet technologies develop rapidly, but not extensively. The Indonesian Ministry of Communication and Information recorded 45 million Internet users[55] (an Internet penetration rate of 18.7%) in 2011, a near tripling of the online population from 2005 (*The Jakarta Globe* 2011). Though its Internet penetration remains much lower than all other Southeast Asian competitive polities except Cambodia, Indonesia is home to the second largest group of Facebook users and fourth largest group of Twitter users worldwide.[56]

(1) Moderate online transgressiveness

The rapid development of the Internet in Indonesia facilitates massive social movements that pose a political challenge to the ruling elites. Two cases — the case of Prita and that of the KPK (Corruption Eradication Commission) — will be introduced here to illustrate this point. The first case saw a Jakartan housewife, Prita Mulyasari, being jailed in 2009 after she lost a civil defamation suit involving a complaining email she sent to discredit a public hospital. This case, the first under the newly passed Information and Electronic Transaction law, provoked an extensive public outcry (Heru Sutadi, interview by author, June 13, 2011). In December 2009, a mailing list as well as a Facebook group called "KOIN UNTUK PRITA" (Coin for Prita) were established which started raising money to support her. Within a startlingly short period of ten days, from December 5 to 14, the movement had collected Rp 650 million from people around the country (*The Jakarta Post* 2009). Facing strong pressure from the public, the Omni Hospital withdrew the civil lawsuit. The Prita case demonstrates how the Internet enables civil society to defy higher authority — in this case, the Omni Hospital — and to affect state regulation and law framework.

The KPK case in 2009, popularly known as the battle of the "gecko vs. the crocodile", witnessed a similar antagonism between ordinary netizens and state authority, but is far more politically influential. In this case, the National Police and the Corruption Eradication Commission (KPK) investigated each other in a retaliatory manner, resulting in the arrest of two KPK deputies who were accused by the police of power abuse and extortion (Kimura 2011, 188–9). This incident, seen by many as unjust to the KPK, invoked strong public outrage. Demonstrators in several cities organised massive rallies with appeals such as "Don't kill the KPK" and "Keep fighting" to support the arrested KPK deputies (*The Jakarta Post* 2009). Accompanying street demonstrations were online movements on Facebook and Twitter on a yet larger scale. In November 2009, Usman Yasin, a lecturer at Muhammadiyah University in Bengkulu, created a Facebook group to mobilise support for the KPK. It soon reached the target number of one million supporters, showing strong discontent over the case (*Bloomberg* 2009).

Unlike the case of Thailand where the Red Shirt movement largely involve new political groups, in Indonesia the massive movements mentioned above mostly mobilised established political actors, such as the urban middle-class. However, to a lesser extent, the Internet technologies have still empowered political actors who are previously inactive or marginalised. For example, formerly marginalised ethnic groups and secessionists have found the Internet to be a valuable tool in advancing their positions. On this score, Hill and Sen (2005) recounted how the Internet was employed by local politicians and activists to seek independence in East Timor and foster primordial identities during the Maluku sectarian conflict. When religious conflicts broke out between Christian and Muslim groups in the Maluku islands, both groups used cyberspace (by creating mailing lists and websites) to elevate local information and discourse onto a global level. The Internet also strengthened both groups' identity politics and formed solidarity networks as they used cyberspace to connect themselves with international diaspora and religious communities (Bräuchler 2004). In addition, political groups promoting Islamic radicalism also resorted to cyberspace (such as the Laskar Jihad Online) to disseminate radical ideas and incite hatred against Christians. Their messages even reached some of the country's leading universities (Lim 2005).

With regard to the content of online transgression, political contentiousness in Indonesia mainly targets particular features or institutions of the regime, thus posing less systemic threats. The Internet-facilitated social movements, as mentioned above, defied state authority and redefined the state–society relationship. But the grievances associated with these movements were centred on how state institutions abused or misused their power. The fundamental aspects that sustained the socio-political order, such as the religious authority or the oligarchic power structure, were seldom challenged by major online contentiousness.

Except for mobilising massive movements, online information also exposes corruption and other irregular or illegal activities of bureaucrats and military officials, unnerving Indonesia's traditional elites and producing public pressure for institutional reforms. For instance, in May 2010, a ten-minute video shot on a cellphone camera showed five military soldiers torturing two Papuan civilians. The short film was uploaded on the Internet and soon aroused nation-wide public outrage (Sihaloho and Rayda 2010). Although the National Commission on Human Rights chose to play down the issue without any substantial investigation — a normal practice, given the privilege enjoyed by the military— this incident further damaged the military's image and aroused more public appeals for institutional reform. In another case, online criticism and satire sprang up after Gayus Tambunan, a former tax official arrested for corruption, was found to have bribed his way out of jail. A satirical song named "Andai Aku Jadi Gayus Tambunan" ("If I Were Gayus Tambunan") soon prevailed on the video-sharing website YouTube and received 300,000 views within two weeks (Barley and Thee 2011). A number of Facebook pages were also established to mock, ridicule, and slam the Gayus Tambunan's case and Indonesia's justice system as a whole (Barley and Thee 2011). As corruption in Indonesia remains rampant (see previous discussion), the Internet would become increasingly important in supervising elites' behaviours. As Ramadhan Pohan, a member of parliament, argued, this trend has "deeply unsettled politicians [and] bureaucrats … unused to such direct challenges to their authority" (Onishi 2010).

To summarise, online political contentiousness in Indonesia has met the criterion of massive, Internet-empowered social movements. However, new political actors (such as marginalised ethnic groups) are not the backbone of these movements, but are instead involved in other forms of online contentious activities which are smaller in scale and less influential. Moreover, political claims associated with these movements are less systemic, concerning, for the most part, the discrete features (such as clientalism and corruption) and institutions (such as the police and judiciary) of political regime rather than the fundamental dimensions of the political order. In this sense, online transgression in Indonesia remains moderate. Its impact on Internet control outcome will be analysed in a later section. Prior to that, we will examine the capacity of Indonesia's online civil society.

(2) Moderate capacity of online civil society

Internet development is less impressive in Indonesia than in many other Southeast Asian countries. The estimated 18–22% penetration rate (see the introduction part of this section) is substantially lower than the Asian average (26.2%). Geographical dispersion of the archipelago inevitably confines the Internet service to a few city centres and impedes the expansion of network infrastructure to peripheral areas. Nonetheless, the huge population base in Indonesia suggests that it has the largest online community in Southeast Asia. In addition, social networking sites are widely used in Indonesia, with Facebook penetrating 17.7% of its population in 2012.[57]

Political linkage between online movements and offline political organisations is not well developed. For instance, with regard to the Prita case, although during the electoral campaign period of 2009, some presidential candidates expressed sympathy or concern over the case, the movement supporting Prita was not linked with any political parties or prominent NGOs (Rapin, interview; Juni Soehardjo, interview by author, June 14, 2011). This Internet mobilised movement, despite its enormous influence in that year, was organised at grass-root level and lacked institutional support. In a similar vein, the movements supporting the KPK were organised spontaneously by ordinary citizens and netizens, without much involvement of political parties and other organisations (Rapin, interview).

Moreover, the underdeveloped linkage between online communities and offline politics can also be seen by briefly examining the features of political parties' websites. The official websites of all three major political parties, the Democratic Party (PD) (http://www.demokrat.or.id/), the PDI-P (http://www.pdiperjuangan.or.id/), and the Golkar (http://www.golkar.or.id/), have very limited interactive functions. The first two do not contain an online forum or discussion board, while Golkar's website carries a message board that allows its party members to leave comments, but the comments are only one-time messages without further feedback and discussion. In general, these party websites feature a unidirectional, downward information provision, mainly introducing policy orientation and major party events. Such characteristics make these websites an exhibition board for propaganda rather than a meaningful channel that links netizens with political organisations.

It should be noticed that although political linkage can not be cultivated overnight, a positive trend has occurred that top politicians are increasingly engaging with the online community. For instance, during the Jakarta gubernatorial election in 2012, the two major candidates, the incumbent Governor Fauzi Bowo and his rival, Joko Widodo, changed the conventional electoral campaign tactics to an Internet-based strategy which extensively mobilised supporters through online social media (Mann 2012). The use of social media was unprecedentedly intensive during this election, as statistics recorded between 20,000 and 40,000 tweets (messages on Twitter) about the governor candidates being sent per day (*The Jakarta Globe* 2012). This change indicated the ruling elites' rising awareness of the critical role played by the Internet and their intentions to build up ties with online communities. As this trend continues and the next general election looms, politicians and political parties would more actively develop their connections with the online civil society and thus enhance the capacity of the latter.

Online media in Indonesia has yet to gain prominence and credibility in comparison with the traditional media. On the one hand, traditional mainstream media still dominates in political communications and the politicisation of the Internet remains rather preliminary. A 2010 survey of Indonesian youth (15–25-year-olds), conducted jointly by the Lembaga Survei Indonesia and the Goethe Institut (2010), indicates that, when asked about their primary information sources of politics (multiple choice), 71.4% of the respondents nominated television and 26.7% chose newspaper. Only 19.6% use the Internet to explore political issues. As we have already mentioned in Chapter 4, the Edelman Trust Barometer (2012) has found that Indonesian interviewees had a much stronger trust in the media (80%) than Malaysian (47%) and Singaporean (68%) candidates did. In this sense, the Internet and the new media are not particularly significant in providing credible information and alternative viewpoints.

In contrast to the situation in Malaysia, where blogs and independent online news sites offer otherwise inaccessible information and become politically important, online journalism in Indonesia appears to be relatively underdeveloped. On this score, a study based on Indonesian university students shows that 47.8% of students disagree with the argument that the Internet news offer different perspectives of each story compared with mainstream media, while 63% do not believe online news content is more neutral than traditional media content (Muliana 2008). In a survey that covered over 219 Indonesian bloggers, a prominent blogger admitted that "citizen journalism is not yet trusted, because we don't have any standard for posting information online" (Indo Pacific Edelman 2009).

Illustrated in Fig.5-1 below, the same survey also found that among the topics written by these bloggers, political content only accounted for 16%, well below the share of other content such as social and human interest (34%), technology (33%), entertainment (31%), and travelling (28%) (Indo Pacific Edelman 2009). Therefore, the complaint made by the Minister of ICT, Tifatul Sembiring, that Internet users in Indonesia dedicate too much to "unproductive pursuits such as games and social media" (*The Jakarta Globe* 2011) rather than political and other meaningful content is not groundless.

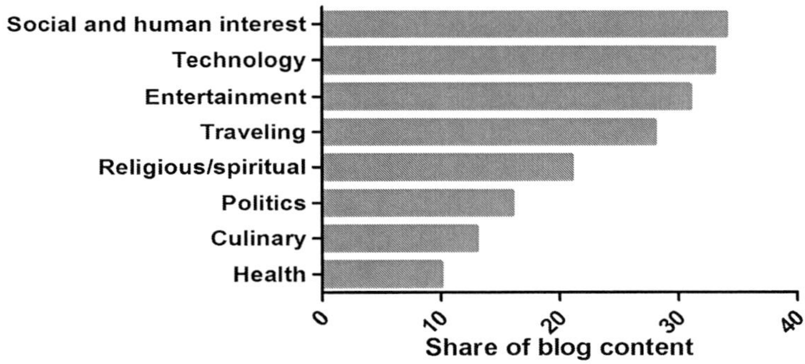

Fig. 5-1: Popular topics in Indonesian blogs
Source: Indo Pacific Edelman 2009

Last but not least, in general, there is no evidence of major counter-movements in cyberspace, which boosts the cohesiveness of Indonesia's online civil society. However, to a less extent, the ascending influence of conservative Islam still creates cleavages among online communities with regard to the issues of Internet control. A number of recent surveys and opinion polls, together with continuous religious violence and conflict, have revealed a rising trend in Indonesia that favours conservatism as well as radicalism (Mostarom and Arianti 2009; Kimura 2012). Such a trend is not only beginning to unfold in Indonesian society, but is also penetrating the nationalist, secular political parties which become the new vehicle for Islamic aspirations (Tanuwidjaja 2010). The resurgence of conservatism has, to some extent, shaped a norm of "political permissiveness" (Marthinus 2011) under which ruling parties and intellectuals are silent on controversial issues such as the purge of the unorthodox Ahmadiyah sect and the passage of the Anti-Pornography Bill. By the same token, as we will see later, this resurgence of conservatism is also associated with, and in fact propels forward, government attempts to regulate cyberspace. It not only impels some politicians and government officials to actively pursue

Internet control policies in order to win over the conservative electorate, but also makes Internet control practices easier to be justified and to garner public support.

To conclude, the political use of Internet technologies presents a moderate level of transgressiveness. It targets particular features and institutions of the regime, but falls short of posing fundamental threats to the political order. Meanwhile, the moderate capacity of Indonesia's online civil society, caused by insufficient development of all the four dimensions, has reduced the costs for Internet control. The combination of moderate transgressiveness and moderate online civil society leads to a medium level, as well as a specific approach, of Internet control in Indonesia, which we now turn to.

Explaining Indonesia's Internet control outcome

As discussed above, Internet technologies have created moderate political transgression in Indonesian politics. Certain groups of elites and the conservative pact of the regime are facing increasing pressure from online information flows that both demand larger accountability and transparency and defy vulnerable social values. Yet the online threat is not systemic, meaning that political elites may lack adequate impetus to undertake effective collective action against it. Meanwhile, collective actions from online communities to resist Internet control also remain inadequately developed, due to the moderate capacity of online civil society. The Internet control practices in post-Suharto Indonesia are clearly outcomes of such mixed impacts.

(1) Legal framework

Since 2004, Indonesian governments, especially under the Yudhoyono presidency, have been seeking ways to control the Internet. In 2008, two laws were passed that have direct reference to Internet usage. The Bill on Information and Electronic Transaction (Law 11 of 2008) defined illegal actions and corresponding punishments concerning the use of the Internet. Many actions are deemed to be criminal under this law, including distributing, transmitting and making accessible electronic information/documents which are contrary to moral norms in Indonesia, or related to gambling, insulting, blackmailing or threatening other people (Edmon Makarim, interview by author, June 10, 2011). However, not only are those criminal acts defined ambiguously, easily subject to partisan interpretation, but the sanctions for those online crimes are also disproportionally harsher than the ordinary criminal codes (Josua Sitompul, interview by author, June 13, 2011). The power of the EIT law, however, is not merely limited to pornographic issues. As mentioned earlier, Prita became the first netizen charged under the EIT regulation for her alleged defamatory email. According to a government official in the Ministry of ICT, most cases under the EIT law were related to defamation, with some involving government officials, though the overall number of EIT cases numbered only a few dozen (Josua Sitompul, interview). It shows that despite government efforts to regulate pornographic content, the Information and Electronic Transaction (EIT) bill was used principally to protect personal secrecy and reputation, especially those of elite personnel and institutions.

Another law, the Bill of Anti-Pornography (Law 24 of 2008), laid out other specific prohibitions and criminal codes with regard to pornographic affairs online. This document covered the content, as well as the behaviour, of both traditional and new media outlets, such as books, newspapers, magazines, DVDs, film, radio, television, SMS, telephone, multimedia messaging service, the Internet, as well as various forms of artistic creation (Allen 2007, 102).

(2) Internet filtering and blocking

Following this legislation were a series of attempts to censor online content and block websites by the government, though on a small scale. The video-sharing website YouTube was blocked by some Indonesian ISPs due to the spread of the "Fitna" movie,[58] although not all Internet providers obeyed the government order. Later that year, the government asked a blogging website and subsequently the country's ISPs to remove and block the prophet cartoon that was deemed "very unethical and very inappropriate" (*BBC News* 2008). In May 2010, the government, again, ordered a block on the fan page of "Everybody Draw Mohammed Day" (EDMD) on Facebook, which advocated freedom of expression around the world. The site was also blocked in India, Pakistan, Turkey and some other countries (Open Net Initiative 2010).

After the Ariel sex scandal[59] in June 2010, the stance of the Indonesian leadership became harsher. President Susilo Bambang Yudhoyono was recorded as saying: "We have increasingly realized that our nation should not stay naked and be crushed by the information technology frenzy, because there will be many victims. The scandal highlighted the need for further regulation of the Web" (*Agence France-Presse* 2010). ICT Minister Tifatul Sembiring also stated that a special team would be established to monitor and blacklist websites that contained pornographic or other unlawful content (*Agence France-Presse* 2010). The blocking and filtering practices were extended to other information technologies as well. In early 2011, Research in Motion Ltd, the company that designed the BlackBerry smartphones, promised to block its cell phone customers in Indonesia from browsing websites that had pornographic content, making Indonesia the first country to filter BlackBerry (*The Wall Street Journal* 2011).

Moreover, while the filtering practices mentioned above are mainly related to pornographic and religious content, some ISPs in Indonesia have been found blocking political content. In this regard, the Open Net Initiative tested seven Indonesian ISPs between 2009 and 2010. It revealed that two major ISPs, Indosat and XL Axiata, blocked a small number of websites that either advocate free speech (such as http://freespeech.org), or contain political criticism (such as http://indonbodoh.blogspot.com), or provide circumvention tools (such as http://surfsecret.com) (Deibert et al. 2012, 315–317). However, the source of the authorisation of such political blockings (from government agencies and politicians or merely from the board of directors of these ISPs) remains unclear.

Therefore, Internet control in Indonesia operates at a level similar to, or even higher than, that in Malaysia. While Indonesia selectively censored pornographic, religious, and, to a lesser extent, political content on cyberspace, Malaysia selectively intimidated and prosecuted several prominent bloggers. Neither of them sufficiently institutionalised Internet control measures as was done in Thailand. The scale of their Internet control practices was also comparatively lower than the Singaporean case in which the ruling party and elites frequently used libel suits to deter online criticism and set up obstacles to deter online political campaigns. In addition, covert strategies — without evident government involvement — to politically control the Internet were found in both Indonesia and Malaysia, in the form of ISP-conducted blocking in the former and anonymous attacks on critical websites in the latter. It should also be noted that Internet controls in Malaysia have subsided after the shock of the 2008 electoral wave gradually declined, while such practices in Indonesia are, in general, intensifying.

(3) Interpreting the Internet control outcome

So how are these Internet control measures associated with the moderate transgressiveness and online civil society capacity in Indonesia? There is substantial evidence that the level of collective action among Indonesian elites to control the Internet remains low, while controlling the

Internet mainly serves personal and organisational interests. For instance, the proposal of the Information and Electronic Transaction law was raised in parliament as early as 2001, initially in the context of global anti-terrorism campaigns. The Ministry of Trade and the University of Indonesia were asked to make respective versions of the draft. But it took a long time, around six to seven years, for parliamentary members to reach a consensus, and to finalise and put the law into force (Zulfiani Lubis, interview by author, June 14, 2011). By contrast the equally controversial Anti-Pornography Bill was resurrected in 2005 (it had been proposed but aborted in the 1990s) and promulgated in less than three years.

With regard to Internet filtering and blocking practices, all major decisions and actions on Internet control are made by the Ministry of ICT whose current minister, Tifatul Sembiring, is the former leader of the conservative Islamist Prosperous Justice Party (PKS) and thus has strong feelings about the threat the Internet might bring to the Islamic community. As the former Minister of Information, Alwi Dahlan, suggests, Tifatul enthusiastically adopts Internet control policies mainly in order to "enhance his political popularity by turning to Islamic values" (Alwi Dahlan, interview by author, June 16, 2011). In fact, the ministerial plans to censor the Internet are welcomed by a number of NGOs, mostly Islamists, including a child protection organisation run by Tifatul's first wife (Ndaru, interview by author, June 11, 2011).

Generally the increasing level of Internet control in Indonesia corresponds to a trend of Islamisation in which resurgent religious interests start to force their way into politics. The passage of the Anti-Pornography Bill has already indicated the militant Islamic interests among Muslim parliamentary members, such as the Front Pembela Islam (FPI, Islamic Defenders' Front), "which campaigns for Islamic law and mobilises protestors against perceived violators of Islamic rules" (Allen 2007, 103). However, it is noticeable that not only religious interests are presented in Indonesia's Internet control practices. During a forum held under the Council of National Defence this year, some participants from the military sector expressed serious concern over the Internet in terms of freedom of expression and anonymity (Ndaru, interview).

On the other hand, Indonesia's online civil society often fails to present a more cohesive force when facing Internet control practices. Although some form of coalition among NGOs, such as the National Alliance for Cyber Law Reform in Indonesia, has been established to advocate against Internet censorship, there are also conservative groups that support and even promote such censorship, thus reducing societal pressures upon government decisions on Internet control. For instance, protesting against the "Draw Mohammed" movements on Facebook, some organisations, including the Islamic Group Forum and the Indonesian Student Action Muslim Union, strongly urged the SBY administration to block the website (Freedom House 2011b, 178).[60] In fact, a 2008 survey of public opinion on the freedom of media has found that only 65% of Indonesian respondents supported the freedom to access the Internet, substantially lower than in other surveyed countries and regions such as Hong Kong (80%), China (71%) and South Korea (69%), while 24% of Indonesians supported government control of the Internet (World Public Opinion 2008).

Moreover, deficiencies in political linkage and online media also whittle down collective resistance against Internet censorship. The National Alliance for Cyber Law Reform in Indonesia (ANRHTI), for instance, is composed of several prominent NGOs, including Indonesian Legal Aid and Human Rights Association, Legal Aid Centre for Press, Benteng Cisadane Blogger Community, and Alliance of Independent Journalists and so on. But there are no political parties or party-affiliated organisations in its membership.[61] Perhaps the only major political party that strongly opposes tighter Internet regulation is the Indonesian Democratic Party of Struggle (PDI-P) (Juni Soehardjo, interview) which rejected the government's plan in 2010 to regulate multimedia content (*The Jakarta Post* 2010). However, it is also noticeable that the PDI-P is the party whose popularity has plunged most significantly over the past decade: its share of votes dropped sharply from 33.7% in 1999 to 14.0% in 2009, and its share of seats from 153 to 94 accordingly (Tomsa 2010).

In brief, this chapter argues that, for now, Internet control in Indonesia is mainly advanced by personal and sectarian interests, which clearly reflects the non-systemic nature of online transgression. Although some actions have been taken to regulate the online content, direct actions against Internet users are quite rare, except for a few examples such as Prita's case in 2009; no particular group of Internet activists or particular type of online political ideas are being targeted, indicating a relatively moderate level of Internet control; stimuli among political elites to collectively act against online threats remains underdeveloped. Meanwhile, the online civil society in Indonesia is not highly cohesive, not well associated with offline political organisations, and lacks prominent and independent online media, which has reduced the cost of Internet control. Further politicisation of the Internet may bring a change to this. Before the 2009 election, political parties in Indonesia made little effort to exploit cyberspace. But as the Prita case and other cases, as well as Obama's electoral success, demonstrated the political power of the

Internet, many political parties are realising the significance of the Internet as an electoral tool (Alwi Dahlan, interview). In this context, it is reasonable to anticipate an upgraded media war on cyberspace among political elites before the next general election in 2014. This may help to strengthen the capacity of online civil society as politicians and parties actively penetrate the Internet space.

Conclusion

Indonesia's democratic transition was initiated amid a turbulent political crisis and massive social unrest. Although the factors that brought down the "New Order" varied, and the Internet at that time penetrated Indonesian society only at a relatively low level, information technologies, to some extent, contributed to Suharto's fall and to the subsequent democratic transition. The Suharto regime, which was busy at the time dealing with street protesters and internal ruptures, failed to contain the subversive information flows in cyberspace and prevent the system from eventual collapse. However, despite the new democratic format, the post-Suharto regime accommodated the political elites in the "New Order" and maintained the enduring practices of money politics and patronage networks. Civil society in Indonesia was still fragmented and, more importantly, somehow isolated from top-level politics. These characteristics defined the way in which the Internet was used to facilitate social movements and contentious politics. The political threats of the Internet were mostly associated with personal and organisational interests, instead of systemic ones. Consequently, the pattern of Internet control in Indonesia's electoral democracy reflected the conflicts between the vibrant yet disarrayed civil society and political elites, and among those elites themselves.

In comparison, online transgressiveness in Indonesia is substantially lower than that in Thailand where online political claims are directed against the fundamental aspects of the political order. It is also slightly weaker than Malaysia where new political actors are, to a greater extent, involved in online contentiousness. But at the same time, Indonesia's online civil society capacity is not as strong as Malaysia's, reflected in the smaller size of the online community, weaker political linkage and online media, and the cleavages (though not severe) within the online society. The discrepancy in the capacity of online civil societies in Indonesia and Malaysia has, to some extent, offset the different degrees of online transgressiveness between them, which would otherwise lead to a more temperate Internet control approach in Indonesia than in Malaysia. In fact,

Freedom House's (2011b) recent report on Internet freedom has ranked the two countries in similar positions. In other words, the aggregation of different transgressive levels and online civil society capacity has resulted in a similar extent of Internet control practices in Indonesia and Malaysia.

The political context in Indonesia is also transforming. Elites and political parties are gradually realising the political power of the Internet. On the one hand, increasing use of the Internet in political campaigns may contribute to the connections between online community and political parties and the development of critical, independent online media. But on the other hand, further politicisation of cyberspace may bring about new forms of online transgression that lend an impetus to greater Internet regulation. In the short term, the mixed impact of contextual change may result in a slight fluctuation of Indonesia's Internet control practices.

CHAPTER SIX

INTERNET CONTROL IN SOUTHEAST ASIA: CONGRUENT CASES OF COMPETITIVE POLITICAL REGIMES

Introduction

In previous chapters, cases studies of Malaysia, Thailand, and Indonesia demonstrated an evident mismatch between regime type and Internet control. Competitive authoritarianism in Malaysia, although amounting to less democratic politics than in the other two countries, is accompanied by a low-medium intensity of Internet control practice. Unstable democracy in Thailand is associated with the most repressive environment for the Internet. Finally, electoral democracy in Indonesia, currently the most democratic state in the region, implements Internet control policies at a medium level. This mismatch refutes the commonly perceived "regime–repression" causal mechanism, and thus, necessitates an alternative framework to analyse the phenomenon of Internet control. In fact, as these case studies indicate, our proposed model, based on online transgressiveness and online civil society capacity, has shown substantial power in explaining Internet control. The outcomes of Internet control in these countries are in accordance with what our model would predict.

By contrast, the remaining three Southeast Asian countries, Cambodia, Singapore, and the Philippines, operate authoritarian and democratic regimes within the competitive spectrum that correlate, and can indeed be expected to correlate, with the level of Internet control. Cambodia constitutes an increasingly hard form of electoral authoritarianism which risks, if the authoritarian trend continues, slipping out of the competitive spectrum. But while Internet controls have not yet been imposed, one can readily speculate that they would be were the very low level of Internet penetration (currently 0.5% of the population) to rise. The treatment given to opposition figures and the extrajudicial killings of civil society activists lead one to expect, then, that harsh controls will gradually be extended to cyberspace. Further, Singapore's resilient electoral authoritarianism corresponds with the medium-to-high level of Internet controls that would be expected. Electoral democracy in the Philippines correlates with the country's unfettered Internet freedom.

Hence, in the country-cases of Cambodia, Singapore, and the Philippines, regime types match the intensity of Internet controls. In appearing to lend themselves, then, to conventional explanation, these cases are given less attention in this book. No in-depth research or fieldwork was carried out — it is the anomalous cases that this project has sought most to explain. However, it may be that while regime types correlate with Internet controls, they are endogenous, suggesting that the explanation for controls is partly located elsewhere. Accordingly, the sections below investigate, at least cursorily, the possibility that in these cases, regime type masks the Internet transgressiveness and online civil society capacity that are more fundamentally at work.

For this reason, this chapter briefly investigates whether similar mechanisms of the "transgression–opposition–repression" model can be found in Cambodia, Singapore, and the Philippines. It relies mainly on secondary information, collected from credible sources including various media, academic, and government reports. In addition, some information from secondary sources has been double-checked through personal communication with a small number of bloggers in these countries.

This chapter is divided into two parts. The first part analyses the political contexts of Cambodia, Singapore, and the Philippines, which provide the contextual sources for agency-level variations. The second part applies our model to these cases. In fact, the level of transgressiveness and the capacity of online civil society demonstrate explanatory power in these peripheral cases. In Cambodia, the underdeveloped status of Internet control results principally from the relatively low transgressiveness in cyberspace. At the same time, the weak online civil society there suggests that government repression on the Internet would be easily increased if online transgression rises. In Singapore, the combination of modest online transgression and a weak modest civil society capacity gives rise to restrictive Internet control policies. Moreover, the combination of low-to-moderate transgressiveness and strong civil society capacity in the Philippines leads to the relatively low level of Internet control, also in accordance with what our theoretical model suggests. Meanwhile, the sequencing of analysing the three cases is based on their degree of democraticness, in the same order of the core cases, from Cambodia, the lowest, to the Philippines, the highest.

Contextual Conditions and Political Systems in Cambodia, Singapore and the Philippines

Historical development

For many comparative historical analyses, colonial experience is a starting point to assess the divergent pathways of nation building, state building, and economic development. Colonial experience and post-colonial turbulence in Southeast Asia, despite its pervasiveness across the region, has left different political legacies for Cambodia, Singapore, and the Philippines.

Since the late eighteenth century, Cambodia has lived in the shadow of great regional power struggles, which led to national instability and institutional weaknesses (Steinberg 1987, 123). Alternative and overlapping pressures and occupations from Siam, Vietnam, France, and Japan undermined effective control of Cambodian authority, no matter whether monarchical or republican. David Steinberg (1987, 375) observes that, "by the middle of 1953, more than half of the countryside was effectively under insurgent control". Instability was exacerbated by the regional crisis of the Vietnam War, followed by the devastating rule of the Khmer Rouge. The post-colonial history of Cambodia was thus characterised by "a protracted period of conflict" (Kim 2007). Even with a UN-assisted transition that returned Cambodia to more stable politics in the early 1990s, important elements for constructing a nation-state, such as political institutionalisation and economic modernisation, remained largely underdeveloped.

By contrast, the colonial experience in Singapore and the Philippines, though in different ways, imparted more favourable legacies. Established by the British as a free trade port, Singapore was featured by its laissez-faire economy. With initial aims to support its economy, modern political institutions were implanted and nurtured by the colonial government, including the Civil Service, the judiciary, and, from 1867, the Legislative Council (Lee 1989, 39), which laid a strong framework for Singapore's efficient bureaucratic system. Moreover, when endemic urban tension and conflict broke out after 1945, Britain helped to strengthen the state fiscal power by extractive taxes such as the Central Provident Fund. It means that, according to Dan Slater (2010, 234–6), when a unified ruling party, the People's Action Party (PAP), emerged to seize the state, it gained abundant revenues and "a well-organized state apparatus willingly serving as a close handmaiden of the party".

In the Philippines, political development appeared, initially, to be promising. Free education was provided by Spain in 1863, producing an important class of educated elite. Spain's colonial successor, the United States, replicated its bi-cameral legislative system in the Philippines, making it one of the democratic trailblazers in Southeast Asia. In addition, compared with other countries in the region, transition to a full sovereign state was smooth in the post-war period. But deep in the new country's social structure, the highly personalised and localised patron–client relationships and bossism inherited from the colonial time weakened the state institutions and put off the vertical penetration of democratic rule, which became a lingering feature of Philippine politics (Anderson 1988; Sidel 1997).

Political regimes

The political systems built upon these colonial legacies and post-colonial disturbances have seen, in Cambodia and Singapore, a "pathway of domination" in which powerful political organisations have (re)centralised the state apparatus (Slater 2010, 22–23). In both countries, a well-entrenched dominant party emerged that retained its power within democratic institutions and through authoritarian repression, cumulating in features of electoral authoritarianism.

In Cambodia, the Cambodian People's Party (CPP), which was the sole legitimate party under the Vietnamese-fostered People's Republic of Kampuchea, gradually dominated the political arena. The first democratic election in 1993 (in which 90% of voter turnout was recorded and twenty political parties registered), however, saw the royalist party, the National United Front for an Independent, Neutral, Peaceful, and Cooperative Cambodia (FUNCINPEC), gain a majority of seats in the Constituent Assembly (Kingsbury 2005). But the CPP quickly re-seized political power by joining the coalition government, confronting FUNCINPEC in an armed showdown in 1997, and forcing FUNCINPEC's leader and its key supporters into exile.

In the subsequent decade, the CPP, by controlling the state institutions and "through a grand program of decentralization and deconcentration of power" (Hughes 2009, 207), consolidated its power in the electoral system, especially at the expense of the FUNCINPEC. In 2006, it successfully coerced FUNCINPEC and the Sam Rainsy Party to lower the constitutional restriction for forming a government from two-thirds to a simple majority vote in parliament. A split in FUNCINPEC also weakened its challenge to the CPP, with the latter winning 90 out of 123 National

Assembly seats and all ministerial positions in the 2008 election (Hughes 2009).

However, unlike the Barisan Nasional (BN) ruling coalition in Malaysia and the PAP in Singapore, CPP's de facto single-party rule was far less solidified. Firstly, the three elections preceding the 2008 contest saw the CPP grow in power, yet fail to impose dominance. With all the bargains and compromises, it took respectively six months and 12 months in the 1998 and 2003 elections to form a coalition government between the rival CPP and FUNCINPEC. Secondly, compared with the PAP in Singapore, the CPP is still in the process of consolidation. Only in the most recent election in 2008 has the CPP convincingly demonstrated its dominance, especially in terms of the popular votes it won (Table 6-1). Therefore, while its counterparts in the Malay Peninsula have already established their electoral monopolies and are seeking ways to retain their hegemony, the CPP is concerned in, at least equally, both entrenching its power base nation-wide and enhancing electoral performance.

Table 6-1: Electoral performances of hegemonic parties in recent three elections

(Cambodia: 2008, 2003 and 1998; Malaysia: 2008, 2004 and 1999; Singapore: 2011, 2006 and 2001)

	Cambodian People's Party		Barison Nasional		People's Action Party	
	Seats (%)	Votes (%)	Seats (%)	Votes (%)	Seats (%)	Votes (%)
Most recent election	73.2	58	63	50.1	93.1	60.1
Next to last election	59.3	47.3	90.87	63.9	97.6	66.6
Third to last election	52.5	42.4	76.6	56.5	97.6	75.3

Source: Hughes 2009; Moten 2009; Singapore Elections Department[62]

Meanwhile, accompanying the power consolidation process emerged a "worrying authoritarian trend in Cambodian politics" (European Parliament 2010). In a report released by Reporters without Borders (2010), Cambodia dropped by double digits from 2009 with regard to the global index on freedom of press, with journalists increasingly being arrested and imprisoned for political reasons. A new penal code that makes defamation a criminal offence was enforced in 2010, further strengthening the authoritarian apparatus (Um 2011). With the help of a CPP-controlled judicial system, Hun Sen frequently resorted to lawsuits "to silence or intimidate some of his opponents", such as the harassment against Sam Rainsy Party's member, Mu Sochua, in 2009 (Chandler 2010). In fact, the leader of that party, Sam Rainsy, has been in self-imposed exile and was sentenced in absentia to twelve-year imprisonment in early 2010 if he would return (Freedom House 2011). Human rights violations against ordinary citizens also worsened, especially in cases of relocation in which around 30,000 families are expelled, with little compensation, from their homes every year (Un 2012, 204). All these incidents show the Cambodian regime's decreasing political tolerance and increasing use of political repression.

By contrast, as Table 6-1 indicates, electoral authoritarianism in Singapore is far more consolidated. Opposition parties did not win a seat in parliament until 1981. Even with its best electoral performance in 2011, the opposition only managed to capture six out of 87 seats in parliament. Four factors are often attributed to PAP's durable dominance. The first factor points to the dramatic economic modernisation achieved under the PAP's rule which buttresses the latter's legitimacy. Even during the economic crisis of 1997–98, a 2006 study portrayed how the PAP exploited its discursive power, deliberately framing the crisis as a regional one and thus shifting responsibility in order to avoid a larger political crisis (Sim 2006). Some scholars, however, claim an opposite causation. On this score, Dan Slater (2010) highlights how the PAP solved the endemic and seemingly unmanageable mass threat and restored order to a turbulent society and polity in the post-colonial period. Its initial coalitional strength, achieved from the perceived threats and necessity for elite quiescence, was parlayed "into revamped state and party institutions" (Slater 2010, 237) which predated, if not determined, successful economic performance and regime durability.

Meanwhile, equally important is the PAP's ability to maintain elite unity and societal quiescence after the state-building stage. The PAP drew its major support from the English-educated middle class which formed the backbone of state institutions (Case 1996). While the BN in Malaysia experienced catastrophic elite fissures, especially in the late 1980s, Singapore's ruling party has never undergone such disunity. The absence of elite disunity has largely diminished the opportunity with which a powerful opposition could emerge and challenge PAP's hegemonic position (Case 2002), thus substantially dampening the competitiveness of Singapore's political system. Furthermore, societal grievances, which could have given an opposition force greater support, were suppressed by institutions such as the Citizens' Consultative Committees and the

Housing Development Board (Slater 2010), and by incentives such as education and health care subsidies (Case 1996). Political quiescence is also achieved by harnessing the media, whose supposed watchdog role has been replaced by functioning as a mouthpiece. On this score, Cherian George (2007) has detailed how the PAP controlled the press via "calibrated coercion" that effectively integrated covert strategies with overt repression. In fact, criticism of the government and the ruling elites (even their families) remains hazardous, since the PAP does not hesitate in resorting to defamation suits which cost the defendant badly.[63]

Last but not least, a number of manipulative methods are employed to ensure the PAP's electoral hegemony. Its "menu of manipulation" (in Schedler's words) includes the gerrymandering of electoral constituencies to incorporate anti-government areas into prevailingly pro-government electorates, the changing of electoral rules — often announced prior to elections or even during the campaign period — in favour of the PAP, and the surveillance of the electoral process in order to create a degree of fear in the electorate (Kingsbury 2005, 332–333). The government also maintains control over the Elections Department, leaving virtually no space for an independent electoral authority (Freedom House 2011). In summary, the PAP has perpetuated in Singapore an electoral authoritarian system less competitive, more resilient, and with higher level of state capacity than the Malaysian regime.

In the Philippines, the political system is best characterised as a low-quality electoral democracy. While ruling parties in Singapore and Cambodia gained domination, the Philippines had fallen into fragmentation (Slater 2010). Even under the martial law of the military dictatorship during 1972–86, Ferdinand Marcos could not effectively concentrate national power into his hands and build capable institutions. With its inability to order power from elites, middle classes and state officials, Dan Slater (2010, 163–164) observes that, "the Marcos regime failed to gain a preponderance of coercive, remunerative, and symbolic power, and stood — from day one of martial law — on shaky coalitional ground". Although a "People Power" movement in 1986 brought the Philippines back to a democratic course, weak state capacity, manifest for instance "in uncollected taxes and uncontrolled crime, bloated bureaucracies and denuded forests, low teacher salaries, and high emigration rates" (Abinales and Amoroso 2005, 2), remained a critical political problem.

In the post-Marcos era, elections are regularly held and political competitions are genuine. But these polls are often accompanied by serious flaws such as electoral fraud and political violence. In regard of the latter, an election-related massacre in November 2009, committed by a local political clan in the Province of Maguindanao, killed 57 people, including many journalists, and shocked the international community (Kraft 2010, 239). An important factor for such local violence is that state institutions, such as bureaucracy and the party system, are subordinate to, or trapped by, cacique politics characterised by local power clans and clientelistic behaviours. Elected presidents in the post-Marcos period are often vulnerable to oligarchic local powers and involved in predatory networks. Though she made little progress in political reform, Corazon Aquino suffered from a total of nine coup attempts, two of which came close to toppling her from office (McCoy 1999, 259). A later president, Joseph Estrada, won unprecedented popularity for his populist rhetoric, but he revived relationships with many of Marcos' cronies (Kingsbury 2005, 314–315). Hence, most of his redistributive efforts benefited his political allies and families instead of the public (Hutchcroft and Rocamora 2003, 281). In 2001, he was forced to resign amid massive protests, labelled as a second "People Power" movement, having served only half of his tenure. His successor, Macapagal-Arroyo, faced even more legitimacy crises including corruption scandals, impeachment attempts, as well as "a botched military mutiny" (Hutchcroft 2008, 141). In addition, the regional and local basis of national politics has also made the political party system fragmented. Hutchcroft and Rocamora (2003, 278) argue that in the post-Marcos era "the new parties that did emerge remained remarkably similar in their orientation toward patronage, reliance on coalitions of local elites, nonideological character, and shifting membership".

On the other hand, civil society is much empowered after the collapse of the Marcos regime as two rounds of "People Power" movements have demonstrated. Non-governmental organisations (NGOs), together with various kinds of civil rights groups, mushroomed after the lifting of martial law, which also weakened the state power vis-à-vis the society. But the strength of civil society is, to some extent, blunted by the fact that citizen activism faces intimidation, kidnappings, and even extrajudicial killings (Freedom House 2011). Moreover, as Mark Thompson (2008, 381) argues, civil society in the Philippines is composed principally of urban big businesses, allied with the urban middle class, which have refused to accept the verdict of the electoral majority. Rather than consolidating the democratic system, the massive campaigns mobilised by the "uncivil society" have "degenerated into an assault on democracy" (Thompson 2008). Therefore, in the Philippines, the political system, though cast as an electoral democracy, is debased by electoral manipulation, weak state institutions, and an urban-based, vibrant yet sometimes "uncivil" society. Compared with Indonesia, the Philippines is weaker in its state capacity. But political elites, except for populist leaders, are less vulnerable towards public criticism as long as they can appease urban business interests and local patronage networks.

In summary, the three countries studied in this chapter have different political contexts. Cambodia is recovering from decades of internal conflict, foreign occupation, and economic impoverishment, and consolidating an increasingly hegemonic political system. With major opponents sidelined, repressed, or exiled, Hun Sen's CPP is now facing an opposition force — which has failed to forge a cohesive alliance (Un 2012, 202-203) — even weaker than it was a decade ago. By contrast, electoral authoritarianism has been much more consolidated in Singapore, where political power and state apparatus are in the PAP's firm grasp, though recent political development has suggested a minor increase of electoral competitiveness (Ortmann 2011; Tan 2012). Meanwhile, the Philippines has perpetuated a democratic system, though with serious defects. State capacity remains weak, with political power decentralised and domestic conflicts protracted. The different characteristics of these political contexts have provided sources for the Internet politics in these countries.

Transgression, Online Civil Society and Internet Control

The last section briefly reviews the major characteristics of political systems in Cambodia, Singapore and the Philippines. As previously discussed, political regimes do not directly result in the virtual outcomes of Internet control. Instead, they provide contextual sources for the formation of online transgression and online civil society, which further determine Internet control policies. This part analyses these agency-level variables and the resultant Internet control situation in Cambodia, Singapore, and the Philippines respectively.

Cambodia

Internet politics in Cambodia possess both a low level of transgression and weak capacity of online civil society. Massive social movements organised via Internet technologies have been extremely rare in Cambodia. On this score, a political commentator recently remarked that it would be "premature and unrealistic" to imagine a social media revolution (like that in Egypt and Tunisia) breaking out in Cambodia, because "Cambodia's majority rural population has a long way before they can utilise social medias to create social changes to their local and national governments" (Pan 2011). The absence of large-scale online movements is not because Cambodian activists and civil society groups lack necessary motivation to organise transgressive events on cyberspace. Instead, low transgression (as well as weak online civil society) results from the underdeveloped status of Cambodia's Internet system. As *Freedom in the World* (Freedom House 2011) states briefly, (in Cambodia) "the Internet is fairly free of government control, but access is largely limited to urban centers". A country ravaged by enduring civil wars and external threats, Cambodia lags behind most of its neighbours in terms of political, social and economic development. Particularly devastating was the totalitarian rule under the Khmer Rouge which, with its radical programmes, caused millions of civilians' death and severe destruction of state infrastructure. Development and popularisation of Internet technologies, which normally rely on fixed-line transmission, become difficult to introduce as the state communication network has been largely wrecked. In fact, Cambodia was the first country in the world where mobile phone subscribers surpassed fixed landline users (International Telecommunication Union 2002), an anomaly that reflects its infrastructural underdevelopment.

According to Internet World Stats,[64] in 2010, there are only 78,000 Internet users among the 14-million population in Cambodia, representing a poor Internet penetration rate at 0.5%. Limited Internet usage suggests that the influence of Internet-facilitated contentiousness remains inconspicuous for the ruling elites. On this score, a report by the International Telecommunication Union (2002) claims that "one of the reasons the government has not felt the need to interfere [with the Internet] is that there are so few Internet users".

Moreover, the limited Internet usage in Cambodia could also be found in political parties' Internet involvement. Here a comparison is drawn between the Cambodian People's Party and its major rival in 2008 election, the Sam Rainsy Party. Both parties have established their official websites (CPP: www.cpp.org.kh; SRP: www.samrainsyparty.org), but the major function of their sites is to provide basic information about the parties, such as their activities, organisational structure and internal statutes, as well as hyperlinks to other affiliated websites. While the SRP website is more technically complex, since it uploads on the site video podcasts about the rallies, speeches and other SRP-organised events, neither site offers a section, such as forum or comment, which allows interaction between the party and its supporters (electorate). It is noteworthy that two overseas websites of SRP — SRP in Australia and

New Zealand (http://samrainsyanz.org/) and SRP in North America (www.srpna.org) — have an online forum section and a section for online donation respectively. This also indicates the lack of demand in domestic political communications.

Online media in Cambodia are also underdeveloped. Major websites that provide news in Khmer and English are the online versions of traditional media, such as Koh Sante Pheap and Phonm Penh Post, which are under control of the government or individual politicians. Critical online media do exist, but their influence is minor. For example, KI Media — an independent news blog site critical of the government — only ranks 150th among the most visited websites in Cambodia, and 54.2% of its readers reside in the United States.[65] Its relative low ratio of domestic readership (40.1%) indicates its limited influence in Cambodia.

Meanwhile it should be noticed that Cambodia has a heavy reliance on foreign aid which may, to some extent, restrict government's repression. This situation, however, is changing with increasingly unconditional investment coming from China and Vietnam. According to the CRS Report for Congress (Lum 2007), over half of the Cambodian government budget is derived from external funding. Its largest providers of official development assistance include the European Union, Japan, Australia, and the United States. These donor countries, together with international financial organisations, were grouped in 1996 into a consortium — the Consultative Group for Cambodia — under the auspices of the World Bank, which hold annual meetings to formulate economic and political reform guidelines for the Cambodian government (Lum 2007). Therefore, dependent on foreign assistance, the Cambodian authority has faced considerable external pressure to abide by international norms of democracy and human rights. For instance, when a political crisis broke out in 2003 that prevented the CPP from forming a government after the election, donors such as the World Bank and the Asian Development Bank shelved any new projects until the deadlock was solved twelve months later (Sjöberg and Sjöholm 2006). The Western leverage, however, would be further reduced and offset by the expanding inflows of unconditional aid and investment from China and Vietnam (Um 2011). By 2011, the two authoritarian states had become, respectively, the first and second largest investors in Cambodia (Un 2012, 207). Vietnam even began to dominate Cambodia's telecommunication services such as mobile phones and the broadband Internet.[66] In this sense, we should not overestimate the extent to which foreign leverage may continuously prevent the Cambodian government from deploying Internet control strategies.

Therefore, in Cambodia, the underdeveloped nature of cyberspace poses little political transgression for Hun Sen and his hegemonic party. There are few urgent needs, in this sense, for the ruling elites to tighten up Internet regulations. On the other hand, however, limited Internet expansion also leads to weak capacity of online civil society. This implies that when online transgression increases and the government feels challenged, online communities will be unable to mount effective resistance against the government responding with suppression. In fact, Cambodia's technical capacity for Internet control is steadily rising, as an increasing number of Cambodian officials have received training in Internet control tactics from China, through various exchange programmes (Cain 2009; Kurlantzick 2011). An incident occurred in early 2011 in which the KI Media was blocked temporarily by some ISPs,[67] which may well imply such a trend. Therefore, it is reasonable to argue that, as the ruling CPP consolidates its power, pushing the political regime into a more stable form of electoral authoritarianism, and as the Internet penetration steadily expands over the country, especially into the countryside, the government will be likely to adopt a harsher stance toward the Internet usage.

Singapore

In Singapore, online transgression has been intensifying steadily over the past decade, but has never exceeded moderate levels. Although massive movements calling for political change, like the Red Shirt movements in Thailand and Bersih movements in Malaysia, are hardly found in Singapore, the Internet technologies do enable opposition parties to galvanise large number of supporters into massive rallies. For instance, during the 2011 general election, tens of thousands of people, demonstrating the highest turnout in Singapore's history, were mobilised to attend the political rally in support of the opposition Workers' Party. The Internet has played such a significant role in the mobilisation process that the *Guardian* (2011) describes the driving force of the rally as being "electric".

Therefore, for Singapore's ruling elites, the most serious challenge posed by the Internet exists in the electoral battlefield where, similar to the Malaysian case, if to a lesser extent, social media and other Internet tools facilitate greater public participation, empower opposition forces, and produce a more competitive electoral outcome (Smith 2007; Lee and Kan 2009). Such a threat became evident in the 2011 general election when alternative online portals such as the *Online Citizen* and the *Temasek*

Review offered independent information and analyses about the election, and social networking sites were used to organise online campaigns and disseminate information about opposition activities (Ortmann 2011). Nonetheless, political transgression generated by these online activities remains moderate, since contentiousness is centred on particular features and processes, instead of the fundamental dimensions, of the political system. In addition, even with the opposition's best electoral performance, the PAP still retains 90% of parliamentary seats in the 2011 general election. A Malaysian 2008 tsunami has not occurred in the southern city-state.

On the other hand, in contrast to the Malaysian situation, the capacity of online civil society in Singapore is not strong. Despite the highest rate (77.2% in 2010) of Internet penetration in Southeast Asia and increasing collaboration between online communities and opposition parties, Singapore lacks prominent and independent online media, which are more vibrant and influential in Malaysia. For example, while *Malaysiakini* is featured by its professionalism and ranks among the top ten most popular websites in Malaysia, the *Online Citizen*, arguably the most influential alternative news site in Singapore, is based on voluntary contribution rather than professional journalism and only ranks 320th in terms of Internet traffic domestically.[68] More importantly, online media are perceived to be less credible in Singapore than in Malaysia. In this regard, a 2010 survey of media and public relation professionals in the two countries found that Singaporean respondents tended to prefer traditional media to online media, as they believed that traditional media were of higher quality of analysis and more balanced and unbiased (Media Monitor 2010).

Compared with that in Malaysia, cohesiveness in Singapore's online community is only moderate. A sense of caution, or the "culture of self-censorship" as Terence Lee (2010) phrases it, has been instilled in Singaporean cyberspace. The fear of lawsuits and other sanctions, already substantiated in a number of incidents, would inevitably weaken collective action organised through the Internet. According to a 2000 survey named the Singapore Internet Project (SIP), a considerable proportion of respondents did not believe that the Internet would provide political empowerment (Kuo et al. 2002). It showed that only 13.6% of Internet users agreed that with the Internet, people could have more political power, while 51.8% of them disagreed. A similar gap also existed (18.7% vs. 41.5%) on the proposition that "people will have more say about what the government does" with the help of the Internet. Moreover, there are even some pro-establishment bloggers who defend the government and rebuke the opposition through their blogs (Ortmann 2011, 161), further splitting Singapore's online communities.

As a result, Internet control in Singapore appears much more repressive than that in Malaysia. Although the Media Development Authority (MDA) in Singapore claims that the government has only imposed on the Internet a "light-touch" regulatory framework, one that simultaneously promotes responsible use while giving industry players "maximum flexibility" (Open Net Initiative 2007), the Internet control practice in Singapore is, in fact, more remarkable than many other competitive regimes in terms of its early implementation and efficiency. In 1994, when public Internet access was first made available in Singapore, reports disclosed illegal file scans on Internet users' private email accounts, conducted by the government-linked Internet Service Provider (ISP). As Garry Rodan argues (1998, 77), despite the government's promise that no unannounced searches would be further conducted, "its demonstrated capability to search files on this vast a scale may in itself and by design have a suitably chilling effect". Such psychological pressure was further amplified by the fact that in 1998 a unit of the Singapore Police Force had been established to "patrol the alleys of cyberspace" (Chong 1998).

Another important element of deterrence rests on the extensive regulatory framework. The national Broadcasting Act stipulated a class licence scheme under which all ISPs and the Internet content providers (ICPs), which are determined to be political parties or persons "engaged in the propagation, promotion or discussion of political or religious issues relating to Singapore", must register with the MDA (Open Net Initiative 2007). The MDA also formulated an Internet Code of Practice which, if ICPs failed to comply, indicated sanctions such as fines and licence suspensions or terminations. Other laws curbing offline civil liberties, especially the Sedition Act, have been gradually expanded into regulating the online space. For instance, a Singaporean doctoral student in the United States was threatened with a defamation suit in 2005 due to his online posts criticising the state-funded agency A*STAR (*Singapore News* 2005).

More importantly, in order to maintain the PAP's hegemony in elections, the Singaporean government restricted the use of the Internet during election campaigns. In the 1997 election, political parties were banned from displaying any posters, biodata, party platforms, speeches or policy positions on their websites (Rodan 1998). While these restrictions were removed ahead of the 2001 election, posting opinion poll results was still prohibited and political parties were required to appoint moderators in the chat rooms and forums on their websites to take responsibility for the content (Smith 2007). Websites not belonging to opposition parties but active in political discussion were also harassed in the 2001 election, resulting in the shutdown of the discussion forum section of the Think Centre, established by James Gomez, and the whole site of Sintercom (Gomez 2002). Shortly before the 2006 election, the government once again warned that Internet users engaging in online political debates around the electoral period could be prosecuted if they fuelled dangerous discourse and misled the public. Podcasting and videocasting of political materials were banned, along with a warning, as the result of opposition parties' (especially the Singapore Democratic Party) active use of these technologies (Smith 2007). Even when bans on online campaigning were substantially lifted ahead of the 2011 election, the government continued its control of the Internet. For example, the government in early 2011 "gazetted" one of the major socio-political blog sites, the *Online Citizen*, as a political association and brought it under the jurisdiction of the rules that govern other political organisations such as political parties (*The Economist* 2011). In this sense, the "light-touch" approach labelled by the government was indeed restrictive in favour of the PAP.

Moreover, with online transgression only moderate, the PAP even has space to relax Internet regulations for electoral purposes. Ahead of the 2001 election, previous bans on online posters and other information by opposition websites were lifted, which was claimed by the government as a liberalising concession (Smith 2007). In the election held in 2011, a similar strategy was employed with the government permitting campaign recordings and video about election rallies to be uploaded on the Internet (Mydans 2011). In such way, the PAP could strategically yet slightly loosen Internet control in order to garner public support in elections.

The Philippines

To date, the Philippine government has, in general, left the Internet uncontrolled. According to a recent report by Freedom House (2011), "while the censorship board has broad powers to edit or ban content, government censorship is generally not a serious problem. The Internet is widely available and uncensored [in the Philippines]". In terms of availability, the number of Internet users has grown exponentially from two million in 2000, or 2.6% of total population, to 29.7 million a decade later, around 29.7% of its 99.9 million population.[69]

The freedom that the Philippine cyberspace has enjoyed owes less to the democratic regime than to the low-to-medium transgression generated by Internet usage. Firstly, after the second "People Power" movement that ousted Estrada from presidency in 2001, massive social movements with direct political objectives are infrequent. Moreover, the Internet has so far exerted an unimportant influence upon the Philippines' party and electoral systems, often characterised by patrimonialism and clientelism (Quimpo 2005; Ufen 2012). Based on a survey of presidential aspirants' Internet strategies ahead of the 2010 election, Mary Mirandilla (2009) argues that most presidential candidates employ the Internet merely to supplement their campaigns on traditional mainstream media, with content and strategy hardly varying online and offline. An online survey conducted in the same study (Mirandilla 2009) shows that Internet users in the Philippines "have little expectation from cyber campaigning platforms and see them as just a source of more detailed information about candidates". The lack of public participation in the online campaign may well reflect the nature of the Filipino democracy which rests on "its capacity to rotate power at the top without effective participation of those below" (Hutchcroft 2008, 143).

Secondly, although the Internet becomes increasingly useful in exposing elite corruption and enhancing executive accountability, the oligarchic political system remains generally immune to this new challenge. For instance, when the Arroyo–Garcillano scandal was leaked in 2005, the National Telecommunications Commission prohibited the broadcasting on mainstream television and radio of the audio tape that identified the President Macapagal-Arroyo as being involved in electoral manipulation. It was a weblog, the blog of the Philippine Centre for Investigative Journalism (PCIJ), which circumvented the ban and uploaded the audio file on its website. Within less than two years, the file had been downloaded by a total of 1,076,913 users and evoked nation-wide debate over the scandal (Montemayor 2008). However, even if these scandals were revealed by both new and traditional media (Hicken 2008; Hutchcroft 2008), the pro-government coalition, named TEAM Unity, still managed to capture 142 out of 218 contested seats in the House of Representatives (Hicken 2008). And it seems that what further determines the development of Arroyo's case lies in the current president's political calculation as well as the struggle over the judicial system (Whaley 2012), instead of lying in the public pressure from both online and offline worlds.

On the other hand, the capacity of online civil society in the Philippines is at a moderate-high level. Around 33% of the Philippine population gets access to the Internet, indicating a penetration rate higher than that in Indonesia and Thailand.[70] Although political linkage between online community and political parties is far from extensive, the vibrant and well-organised NGO community in the Philippines is increasingly engaging with online society in pursuing specific policy reforms (Soriano 2008). With regard to critical online media, while most of the influential news websites, such as *Philippine Daily Inquirer* (inquirer.net) and *ABS-CBN News* (abs-cbnnews.com),[71] are operated by traditional media groups, many of these traditional media are privately owned and they offer a wide variety of views (Freedom House 2010). In addition, unlike the situation in Indonesia and Singapore where traditional media are much more trusted by the public, there is only a minor discrepancy between traditional and online media in their perceived credibility. According to a 2011 survey conducted under the Philippine Trust Index project, online news sites (68%) are less trusted than televisions (74%), but are more trusted than newspapers (66%) and radio stations (66%) (Medina 2011). The same survey also finds that media, in general, is the second most trusted institution (following the Church), outstripping NGOs, businesses, and the government. Last but not least, there is little evidence of major counter-movements in cyberspace. In fact, civil society organisations in the Philippines are strongly connected to each other through coalitions and networks, indicating a high degree of cohesion (Jose 2011).

Therefore, online civil society in the Philippines enjoys greater capacity than that in Indonesia. The difference may relate to the different trajectories of democratisation in the two countries. As Vince Boudreau (2009) argued, democratic transition in the Philippines was built upon the already organised and mobilised popular movements, thus leaving a strong societal force in the post-Marcos politics, while in Indonesia the transition was a pact among elites, thus constraining and fragmenting the anti-regime movements. As a result, the Philippine civil society had already gained considerable organisational power even before the advent of new information technologies. More importantly, succeeding governments in the Philippines also had to respond to such social force by adopting liberalising programmes (Magadia 2003). In this sense, it would be more difficult for the Philippine government than its Indonesian counterpart to deploy any repressive measure upon cyberspace. In fact, as Garry Rodan (1998, 87) notices, when the Association of Southeast Asian Nations (ASEAN) Committee on Culture and Information met in Singapore in September 1996 and agreed to collaborate on finding ways to control activities on the Internet, the representative of the Philippines was the only one who rejected the idea of political control.

Conclusion

In this chapter, the cases of Cambodia, Singapore, and the Philippines have been treated separately and less comprehensively, because although they are also competitive regimes, their regime types correspond closely to the level of Internet control. It is the anomalous cases that most require explanation. However, even in Cambodia, Singapore and the Philippines, it may be that regime type is spuriously correlating with Internet controls, hence masking the fact that causality in these cases is much the same as in the previous cases, involving transgressiveness and civil society capacity. Therefore, this chapter reviewed online transgression, online civil society and their respective impact on government Internet control strategies in Cambodia, Singapore, and the Philippines, the remaining Southeast Asian countries with competitive political systems. In general, the empirical finding accords with our theoretical model which underscores the role of transgression and civil society, instead of regime type (whether electoral authoritarian or electoral democratic in form).

The underdeveloped Internet system in Cambodia brings about a low level of political transgression that the ruling elites feel little urgent need to confront. But the weak capacity of online civil society, another product of the infrastructural underdevelopment, makes such Internet freedom vulnerable to potential repression as online transgression increases. By contrast, online transgression is greater in Singapore's case, but not as much as that in the Malaysian case where the government confronts effective online activism and large-scale street protests. Moreover, online civil society in Singapore appears less cohesive than its counterpart in Malaysia, thus imposing fewer constraints upon the government's Internet control practices. As a result, Internet control is implemented in a far more extensive and systemic way by the PAP government. The case of the Philippines, meanwhile, involves a low-medium level of online transgression and a relatively strong online civil society. Since transgression is lower and online communities stronger, the Philippine government allows greater freedom on cyberspace than Indonesia does. In other words, the low quality of the Philippines' electoral democracy does not necessarily translate into political repression on cyberspace. Table 6-2 below briefly summarises these findings.

It is also necessary to point out the role of political contexts which cause the variation of online transgression and online civil societies. For instance, the underdevelopment of Cambodia's Internet infrastructure is related to the enduring internal conflicts that ravaged its economy and society, while the capacity of Philippine online civil society stems mainly from its offline counterpart that has been significant in the democratic transition process in the 1980s. Such discussion enables us to better understand why different levels of transgression are formed across country-cases and why the capacity of online civil societies varies. The final chapter will further explore the theoretical implications of our empirical findings.

Table 6-2: Explaining Internet control in the peripheral cases

	Transgressiveness	**Civil-society Capacity**	**Internet Control**
Cambodia	Low	Low	Low
Singapore	Medium	Medium	Medium-High
Philippines	Low-Medium	Medium-High	Low

CHAPTER SEVEN

CONCLUSION

Major Findings of this Book

Over the past decade, Internet technologies have deeply penetrated society and, in various aspects, become intertwined with political institutions and processes. This book examines one important aspect of such a relationship — the political control of the Internet. Looking beyond hard authoritarian polities which are the usual subject of research on Internet control, it focuses on more competitive political regimes (in Southeast Asia) and aims to identify, under electoral authoritarian or democratic conditions, the major determinants of Internet control practices. Three in-depth cases, including Malaysia, Thailand, and Indonesia, were chosen to test a theoretical model which addresses the intensity of political contentiousness and the capacity of civil society. In addition, the remaining competitive regimes in Southeast Asia, namely Cambodia, Singapore, and the Philippines, were also examined, though briefly, to confirm the validity of our propositions.

This book raises two major hypotheses, the first of which concerns the relationship between regime type and Internet control. It suggests that, contrary to previous studies that implicitly or explicitly attribute Internet control to the authoritarian or democratic nature of a particular regime (Rodan 1998; Taubman 1998; Kalathil and Boas 2003; Calingaert 2010; Morozov 2011a), this dimension (the degree of democraticness) has only minor effects upon the extent of Internet control. It is true that liberal democracies tend to impose far fewer Internet control measures and that politically closed regimes appear to be most repressive in this regard. However, an increase along the democracy index does not necessarily accompany a decline in Internet controls, especially in the intermediate range of the political regime continuum. Instead, in some cases, countries with more democratic regimes may repress cyberspace in a more systematic way than those with conspicuous defects in democracy. On this score, the three country-cases in our study demonstrate this: Indonesia features a consolidated electoral democracy, indeed the most democratic regime in Southeast Asia, but it implements Internet control policies to an extent similar with, or even greater than, Malaysia where competitive authoritarianism has been entrenched and resilient. Further, Thailand's unstable democracy sits in between these two countries in terms of regime democraticness (less democratic than that in Indonesia but more so than Malaysia), but it adopts a highly repressive approach to regulating cyberspace through extensive Internet monitoring and blocking. Even as a nation-wide election held in 2011 has plausibly brought the country back to democracy, the newly elected Yingluck government continues, if not escalates, the war against Internet freedom.

Therefore, regime type per se arguably does not determine the pervasiveness of Internet controls. In fact, even some full democracies, such as South Korea and the United States, attempt to control cyberspace, while some deeply authoritarian states, especially in Africa, have so far left the Internet generally unfettered (York 2011). Democratic and authoritarian regime types do not in themselves determine the internal political dynamics that may shape the cost and benefit (from the perspective of decision-makers) of Internet control. For instance, the Internet in some political contexts may pose grave threats to the country's traditional culture, dominant ideology, or hierarchical power structure, and may pose a serious challenge through empowering massive social movements or exacerbating inter-ethnic (inter-religious) conflicts. But, in another context, the use of the Internet may be largely apolitical, with online activism only sporadic and un-coordinated. The contrast between these scenarios poses different levels of political threat to national governments, thus indicating different potential benefits (or the urgency) of Internet control practice.

On the other hand, the cost of Internet censorship also varies. It substantially increases when civil society groups, opposition parties, and/or private sectors mount cohesive and effective resistance (through boycott, protest, petition, voting, and other means) against Internet control policies. And it will dwindle when such societal resistance is weak and fragmented. Taking these interactions into account arguably provides a better understanding of when, and to what level, Internet controls are imposed. Accordingly, this study has been guided by a two-dimensional model that highlights the level of online transgressiveness (as an indicator of Internet control benefits) and online civil society capacity (as an indicator of Internet control costs). It argues that these two variables, rather than regime type, best explain Internet control practices in the competitive political systems.

This second hypothesis has also been borne out by our case studies. Internet politics in Thailand has involved a high level of transgressiveness and a fragmented online civil society. On the one hand, ex-Prime Minister Thaksin Shinawatra and his supporters have actively employed Internet tools to sustain their struggle, through mass demonstrations, against the political establishment. The socio-political order has been fundamentally threatened by a growing anti-monarchy discourse in cyberspace. On the other hand, because Thai online communities are polarised between pro-Thaksin and royalist forces, collective resistance against Internet censorship appears weak and ineffective. Under such circumstances, government authorities, under both Abhisit and Yingluck administrations, can even effectively garner substantial public support in their campaign against "illegal" online activities. As a result, the Internet in Thailand suffers from extensive and systematic control measures, including massive website blocking and harsh suppression of critical Internet users.

By contrast, Malaysia faces a moderate-to-high level of transgressiveness. The Internet facilitated massive social movements which empowered the opposition force to deprive, for the first time since the late 1960s, the ruling coalition of its two-thirds parliamentary majority in the 2008 elections. The hegemonic status of the BN has thus been severely undermined, and it may even be broken if the Internet continues to perform its significant role in the upcoming elections. However, even if the government's anxieties over the Internet mount, the online civil society in Malaysia, which often coordinates (allies) with the opposition parties and other social forces and has independent online media outlets, has effectively prevented the government from upgrading its Internet control arsenal. Therefore, harassment against netizens and online media takes place sporadically, together with some covert strategies being deployed to soften the Internet threat. But none of these methods have grown consistent and systemic, as most plans to institutionalise Internet control have been shelved shortly amid strong public resistance.

Meanwhile, online transgressiveness remains at a moderate degree in the Indonesian case. The political threats of the Internet, though potent, are mostly parochial, specific to particular persons and organisations. However, while political transgression in Indonesia is somewhat lower than that in Malaysia, the former's online civil society is also weaker than that of Malaysia. Its weaknesses exist in the underdeveloped linkages between online communities and offline political organisations, the lack of critical online media, as well as in the cleavages of social values between conservative and liberal groups. The discrepancy in the capacity of online civil societies between Indonesia and Malaysia has, to some extent, offset the different degrees of online transgressiveness which would otherwise lead to an Internet control approach in Indonesia more modest than that in the Malaysian case. In fact, the two countries implement Internet control practices, though by different means, at a similar level. This finding bears out this study's theoretical framework.

This model also applies to our other cases of Southeast Asian competitive systems. The combination of low transgressiveness and weak civil society capacity in Cambodia, mainly caused by infrastructural underdevelopment, has led to considerable Internet freedom in the country, although such freedom is vulnerable to potential repression if online transgression increases. By comparison, Singapore has stronger online transgressiveness, as reflected in the outcome of the 2011 general election, and moderate online civil society capacity. It has carried out systemic Internet control since the late 1990s, thus serving as the vanguard of cyber censorship in the region. But as online civil society gains strength, the ruling party in Singapore strategically dismantles Internet regulations, piece by piece, to meet its electoral needs. Finally, Internet freedom in the Philippines stems from low transgressiveness on cyberspace and the relatively vibrant and cohesive online civil society. Not only does the Philippine government lack sufficient impetus to promote Internet control policies, but sporadic attempts to do so have raised fierce public outcry and been subsequently aborted. In general, these supplementary cases have met our propositions. Table 7-1 below briefly illustrates the different combinations of variables among these countries.

Table 7-1: Combination of variables and outcomes

Country	Level of Transgressiveness	Capacity of Online Civil Society	Expected Level of Internet Control	Virtual Outcome
Thailand	High	Low	High	High
Malaysia	Medium-High	High	Medium	Medium
Indonesia	Medium	Medium	Medium	Medium
Singapore	Medium	Medium	Medium	Medium-High
Cambodia	Low	Low	Low-Medium	Low
Philippines	Low-Medium	Medium-High	Low	Low

This model enables us to closely investigate the rationale (cost–benefit calculation) behind Internet control practices. While online transgressiveness serves as the impetus that defines the necessity of Internet controls, online civil society represents an inhibiting force, the capacity of which determines the extent to which societal resistance against Internet control might succeed. In fact, since full democracies are more likely to accommodate political contention (Carey 2006) and are more accountable to civil society groups, Internet regulation in these countries tends to be loose, in general. At the same time, fully closed, authoritarian regimes are readily disturbed by Internet-facilitated dissent and demonstrations, with civil society appearing weak vis-à-vis the state. Under such conditions, Internet control approach escalates and often becomes highly repressive. But regime type does not directly explain Internet control. For instance, transgression in cyberspace grew dramatically in Britain in 2011, as massive civil unrest was effectively organised via online social media. Consequently, the British government responded by cracking down Internet users (*CBC News* 2011) and attempting to censor those social media sites (Abbas 2011). At the same time, China's planned implementation of the Internet filtering programme, named "Green Dam", faced boycott — and was shelved soon afterward — by coordinated online communities that included ordinary netizens, prominent intellectuals, online organised groups, as well as IT companies (Hille 2009). In this sense, our two dimensional model also displays its explanatory power by accounting for Internet control policies in fully democratic and authoritarian contexts.

Furthermore, this research also analysed the contextual conditions that, in the long term, shaped the form of online transgression and the formation of online civil society. It examined the political and economic contexts in the 1990s when Southeast Asian governments first introduced Internet technologies and adopted initial regulations. It found that the presence of liberalising and democratising conditions created, for early Internet development, a political environment characterised by laissez-faire policies and democratic discourse. Under such circumstances, governments would adopt a political-friendly approach — imposing little regulation on Internet content and behaviour — in promoting Internet development. When these conditions are absent, as in the case of Singapore, Internet control policies would be deployed at an early stage, indicating greater levels in institutionalising Internet control practices. Discussion of these contextual conditions supplements our understanding of Internet control by charting the historical process in which the Internet and domestic politics interacts.

Alternative Explanations of Internet Control

Although discussions above have demonstrated our model's potential application to a larger range of country-cases, thus enhancing its universality, there is still the possibility that other factors may also affect government decisions about controlling cyberspace. Therefore, it is worth examining alternative explanations of Internet control before we further gauge the implications of our findings.

External to the socio-political context, one potential factor focuses on the degree of Internet development. It may be argued that a low Internet penetration rate (or weak Internet accessibility) decreases the general volume of Internet usage and thus the necessity of Internet control. Indeed, the level of Internet development is related to the level of Internet control in one of our Southeast Asian cases, Cambodia. Both the low online transgressiveness and weak online civil society there seem to stem primarily from infrastructural underdevelopment of the IT sector. However, the validity of this development hypothesis is not straightforward. Among our country-cases, Thailand and Singapore are the two countries with relatively high levels of Internet control, but their Internet penetration rates differ significantly — 27.4% in Thailand and 77.2% in Singapore respectively. Similar contrasts also exist between Malaysia (58.8%) and Indonesia (16.1%) with moderate Internet control, and between Cambodia (2.2%) and the Philippines (29.2%) with low Internet control.

In its *Freedom on the Net 2011* report, Freedom House (2011a) analysts have compared the scores of Internet freedom with Internet penetration rates in particular countries. The distribution of these two variables (Fig.7-1) demonstrates great divergence — the penetration–freedom correlation is much weaker than the regime–freedom one — among these countries. As Fig.7-1 shows, countries at a similar level of Internet development may impose substantially different levels of Internet controls (for example, compare the triad of Italy, Malaysia and Bahrain, or that of Brazil, Turkey and Saudi Arabia). Especially for those countries under the (Internet) "Partly Free" category, the increase in Internet penetration may result in either greater repression *or* greater Internet freedom (Freedom House 2011a, 18). Internet development can contribute to harsher government regulation since it may bring about stronger online activism, and thus stronger transgressiveness. Conversely, it can contribute to less political repression because it may enlarge and strengthen the online community and induce higher costs for Internet control. On this score, Cherian George (2005, 903) has argued that "a country with lower penetration levels of a medium [i.e., the Internet] may, paradoxically, exhibit superior utilisation of that medium than a country with higher penetration". As a result, while we may find in some cases that rates of Internet penetration have distinctive effects upon Internet control practices, these impacts are retracted through the intensity of online transgression and the capacity of online civil society. Thus, no firm, universal relationship between Internet development and freedom exists.

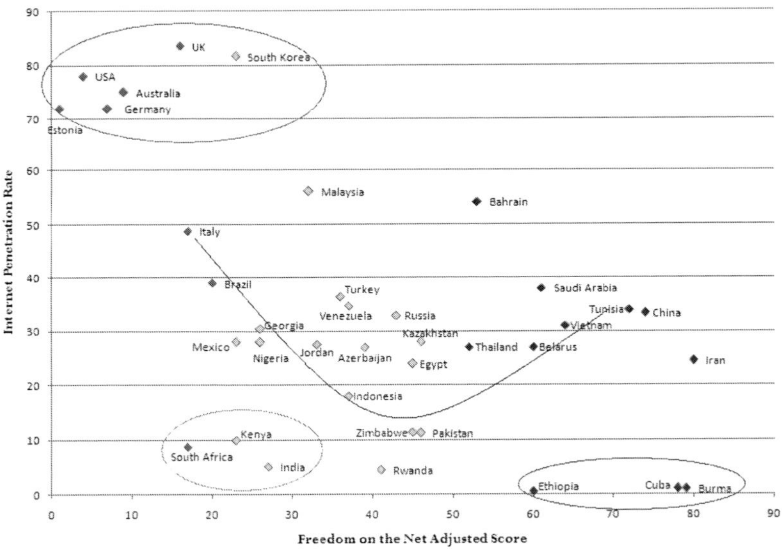

Fig. 7-1: Internet freedom vs. penetration rate

Another alternative explanation considers Internet control as an extension of general media censorship. In fact, a number of studies have situated Internet control within the broad discussion of media politics (Rodan 2004; Wu 2004; Rawnsley 2006; McNair 2009; Freedom House 2011b; Lee 2010). It is true that in many countries state institutions that regulate traditional media and cyberspace overlap to a large extent. It is also true that many government authorities tend to place the online media under the same regulatory framework as mainstream media. But Internet control differs in nature from traditional media control, since technological sophistication matters in the former and ownership plays a significant role in the latter. In this sense, freedom in cyberspace does not necessarily guarantee freedom in the media space or vice versa. For instance, in the *Freedom of the Press 2011* report, four of our regional cases fall into the

"Not Free" class: Thailand receive a score of 62, Cambodia 63, Malaysia 64, and Singapore 68 (the higher the score, the worse the press freedom) (Freedom House 2011b). Yet these countries show great divergence in their respective approaches to regulating the Internet. While Thailand and Singapore impose harsh controls upon Internet usage, the other two adopt far fewer restrictions. More generally, Freedom House's (2011a, 17) recent report has acknowledged this gap between "a relatively unobstructed domain of free expression" on cyberspace and "a more repressive or dangerous environment for traditional media" in a significant number of countries. Given that the Web 2.0 applications facilitate much more civil participation and interaction than traditional media does, to regard Internet control simply as an extension of media censorship may risk overlooking the different political dynamics emerging on the online and offline worlds.

A final alternative explanation involves foreign investment (and/or foreign aid) as a constraining factor in Internet controls. The development of market economy and international capital flows have increasingly called for host governments' transparency and accountability which are associated with the free flow of information. In fact, during my field research, some informants, especially in Malaysia, have cited the concern for foreign investment as a major factor that prevents government authorities from imposing Internet censorship. This argument leads to a hypothesis that countries with heavier reliance upon foreign investment will allow greater Internet freedom, while countries with smaller foreign investment inflows impose more controls.

Table 7-2: Significance of FDI in Southeast Asian economies

Country	Accumulated FDI inflow, 2001–10	GDP in 2010 (PPP)	Proportion
Cambodia	4.377	30.91	14.20%
Indonesia	46.373	1054	4.40%
Malaysia	47.279	424.8	11.10%
Philippines	15.827	375.9	4.20%
Singapore	198.802	299.5	66.40%
Thailand	67.685	600.8	11.30%

Source: Data on FDI are obtained from UNCTAD database; data on GDP are retrieved from CIA World Factbook

To evaluate this hypothesis, we can calculate the accumulated foreign direct investment (FDI) inflows during 2001–10 in our six respective country-cases, and compare the figures with their GDP as of 2010.[72] The resulting FDI/GDP ratio will reflect approximately the reliance on FDI in these countries. However, little evidence can be found for any relationship between FDI dependence and Internet freedom. Among the four countries whose FDI/GDP proportion exceeds 10%, two restrictively control cyberspace (Singapore and Thailand), one imposes modest control (Malaysia), and the other generally leaves the Internet unfettered (Cambodia). For Indonesia and the Philippines, countries that have similar amount of FDI reliance, negative impact on FDI does not seem to be a determinate factor as their Internet control policies diverge substantially. Therefore, even if foreign investment may, to some extent, constrain government policies on Internet control, it can be hardly weighed as a decisive factor. In fact, business interests may even assist in imposing Internet repression, rather than guaranteeing Internet freedom. On this score, a number of studies have identified the negative role of multinational corporations, some of which are Western companies, in facilitating Internet control, through means of technological assistance or compliance with host country's requests (Zittrain and Palfrey 2008; Zuckerman 2010). In this sense, the constraining effect of foreign investors should not be taken for granted.

In summary, none of the alternative explanations canvassed above for explaining Internet controls are convincing after subjecting them to empirical testing. Such tests help to validate our explanation centring on transgressiveness and online civil society. The following part further discusses the theoretical importance of our findings.

Theoretical Implications

This research project presents a new framework for understanding the practice of Internet control, which has become increasingly important in the study of Internet politics and regime type more generally. Unlike previous studies that either technically describe the measures and institutions of Internet control (see, for example, Goldsmith and Wu 2006; Murdoch and Anderson 2008; Deibert and Rohozinski 2010; Morozov 2011b), or empirically describe how Internet control functions in a particular setting (see, for example, Rodan 1998; Wacker 2003; Noman 2011), this study considers Internet control as a political phenomenon across different settings that merits theoretical explanation. It differs from conventional wisdom that simply links Internet control with authoritarianism. Instead, it centres on how online activists deliberately exploit the political opportunities offered by new information technologies to challenge the political establishment, thereby posing different levels and forms of challenges to the government authorities. The Internet threats greatly vary in terms of severity, even between countries with similar political systems. In some cases, the Internet facilitates political dissent against state-sponsored ideologies, institutions, and procedures, and thus imposes fundamental challenges to the socio-political order. Although closed authoritarian countries have higher probability to be exposed to such systemic threats, some democratic states may face similar pressures, since their nation- and state-building processes may be rooted in key political compromises (such as special status for religion) or particular power distribution (such as hierarchical position for a specific institution). Under these circumstances, the Internet may undermine and destabilise the "pact of domination" (Brachet-Marquez 2001) upon which conflicting political and social interests are reconciled. In this sense, the assertion that the Internet overturns authoritarianism and consolidates democracy may be directly contradicted.

Meanwhile, this study also highlights the role of online civil society in affecting Internet control policies. In general, online communities represent a counteracting force against state control of cyberspace. Their alliance with offline political groups, especially opposition parties, media, and prominent NGOs, and their utilisation of critical online media, are important in pressuring the government and safeguarding Internet freedom. However, in societies that are fragmented or polarised along social, ideological, or religious lines, online communities may lack cohesion and, in some cases, break apart in antagonistic factions. Some conservative elements may form alliances with the government, advocate Internet censorship, and even actively engage in suppressing dissenting voices on cyberspace. The existence of this "uncivil society" not only explains why Internet control still prevails even in countries with ostensibly flourishing civil societies, but also indicates the limits in the Internet's assumed powers of liberalisation.

Internet control constitutes a new form of political repression. Some findings in this study have buttressed the existing literature on repression. To a large extent, these findings confirm Davenport and Armstrong's (2004) thesis that within the intermediate range on a continuum of political regime types, the propensity of a government to impose coercion is less likely to be determined by the types of regimes. They also underscore the centrality of threat in understanding political repression, an argument that within this field is unanimously accepted (Davenport 2007). However, as previous studies on state repression have not reached consensus on how to operationalise political threats (i.e. through any typology of threats) or how the "threat–response" process exactly works (Davenport 2007, 8–9), this research offers an approach to analyse political threats by examining the scale and content of online political contentiousness. The case studies investigate in detail how state authorities securitise the Internet threats.

In addition, this research contributes to the study of political repression in two other aspects. Firstly, it identifies the role of civil society in limiting the repression that a government can impose. Previous studies have considered a number of constraining factors such as influence of elections, executive accountability, and economic conditions. This research provides fresh insights to the relationship between civil society and repression. In particular, it finds that the role of civil society is quite ambiguous, since the fragmentation of it may even exacerbate state repression. To what extent this finding could apply to other types of repression remains unclear, but it would be valuable to further explore such relationships. Secondly, this study demonstrates the necessity to disaggregate different forms of repression. States with unfavourable human rights records (such as Cambodia and the Philippines) may not necessarily infringe on Internet freedom. A recent example in Malaysia saw the government violently cracking down the Bersih 3.0 movement by using tear gas and water cannons and arresting hundreds of protestors, but no restrictions was imposed on cyberspace where sharp criticism against police brutality exploded (Gooch 2012). By the same token, it could be expected that a similar gap also occurs between other forms of repression. For instance, a government that faces the exposure of a scandal has a list of choices at its disposal, ranging from filing libel suits to kidnapping the informant. It is important to further identify the specific condition that gives rise to the particular choice of political repression, and to identify the inter-relationship among repression strategies.

Moreover, this study also speaks to the broad literature on political regimes and democratisation. Over the past decade, increasing attention has been paid to the hybridity of political systems that reside somewhere between full democracy and closed authoritarianism (see Levitsky and Way 2002; Ottaway 2003; Schedler ed. 2006). These political regimes are, in general, responsive to public demands but fall short of full democracy. The era of information technologies has altered state power vis-à-vis the society and the way in which state and society interact. Cyberspace not only represents a new domain for such interaction, but also changes the rules and outcomes of other interactions. For instance, state monopoly over traditional media, a means often employed to perpetuate hybrid regimes, becomes less effective as the Internet largely circumvents state information control. In fact, some previously resilient regimes either fall apart or face great pressure for fundamental reform — both types of trajectories are, to some extent at least, caused by political use of the Internet. On this score, our case studies have specified, and differentiated between, the political challenges posed to different states and their respective regimes. It helps us to better understand how (and why) these hybrid regimes persist or change in the new information age.

The Way Forward

With the Internet deeply penetrating more societies and information technologies developing over time, the interaction between the Internet and political system will change further. In this sense, this book serves as only a preliminary step to a more comprehensive understanding of Internet politics. Based on this study, future research could proceed in two directions. The first is to broaden the research area geographically and to test the extent to which findings of this book can be generalised to a larger set of (cross-region) country-samples, thus encouraging statistical analysis. To be specific, we have to use multivariate regression, covering as many countries as possible, to measure the correlation between the level of transgressiveness and online civil society capacity on the one hand, and the degree of Internet control on the other, and to examine more thoroughly whether other potential factors can be controlled and excluded. Such quantitative assessment will demand much effort, since the required data sets, especially those about transgressiveness and online civil society, are not yet available and to date the most extensive data (provided by Freedom House) on Internet freedom (and this may not satisfactorily equal the level of Internet control) include merely 37 countries.

Difficulties in expanding the scope of research also stem from the fact that governments are increasingly adopting covert strategies to monitor, filter, manipulate, and even attack cyberspace. Transparency on Internet control remains quite low, especially in politically closed regimes. On this score, the Open Net Initiative's testing of Internet filtering practices offers valuable experience, although the technical complexity confines its sample size to barely a dozen. Despite these difficulties, a more comprehensive assessment on Internet control, as well as further assessment on the role of transgressiveness and civil society, is still necessary and will be influential in facilitating future studies on Internet politics. Perhaps one way to move forward is to quantify online transgressiveness and online civil society capacity, and combine them with existing data (medium sample size) on Internet freedom.

Following another direction, we may also need to think about the political consequences of Internet control. In particular, does Internet control trigger or hinder democratisation? And if so, to what extent? Previous studies have identified the role of social movements in democratic transitions. Tactics and patterns of political dissent are considered to be influential in changing the coalitional relationship among established power structures (Boudreau 2004). Meanwhile, whether political repression increases or reduces the level of contentiousness remains an open question as either side is supported by statistical and historical evidence (Davenport 2007). Evaluating the political impacts of Internet control may supplement this literature. Some incidents have demonstrated the likelihood of such impacts. For example, if Internet control strategies are implemented and escalate suddenly, most probably amid rising social unrest, it is highly likely that government authorities would face strong resistance from civil society, already established and networked in cyberspace, perhaps summoning pressures from international actors. In Thailand a sharp increase in website blockage during the Red Shirt movement in 2010 was accompanied by the plummeting legitimacy of the Abhisit government. In both Burma and Egypt, government decisions to switch off the entire Internet network when massive social movements broke out only increased the pressure by which they were undermined. All three countries underwent political change after their clumsy manipulation of the Internet: Thailand underwent a transition from a military-backed government to populist leaders; Egypt saw the fall of Hosni Mubarak who has ruled the country for thirty years; Burmese generals took the initiative to liberalise politics, though on their own terms, and organised the first nation-wide election since 1990. By contrast, if authoritarian or semi-authoritarian governments were able to counter the Internet threats more strategically, by employing covert and indirect means rather than suddenly increasing the level of control, they might have a greater chance of surviving in the new information age. These arguments, nonetheless, are still preliminary and require more in-depth research. In this sense, we should re-examine, borrowing Brownlee's (2007) title, authoritarianism in an age of information technologies.

APPENDIX A

NOTES ON INTERVIEW METHODS

1. Purposes of interviews and sample selection

The purposes of using interviews in this research are mainly twofold: (1) gathering first-hand information of the process, rationales, and constraints of Internet regulation and enhancing our understanding of political interactions caused by Internet usage and controls; (2) cross-checking and complementing secondary information with interview materials and guiding work that uses other sources of data. Elite interview, instead of broadly-based survey, is used because the research subject is closely related to policy-making and the target interviewees are expected to have adequate knowledge and experience on Internet regulation.

In order to obtain nuanced opinions, interviewees were selected from four different sectors. The "Government" sector refers to those government agencies and organisations that share responsibility of Internet regulations. The "Media" sector mainly refers to media agencies that operate in cyberspace. The "NGO" sector includes organisations that advocate for freedom of expression and information. It should be noticed that some political bloggers are included in this category due to their similar stance on Internet regulation. Both NGOs and critical bloggers represent strong forces in civil society. The "Academia" sector comprises prominent scholars in political science, communication, and law. Some of them have been directly involved in the process of Internet-related legislations, while others have valuable knowledge of their domestic politics. The "Other" category is created to feature interviewees that are difficult to be placed within the four main categories but are still important for this research. In fact only one interviewee, who is both an opposition politician and a well-known blogger, falls into that group.

Figure-1 below illustrates the distribution of interviewees in each sector. The "NGO" sector has a relatively larger proportion, since it covers both organisations and individual bloggers. Although fewer respondents come from the "Government" sector, they are drawn from government institutions that directly oversee Internet regulation issues. The exact ratio of four categories in each country may vary slightly, due to non-response and different situation in these countries. But in each country I managed to draw interviewees from all four sectors, thus to some extent ensuring representativeness. Moreover, I drew roughly similar amount of interviewees from each country: of the 40 interviewees, 15 are from Thailand, 14 from Malaysia, and 11 from Indonesia. The variance of sample size was, again, caused by non-response and other unexpected problems such as availability and tight schedule that recurred throughout each field trip.

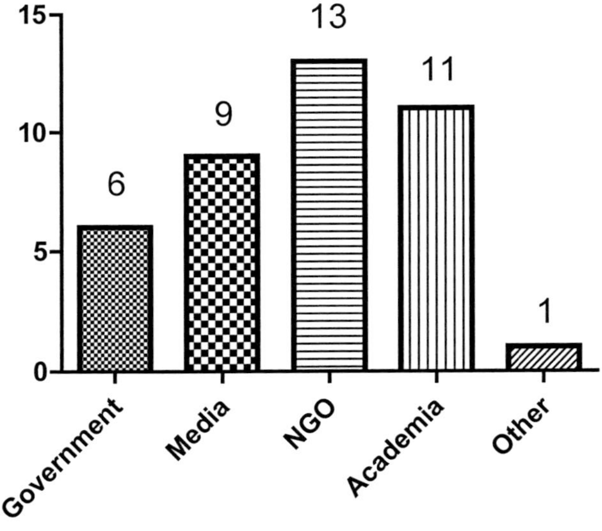

Figure-1 Distribution of interviewees

In order to identify target interviewees, this research built the sampling frame by carefully following Internet politics issues covered by mainstream media in these countries, including the *Bangkok Post*, the *Nation*, the *New Straits Times*, and the *Jakarta Post* and so on. It also relied on other scholarly journals and monographs to identify major organisations and individuals relevant to this research. Most of the online media, NGOs, and bloggers interviewed in this study (such as *Prachathai*, Thai Netizens Network, *Malaysiakini*, and ICT Watch etc.) were selected by these means. Normally the heads of these organisations (for example, the chief editor or the executive director) were invited to interviews, and in some cases their colleagues were also interviewed if deemed necessary. By contrast, although a sampling frame for government sector was easier to create, officials that I was allowed to conduct interviews were often of middle rank. The positive side, however, was that these interviewed officials often had personal and direct experience of handling or implementing Internet control matters, which their superiors may not have. When identified interviewees were successfully reached, I also used snowball sampling to enlarge our contacts and seek for more interviewees. This method was particularly useful when I sought for relevant NGOs which were often well-connected with each other.

In all I conducted 40 interviews in Thailand, Malaysia, and Indonesia, not including those people with whom I briefly chatted. The number of people included in the sampling frame was almost twice as large as the eventual interviews we managed to conduct. Time constraints, unavailability, as well as refusal of invitation inevitably decreased the effective sample size. But as I initially planned, my effective samples had representatives from different sectors and even from different organisations within each sector.

The question list for each country uses semi-structured form. Core questions, mainly concerning impacts of the Internet and regulation issues, are listed in the last section. It should be noticed that these questions are used as guidelines in interviews. Many follow-up questions were raised during each interview. And the exact question lists would be slightly different, depending on the specific sector the interviewee belonged to.

2. Interview questions

Thailand

(1) Political impacts of Internet

Since its birth the Internet technology has been described as a unique force that would bring fundamental political and social transformations. In your opinion, what is the most important effect that the Internet has made in Thai politics? Can you give any example of such impact?

During recent political crisis, what role do you think the Internet has played in facilitating the confrontation between red and yellow shirts?

The popularisation of Internet also incurs malpractices (illegal and immoral) in the cyber space, such as dissemination of pornographic content. Do such Internet-related negative effects also exist in political area? Any example?

(2) Internet control

Across the East Asian region, more and more countries have begun to regulate the Internet system. In Thailand, what methods have been used by government to control the Internet?

To what extent are these methods effective? Why?

Do you have any personal experience of Internet censorship or other types of Internet control? How did that happen?

What are the major obstacles for government to control the Internet? Are they technological, political, or economic? Any example?

In your opinion, what is the most important reason for government to control the Internet? What kind of rhetoric or excuse has the government used to frame that reason?

(3) other related issues

Do you think the Internet control practices in Thailand are affected by other neighboring countries, like China and Singapore? Or the other way round, will its Internet censorship affect decision-making in other states?

Malaysia

(1) Political impacts of Internet

Since its birth the Internet technology has been described as a unique force that would bring fundamental political and social transformations. In your opinion, what is the most important effect that the Internet has made in Malaysian politics? Can you give any example of such impact?

Do you think in what aspects the Internet could contribute to build a democracy in Malaysia?

During 2008 general election, what role do you think the Internet has played in weakening the ruling coalition BN? Any example?

The popularisation of Internet also incurs malpractices (illegal and immoral) in the cyber space, such as dissemination of pornographic content. Do such Internet-related negative effects also exist in political area? Any example?

(2) Internet control

Across the East Asian region, more and more countries have begun to regulate the Internet system. In Malaysia, what methods have been used by government to control the Internet?

Do you have any personal experience of Internet censorship or other types of Internet control? How did that happen?

What are the major obstacles for government to control the Internet? Are they technological, political, or economic? Any example?

In your opinion, what is the most important reason for government to control the Internet? What kind of rhetoric or excuse has the government used to frame that reason?

(3) Other related issues

Do you think the Internet control practices in Malaysia are affected by other neighboring countries, like China and Singapore? Or the other way round, will its Internet censorship affect decision-making in other states?

Indonesia

(1) Political impacts of Internet

(Introduction) Could you describe your early experience with Internet system? (the first time of using Internet; perception of Internet)

The Internet and other information technologies have been considered as important in overthrowing the Suharto's regime in 1998. Do you have any experience of Internet's political impacts at that time?

Can you give any example of such impact?

After the political transformation in 1998, what role has the Internet played in promoting democratisation in Indonesia? In what aspects?

We have seen many events that the Internet was used as an important tool to empower individuals and civil society against the government or other authorities. How did the online mobilization spread into the offline society? What are the mechanisms that connect the online and offline world?

Are the online movements associated with any political parties? Why or why not?

The popularisation of Internet also incurs malpractices (illegal and immoral) in the cyber space, such as dissemination of pornographic content. Do such Internet-related negative effects also exist in political area? Any example?

(2) Internet control

Across the East Asian region, more and more countries have begun to regulate the Internet system. In Indonesia, what methods have been used by government to control the Internet?

To what extent are these methods effective? Why?

The government has attempted several times to impose more rigid regulation on the cyber space. What are the reasons that the government gives to justify its proposals?

Besides the reasons offered by the government, do you think there is other political consideration behind such proposals?

Who are the major supporters of Internet regulation (parties and social groups) and who the major opponents?

What are the major obstacles for government to control the Internet? Are they technological, political, or economic? Any example?

In the near future is it possible for the government to deploy more repressive and sophisticated Internet control system? Such as a filtering system with keywords search.

(3) Other related issues

Do you think the Internet control practices in Singapore, Thailand, and Malaysia will affect the decision of Indonesian government? Is there any evidence that Indonesia is emulating other Southeast Asian countries?

APPENDIX B

MEASURING TRANSGRESSIVENESS AND CIVIL SOCIETY CAPACITY

1. Online transgressiveness

To transgress is to cross the limits or boundaries that political establishment has prescribed in conducting political activities. Transgressiveness refers to the extent to which online political contention and activities stand in contradiction, inversion, or as alternatives to the status quo.

Transgressiveness is measured by its scale and content:

Transgressiveness is scored as **HIGH** if:

(1) Massive social movements (involving at least 10,000 participants) occurred which were (widely believed to be) largely facilitated by Internet technologies (SCALE)
(2) A major proportion of participants of these movements came from political groups that were previously inactive, marginalized, or politically restricted (SCALE)
(3) Core political claims raised by online contentious groups seriously contradicted with the fundamental social order (for example, monarchy, religious authority, and so on), or major ideological or cultural norms, upon which political structure of a given country relied (CONTENT).

Transgressiveness is scored as **MEDIUM** if:

(1) Massive (Internet facilitated) social movements occurred but criteria (2) and (3) above are not met (SCALE)
(2) Core political claims raised by online contentious groups concentrated on rules and/or norms of a particular political process

or institution (for example, electoral system, financial institution, and so on) (CONTENT).

Transgressiveness is scored as **LOW** if:

(1) No evidence of massive Internet-empowered social movements (SCALE)
(2) No evidence of structural or institutional political claims (CONTENT).

2. Online civil society capacity

Online civil society refers to the societal community of associations, initiatives, movements and networks in cyberspace. (Gosewinkel and Kocka 2006)

In this study, the capacity of online civil society refers to the bargaining power that online communities have to forestall, restrain, or resist government repression.

Cases are coded as **HIGH** if:

(1) The Internet is available to over half of the domestic population (PENETRATION)
(2) Online social movements have strong political backing (for example, receiving funding from or being organized by political groups, especially political parties) (POLITICAL LINKAGE)
(3) Domestic online media are critical of and independent from the government, have substantial share of readership, and have equal or higher credibility over traditional media (CRITICAL MEDIA)
(4) There is no evidence of major counter-movements (movements that are antagonistic to each other in terms of political or ideological orientations) in cyberspace (COHESIVENESS).

Cases are coded as **MEDIUM** if:

(1) The Internet penetrates a substantial portion of the population (10% to 50%) (PENETRATION)
(2) Criteria for POLITICAL LINKAGE and CRITICAL MEDIA are only partly met
(3) Criterion for COHESIVENESS is met.

Cases are coded as **LOW** if:

(1) The Internet penetrates only a small portion of the population (less than 10%) (PENETRATION)
(2) Criteria for POLITICAL LINKAGE and CRITICAL MEDIA are only partly met or not met
(3) Criterion for COHESIVENESS is seriously violated (i.e. clear evidence of major counter-movements).

NOTES

[1] "Packet switching" refers to the digital communication method that divides messages into fixed-size units (packets) and transmits them in a shared network. For details of how this process works, see: Abbate (2000, 17–21).

[2] Although titles of these reports indicate different years (2010 vs. 2011), they describe the situation in basically the same period: Freedom House's report surveys Internet freedom in 2010, the Democracy Index 2010 traces the political situation up until November 2010, and the Polity IV report covers the same period.

[3] It should be noticed that besides EIU and Polity IV's reports, Freedom House's annual surveys are also widely used to measure the level of democracy. However, in our "regime–control" comparison we did not include Freedom House's democracy scores, in order to avoid overlapping elements covered both by democracy scores (especially the "civil liberty" dimension) and Internet freedom scores.

[4] Brunei, Laos, Myanmar and Vietnam are thus excluded from this study since their political regimes arguably resemble politically closed authoritarianism.

[5] Here social movements refer mainly to those movements with evident, strong political meanings and demands. Therefore, movements that advocate for generally social and economic issues, such as labour rights, homosexuality, environment protection and so on, are not included in our measurement.

[6] This notion of "audience cost" was first used by scholars in International Relations studies, especially in areas of military crises, models of alliances, economic sanctions and international cooperation in general (Fearon 1994; Schultz 2001; Tomz 2007). But some recent studies have begun to adopt this notion in analysing domestic human rights protection (see Chung 2007).

[7] Singapore was expelled from the Federation and achieved independent status in 1965.

[8] This study follows Levitsky and Way (2010) who distinguish between electoral and competitive authoritarianism and classify the Malaysian regime as one of the latter.

[9] For a more comprehensive account of authoritarian manipulation, see: Andreas Schedler (2002) and William Case (2006).

[10] The data was provided on the MSC website, available at: http://www.mscmalaysia.my/topic/Company+Directory.

[11] Other advantages cited include advanced infrastructure, high quality cosmopolitan living, the educated, multilingual population and so on. See: http://www.mscmalaysia.my/topic/12073058097925.

[12] The full text and sub-provisions of CMA can be retrieved at: http://www.skmm.gov.my/index.php?c=public&v=art_view&art_id=43.

[13] In fact, in 1989, the UMNO split and the formation of Semangat' 46, which soon allied itself with two prominent opposition parties Parti Islam Se-Malaysia (PAS) and Democratic Action Party (DAP), led to a strong electoral challenge in the 1990 general election.

[14] The relevant data for Malaysia's Internet development are retrieved from the World Bank's database, which can be seen at: http://data.worldbank.org/country/malaysia. Meanwhile, it should be noticed that the Internet World Stats reports a higher penetration rate (64.6% in 2010) and larger online population (nearly 17 million in 2010) in Malaysia. The relevant information is available at: http://www.internetworldstats.com/asia/my.htm.

[15] The word "bersih" means clean in Malay. It was adopted from the name of rally organisation, "Gabungan Pilihanraya Bersih dan Adil" (Coalition for Clean and Fair Elections). For further information about the organisation, see: http://bersih.org/.

[16] The state assembly in Sarawak state was not dissolved since the state election there was held in 2006 and subsequently in 2010.

[17] The eight points of Bersih movements' demands can be viewed at their official website at: http://www.bersih.org/?page_id=352.

[18] The data was compiled by the author at Lim Kit Siang's personal blog, available at: http://blog.limkitsiang.com/. His Chinese language blog, at http://cblog.limkitsiang.com/, has fewer posts, but has a similar ratio of topics.

[19] Data on Internet penetration rate in Malaysia can be retrieved from Internet World Stats, available at: http://www.internetworldstats.com/asia/my.htm.

[20] The complete list of endorsees is available at: http://bersih.org/?page_id=360.

[21] See Bersih 2.0's Facebook page at: http://www.facebook.com/pages/BERSIH-20-OFFICIAL/213938935311531.

[22] Bersih 2.0 claimed that 50,000 people attended the July 9 rally, but other independent estimates gauged the figure between 10,000 and 20,000; see Simon Roughneen (2011).

[23] For a comprehensive overview of Internet filtering techniques and related data on countries cases, research by the Open Net Initiative would be instructional. Its various research outputs can be viewed at: http://opennet.net/research.

[24] Relevant information on the corruption of Taib Mahmud and other officials in Sarawak can be found on *Sarawak Report*'s website at http://www.sarawak report.org.

[25] See the self-claimed profile of Radio Free Sarawak at http://radiofreesarawak.org/aboutus/.

[26] The post is available at Rocky's bru blog: http://www.rockybru.com.my/2011/03/sarawak-reports-vs-sarawak-report.html.

[27] The other country that received this status was the Philippines. Both Thailand and the Philippines were dropped from the "free" group after 2005, while Indonesia took their position as the remaining "free" state in Southeast Asia. Freedom House's reports are accessible at http://www.freedomhouse.org/report-types/freedom-world.

[28] The Democracy Index compiled by the Economist Intelligence Unit and used in Chapter 2 was first released in 2006. Therefore this index is not included here for comparison.
[29] Data for this figure are obtained from the Polity IV project. Here we only use Polity IV's data without comparison with other reliable indexes on democracy (such as reports from Freedom House and EIU) because Polity IV's data have a longer time-span than other data sources, thus enabling us to observe the long-term trend of political development in Thailand.
[30] The other one is the Telephone Organisation of Thailand (TOT).
[31] Shin Satellite, Shin Corp, and AIS are the different branches of Shin Corporation.
[32] The exact starting year of this website still needs to be clarified.
[33] However, it should be noticed that the actual composition of red shirts and yellow shirts is much more complex. See McCargo (2009) and Naruemon and McCargo (2011).
[34] In Thailand, yellow is usually used to decorate royal symbols.
[35] ABAC refers to the Assumption Business Administration College, a forerunner of Assumption University (AU).
[36] The detailed information about the poll can be found at http://www.ryt9.com/s/abcp/448833.
[37] Freedom House (2011) scores on political rights in Thailand — the higher the score, the less the political freedom it represents — witnessed a sharp increase (from 3 to 7) immediately after the coup, and remained high in the following years. By contrast, scores on civil liberties in Thailand only slightly changed from 4 to 5 during the same period.
[38] With regard to how mobilising structure affects social movement, see: Tarrow, Sidney. 1998. *Power in Movement: Social Movements and Contentious Politics*. Cambridge University Press.
[39] The full text of the Manifesto can be retrieved from the *Asia Sentinel*: http://www.asiasentinel.com/index.php?option=com_content&task=view&id=1714&Itemid=159.
[40] Data for Internet penetration rates in Thailand and over the region are retrieved from Internet World Stats, available at: http://www.internetworldstats.com/stats3.htm.
[41] It should be noted that rifts between the PAD and the New Politics Party became apparent ahead of the 2011 general election. Subsequently Sondhi resigned from the NPP and the NPP leader, Somsak Kosaisuuk, left the PAD leadership. Therefore, after 2011 the two organisations have in effect divorced. For relevant news about the rupture, see: http://www.bangkokpost.com/news/politics/234340/somsak-vetoes-pad-demand-for-npp-poll-boycott.
[42] Data on popularity of websites in a particular country can be obtained from Alexa.com (www.alexal.com) which offers information about websites including Internet traffic statistics and top website rankings.
[43] The survey is available at: http://research.spu.ac.th/poll/content/1/12362.php.
[44] In fact, on the second day of the coup, the Council for Democratic Reform (CDR), as the de facto supreme authority established by the coup action, announced its Order No.5 that demanded the Ministry of ICT "restrict, control,

stop or destroy information within any given communication network deemed to affect the constitutional monarchy" (*Bangkok Post* 2006).

[45] The English translation of CCA is provided by *Prachathai* news website: http://www.prachatai.com/english/node/117.

[46] The relevant news about this man, Amphon Tangnoppaku, can be found in *The Nation*: http://www.nationmultimedia.com/politics/Lese-majeste-texting-convict-sentenced-to-20-years-30170473.html.

[47] The news story is available at http://www.google.com/hostednews/afp/article/ALeqM5iMwhnHSt36x-Hm-Wm_Y3thBV_t9w?docId=CNG.66922326b86c84d2b0f3ebc395ad2035.1c1.

[48] The relevant news story is available on the *Asian Correspondent*: http://asiancorrespondent.com/72773/campaign-for-a-good-and-moral-government-in-thailand/.

[49] One can review Indonesia's performances in the *Freedom in the World* surveys at: http://www.freedomhouse.org/report/freedom-world/2011/indonesia.

[50] It refers to five principles of "Belief in the One and Only God, Just and Civilised Humanity, the Unity of Indonesia, Democracy Guided by Inner Wisdom in Unanimity Arising out of Deliberation among Representatives, and Social Justice for All the People of Indonesia" (Smith ed. 1974, 174–183).

[51] The two censuses in 1995 and 2000 reported respectively around a 195 million- and a 206 million-population in Indonesia. The population statistics from are available from the Badan Pusat Statistik at: http://dds.bps.go.id/eng/tab_sub/view.php?tabel=1&daftar=1&id_subyek=12&notab=1.

[52] Indonesia's performances in the *Freedom in the World* surveys can be viewed at: http://www.freedomhouse.org/report/freedom-world/2011/indonesia.

[53] It should be noted that radical elements, especially in the form of extreme Islamist groups, still play a role in Indonesian society. But with the government's increasingly aggressive counter-terrorism measures, the influence of these groups has largely subsided (see Rommel Banlaoi 2009).

[54] See CIA Factbook: Indonesia, last updated on March 1, 2012, available at: https://www.cia.gov/library/publications/the-world-factbook/geos/id.html.

[55] By contrast, a research firm suggested that there were 55 million Internet users in 2011. See: *The Jakarta Post* (2011) "Internet users in Indonesia reaches 55 million people", October 28, 2011, available at: http://www.thejakartapost.com/news/2011/10/28/internet-users-indonesia-reaches-55-million-people.html.

[56] The relevant data can be retrieved from: https://wiki.smu.edu.sg/digitalmediaasia/Digital_Media_in_Indonesia.

[57] Data on Facebook penetration rate in Indonesia are obtained from Internet World Stats, available at: http://www.internetworldstats.com/asia.htm.

[58] "Fitna" is a short film largely perceived as anti-Islamic and is thus banned by many Muslim countries (Global Voices Advocacy 2008).

[59] This event happened in 2010 when several private pornographic videos featuring three well-known celebrities in Indonesia were leaked on the Internet which triggered extensive discussions around the country. "Ariel" refers to the famous pop star involved.

[60] In Pakistan, there were even massive social demonstrations against the use of Facebook in the aftermath of the "Draw Mohammed" event. See: http://cnsnews.com/news/article/facebook-accused-hurting-muslims-anti-islamic-sentiments.
[61] For the complete list of members in this coalition, as well as its media partners, see the website http://anrhti.blogdetik.com/tentang-anrhti/.
[62] Relevant statistics are available on the official website of Elections Department: http://www.elections.gov.sg/elections_past_parliamentary.html.
[63] For instance, the *Far Eastern Economic Review* paid 300,000 US dollars in exchange for a settlement with the Lees family in 2009, and the *International Herald Tribune* paid 122,400 in 2010 for similar reason (Freedom House 2011).
[64] Relevant statistics on Cambodia are available at http://www.internetworldstats.com/asia/kh.htm.
[65] Statistics about the KI Media website (ki-media.blogspot.com) are retrieved from Alexa, a web information company, available at: http://www.alexa.com/siteinfo/ki-media.blogspot.com.
[66] The relevant information could be viewed at: http://businesstimes.com.vn/vietnam-fpt-to-invest-us10m-in-cambodia-telecom-market/.
[67] The government, however, denied ordering such block and attributed the inaccessibility to technical reasons. The relevant information was obtained through personal email communication with Kounila Keo, a prominent blogger and reporter in Cambodia.
[68] Statistics about the *Online Citizen* website (http://theonlinecitizen.com/) are retrieved from Alexa, available at: http://www.alexa.com/siteinfo/theonlinecitizen.com.
[69] Relevant statistics are available at http://www.internetworldstats.com/asia/ph.htm.
[70] Data on Philippines' Internet penetration rate are retrieved from Internet World Stats, available at: http://www.internetworldstats.com/asia.htm.
[71] According to Alexa's records, *Inquirer* ranks 23rd among the most popular websites in the Philippines, and *ABS-CBN News* ranks 38th. See: http://www.alexa.com/topsites/countries;0/PH.
[72] We use the 10-year accumulated data for FDI inflows, instead of 1-year figure, to avoid annual fluctuation of FDI volume. In fact, such fluctuation can be considerable, primarily caused by global economic downturn (and upturn).

BIBLIOGRAPHY

Abbas, Mohammed. 2011. "UK may disrupt social networks during unrest". *Reuters*. August 11. http://www.reuters.com/article/2011/08/11/us-britain-riot-networks-idUSTRE77A20C20110811.

Abbate, Janet. 2000. *Inventing the Internet*. The MIT Press.

Abbott, Jason. 2001. "Vanquishing Banquo's ghost: the Anwar Ibrahim affair and its impact on Malaysian politics". *Asian Studies Review* 25(3): 285-308.

—. 2004. "The Internet, reformasi and democratization in Malaysia". In *The State of Malaysia: Ethnicity, Equity and Reform*. Edited by Edmund Terence Gomez. London: RoutledgeCurzon.

—. 2011a. "Electoral Authoritarianism and the Print Media in Malaysia: Measuring Political Bias and Analyzing Its Cause". *Asian Affairs: An American Review* 38(1): 1-38.

—. 2011b. "Cacophony or Empowerment? Analysing the Impact of New Information Communication Technologies and New Social Media in Southeast Asia". *Journal of Current Southeast Asian Affairs* 30(4): 3-31.

—. 2012. "Democracy@internet.org Revisited: analysing the socio-political impact of the internet and new social media in East Asia". *Third World Quarterly* 33(2): 333-357.

Abinales, Patricio and Donna Amoroso. 2005. *State and Society in the Philippines*. New York and Oxford: Rowman and Littlefield Publishers.

Agence France-Presse. 2005. "Thailand to block over 800,000 sites". November 28.

Ainsworth, David. 2001. *Capacity building in civil society: NGO networks in the regions of Mexico*. PhD diss., McGill University.

Allen, Pam. 2007. "Challenging Diversity?: Indonesia's Anti-Pornography Bill". *Asian Studies Review* 31(2): 101-115.

Amnesty International. 1999. "Malaysia: Human rights undermined: Restrictive laws in a parliamentary democracy". http://www.amnesty.org/en/library/info/ASA28/006/1999/en.

Anderson, Benedict. 1983. "Old State, New Society: Indonesia's New Order in Comparative Historical Perspective". *Journal of Asian Studies* 42(3): 477-496.

—. 1988. "Cacique democracy in the Philippines: origins and dreams". *New Left Review* 169: 3-31.
Anek Laothamatas. 1992. *Business Associations and the New Political Economy of Thailand: From Bureaucratic Polity to Liberal Corporatism*. Westview Press.
Anuar, Mustafa. 2005. "Politics and the Media in Malaysia". *Kasarinlan: Philippine Journal of Third World Studies* 1: 5-47.
Aspinall, Edward. 2009. "Combatants to Contractors: The Political Economy of Peace in Aceh". *Indonesia* 87: 1-34.
—. 2010. "The Irony of Success". *Journal of Democracy* 21(2): 20-34.
Athukorala, Prema-chandra. 2010. "Malaysian Economy in Three Crises". *Working Papers in Trade and Development* No.2010/12. Arndt-Corden Department of Economics, Crawford School of Economics and Government, ANU College of Asia and the Pacific.
Baker, Chris and Pasuk Phongpaichit. 2009. *A History of Thailand* (2nd Edition). Cambridge University Press.
Banerjee, Indrajit. 2003. *Rhetoric and Reality: The Internet Challenge for Democracy in Asia*. Singapore: Eastern Universities Press.
Bangkok Post. 1998. "On-line Activists Step up Fight". April 29.
—. 2006. "Council wants clamps on information". September 21.
—. 2010. "Political battles go online". August 1.
—. 2012. "Political prisoners added to compensation scheme". February 26.
Banlaoi, Rommel. 2009. "War against terrorism in Southeast Asia". *The Jakarta Post*. November 18. http://www.thejakartapost.com/news/2009/11/18/war-against-terrorism-southeast-asia.html.
Barley, Tasa Nugraza and Marcel Thee. 2011. "Unleashing Indonesian Anger over the Internet". *The Jakarta Globe*. January 31. http://www.thejakartaglobe.com/lifeandtimes/unleashing-indonesian-anger-over-the-internet/419590.
Barton, Greg. 2010. "Indonesia: Legitimacy, Secular Democracy, and Islam". *Politics & Policy* 38(3): 471-496.
BBC. 2008. "Prophet cartoon row in Indonesia". November 19. http://news.bbc.co.uk/2/hi/7737223.stm.
—. 2010. "Burma hit by massive net attack ahead of election". November 4. http://www.bbc.co.uk/news/technology-11693214.
Blanton, Shannon and Robert Blanton. 2007. "What Attracts Foreign Investors? An Examination of Human Rights and Foreign Direct Investment". *Journal of Politics* 69(1): 143-155.
Boudreau, Vince. 2004. *Resisting Dictatorship: Repression and Protest in Southeast Asia.* Cambridge University Press.

—. 2009. "Elections, repression and authoritarian survival in post-transition Indonesia and the Philippines". *The Pacific Review* 22(2): 233-253.

Brachet-Marquez, Viviane. 2001. *El pacto de dominacion / The pact of domination*. Colegio De Mexico A.C.

Bräuchler, Birgit. 2004. "Public Sphere and Identity Politics in the Moluccan Cyberspace". *Electronic Journal of Communication* 14(3): 1-14.

Brown, Graham. 2004. "Between Gramsci and Graffiti: Opposition Politics and the Impact of the Internet in Malaysia". In *The Political Economy of the Internet in Asia and the Pacific*. Jason Abbott edited. Praeger Publishers.

—. 2005. "The Rough and Rosy Road: Sites of Contestation in Malaysia's Shackled Media Industry". *Pacific Affairs* 78(1): 39-56.

—. 2008. "Federal and state elections in Malaysia, March 2008". *Electoral Studies* 27(4): 740-744.

Brownlee, Jason. 2007. *Authoritarianism in an Age of Democratization*. Cambridge University Press.

Buehler, Michael. 2010. "Decentralization and Local Democracy in Indonesia: The Marginalization of the Public Sphere". In *Problems of Democratization in Indonesia: Elections, Institutions and Society*. Edward Aspinall and Marcus Mietzner edited. Singapore: Institute of Southeast Asian Studies.

Cain, Geoffrey. 2009. "The Cyber-Empire Strikes Back". *Far Eastern Economic Review* 172(2): 50-52.

Calingaert, Daniel. 2010. "Authoritarianism vs. the Internet". *Policy Review* 160: 63-75.

Carey, Sabine. 2006. "The Dynamic Relationship between Protest and Repression". *Political Research Quarterly* 59(1): 1-11.

Carr, Madeline. 2009. "The Political History of the Internet: A Theoretical Approach to the Implications for US Power". Paper presented at ISA Conference 2009, New York.

Carothers, Thomas. 2006. *Confronting the Weakest Link: Aiding Political Parties in New Democracies.* Carnegie Endowment for International Peace.

Carson, Matthew and Mark Turner. 2009. "Popular Perceptions of Political Regimes in East and Southeast Asia". *Democratization* 2: 377-398.

Case, William. 1993. "Semi-Democracy in Malaysia: Withstanding the Pressures for Regime Change". *Pacific Affairs* 66(2): 183-205.

—. 1996. "Can the "Halfway House" Stand? Semidemocracy and Elite Theory in Three Southeast Asian Countries". *Comparative Politics* 28(4): 437-464.

—. 2001. "Malaysia's General Elections in 1999: A Consolidated and High-Quality Semi-Democracy". *Asian Studies Review* 25(1): 35-55.

—. 2002. *Politics in Southeast Asia: Democracy or Less*. Richmond, Surrey: Curzon Press.

—. 2006. "Manipulative Skills: How Do Rulers Control the Electoral Arena?" In *Electoral Authoritarianism: The Dynamics of Unfree Competition*. Andreas Schedler edited. Lynne Rienner Publishers.

—. 2009. "Electoral authoritarianism in Malaysia: trajectory shift". *The Pacific Review* 22(3): 311-333.

—. 2010. "Transition from Single-Party Dominance? New Date from Malaysia". *Journal of East Asian Studies* 10: 91-126.

Castells, Manuel. 2008. "The New Public Sphere: Global Civil Society, Communication Networks, and Global Governance". *The ANNALS of the American Academy of Political and Social Science* 616: 78-93.

CBC News. 2011. "U.K. riot Facebook page authors get 4 years". August 17. http://www.cbc.ca/news/world/story/2011/08/17/britain-riots-sentence .html.

Chambers, Paul. 2010. "Thailand on the Brink: Resurgent Military, Eroded Democracy". *Asian Survey* 50(5): 835-858.

Chandler, David. 2010. "Cambodia in 2009: Plus C'est la Même Chose". *Asian Survey* 50(1): 228-234.

Chandranayagam, Daniel. 2009. "Malaysia: A Step Closer To Internet Censorship?" *Global Voices Advocacy*. http://advocacy.globalvoices online.org/2009/08/06/malaysia-a-step-closer-to-internet-censorship/.

—. 2010. "Malaysia: Insult to Royalty Not So Easily Forgiven". *Global Voices Advocacy*. http://advocacy.globalvoicesonline.org/2010/02/15/ malaysia-insult-to-royalty-not-so-easily-forgiven/.

Chi, Melissa. 2011. "DAP pledges support for Bersih rally". *The Malaysia Insider.* http://www.themalaysianinsider.com/malaysia/article/dap-pled ges-support-for-bersih-rally/.

Chicago Tribune. 1997. "Indonesia's Information Highway Is Too Fast for Suharto". April 23. http://articles.chicagotribune.com/1997-04-23/news /9704230039_1_president-suharto-regime-nationalism.

Chin, James. 2003. "Malaysiakini.com and its impact on journalism and politics in Malaysia". In *Asia.com: Asia encounters the Internet.* Ho, K.C., Kluver, Randolph and Kenneth Yang edited. London: Routledge Curzon.

Chin, James and Wong Chin Huat. 2009. "Malaysia's Electoral Upheaval". *Journal of Democracy* 20(3): 71-85.

Choi, Nankyung. 2009. "Democracy and patrimonial politics in local Indonesia". *Indonesia* 88(October): 131-164.

—. 2011. *Local Politics in Indonesia: Pathways to Power.* London: Routledge.

Choong Pui Yee. 2010. "MCA's New President: From Disgrace to Community Hero?" *S. Rajaratnam School of International Studies Commentaries* 100. http://dr.ntu.edu.sg/handle/10220/6664.

Chung, Kuyoun. 2007. "Explaining International Human Right Compliance: Democracy, Media and Audience Cost". Paper presented at the *annual meeting of the International Studies Association 48th Annual Convention*, Hilton Chicago, CHICAGO, IL, USA, Feb 28.

CNNIC. 2013. *Statistical Report on the Internet Development in China*.

Connors, Michael. 2008. "Thailand: Four elections and a coup". *Australian Journal of International Affairs* 62(4): 478-496.

—. 2009. "Liberalism, authoritarianism and the politics of decisionism in Thailand". *The Pacific Review* 22(3): 355-373.

Crispin, Shawn. 2011. "Royal contradictions in Thailand". *Asia Times Online*. http://www.atimes.com/atimes/Southeast_Asia/ML13Ae01.html.

Crouch, Harold. 1996a. *Government and Society in Malaysia*. Ithaca, N.Y.: Cornell University Press.

—. 1996b. "Malaysia: Do elections make a difference?" In *The politics of elections in Southeast Asia*. Robert Taylor edited. Woodrow Wilson Center Press and Cambridge University Press.

—. 2000. "The Perils of Prediction: Understanding the Indonesian Transition 1998-1999". Unpublished paper.

—. 2007. *The Army and Politics in Indonesia*. Singapore: Equinox Publishing.

Cukier, Kenneth. 2005. "Who Will Control the Internet?" *Foreign Affairs* 84(6).

Dahlgren, Peter. 2009. *Media and Political Engagement: Citizens, Communication and Democracy*. New York: Cambridge University Press.

Dalpino, Catharin. 2011. "Thailand in 2010: Rupture and Attempts at Reconciliation". *Asian Survey* 51(1): 155-162.

Davenport, Christian. 1995. "Multi-dimensional threat perception and state repression: An inquiry into why states apply negative sanctions". *American Journal of Political Science* 39(3): 683-713.

—. 2000. "Introduction". In *Paths to State Repression: Human Rights Violations and Contentious Politics.* Christian Davenport edited. Rowman & Littlefield Publishers, Inc.

—. 2004. "The Promise of Democratic Pacification: An Empirical Assessment". *International Studies Quarterly* 48(3): 539-560.

—. 2007. "State Repression and Political Order". *Annual Review of Political Science* 10(1): 1-23.

Davenport, Christian and David Armstrong. 2004. "Democracy and the Violation of Human Rights: A Statistical Analysis from 1976 to 1996". *American Journal of Political Science* 48(3): 538-554.

Deibert, Ronald and Rafal Rohozinski. 2010a. "Beyond Denial: Introducing Next-Generation Information Access Controls". In *Access Controlled: The Shaping of Power, Rights, and Rule in Cyberspace.* Ronald Deibert et al. edited. The MIT Press.

Deibert, Ronald and Rafal Rohozinski. 2010b. "Liberation vs. Control: The Future of Cyberspace". *Journal of Democracy* 21(4): 43-57.

Deibert, Ronald, John Palfrey, Rafal Rohozinski and Jonathan Zittrain, eds. 2012. *Access Contested: Security, Identity, and Resistance in Asian Cyberspace*. The MIT Press.

Diamond, Larry. 1999. *Developing Democracy: Toward Consolidation.* Baltimore: Johns Hopkins University Press.

—. 2002. "Elections without democracy: thinking about hybrid regimes". *Journal of Democracy* 13(2): 21-35.

Drabek, Zdenek and Warren Payne. 2001. "The Impact of Transparency on Foreign Direct Investment". *World Trade Organization Staff Working Paper* ERAD-99-02.

Dressel, Björn. 2009. "Thailand's Elusive Quest for a Workable Constitution, 1997-2007". *Contemporary Southeast Asia* 31(2): 296-325.

—. 2010. "Judicialization of politics or politicization of the judiciary? Considerations from recent events in Thailand". *The Pacific Review* 23(5): 671-691.

Economist. 2008 (The). "Malaysia's election: Political tsunami? A threat to the prime minister". March 10. http://www.economist.com/node/10833119.

—. 2011. "Singapore's media: A chill in the blogosphere". January 19. www.economist.com/blogs/banyan/2011/01/singapores_media.

—. 2012. "Protest in Malaysia: It's that time of year". May 1. http://www.economist.com/blogs/banyan/2012/05/protest-malaysia.

Edelman Trust Barometer. 2012. "Trust Barometer Global Results". http://trust.edelman.com/trust-download/global-results/.

Elson, R. E. 2010. "Nationalism, Islam, 'secularism' and the state in contemporary Indonesia". *Australian Journal of International Affairs* 64(3): 328-343.
Englehart, Neil. 2003. "Democracy and the Thai Middle Class: Globalization, Modernization, and Constitutional Change". *Asian Survey* 43(2): 253-279.
European Parliament. 2010. "European Parliament resolution on Cambodia, in particular the case of Sam Rainsy". http://www.europarl.europa.eu/sides/getDoc.do?type=MOTION&reference=P7-RC-2010-0550&language=EN.
Farrelly, Nicholas. 2010. "From Village Scouts to Cyber Scouts". *New Mandala*. http://asiapacific.anu.edu.au/newmandala/2010/07/02/from-village-scouts-to-cyber-scouts/.
Felker, Greg. 1999. "Malaysia in 1998: A Cornered Tiger Bares Its Claws". *Asian Survey* 39(1): 43-54.
Ferrara, Federico. 2011. "L'état, ce n'est plus moi: Popular Sovereignty and Citizenship over a Century of Thai Political Development". *Southeast Asia Research Centre Working Paper Series* 110.
Forrester, Geoff. 1998. "A Jakarta Diary, May 1998". In *The Fall of Soeharto*. Forrester and R.J. May edited, 24-69. Bathurst: Crawford House.
Franco, Jennifer. 2001. *Elections and Democratization in the Philippines*. New York: Routledge.
Freedom Against Censorship Thailand. 2006. "Analysis: MICT Blocklist, 13 October 2006". http://facthai.wordpress.com/2006/11/16/analysis-mict-blocklist-13-october-2006/.
Freedom House. 2010. *Freedom of the Press* (2010 edition).
—. 2011a. *Freedom in the World* (2011 edition).
—. 2011b. *Freedom on the Net 2011: A Global Assessment of Internet and Digital Media*. http://www.freedomhouse.org/report/freedom-net/freedom-net-2011.
Gan, Steven. 2001. "Moving beyond racial politics". *Malaysiakini*. March 7. http://www.malaysiakini.com/news/1176.
Ganesan, N. 2010. "Worsening Schisms in Thai Domestic Politics". *Japanese Journal of Political Science* 11(1): 125-147.
Gartner, Scott and Regan Patrick. 1996. "Threat and Repression: The Non-Linear Relationship between Government and Opposition Violence". *Journal of Peace Research* 33(3): 273-287.
George, Cherian. 2005. "The internet's political impact and the penetration/participation paradox in Malaysia and Singapore". *Media, Culture & Society* 27(6): 903-920.

—. 2007. "Media in Malaysia: Zone of Contention". *Democratization* 14(5): 893-910.

Gerring, John. 2004. "What is a case study and what is it good for?" *American Political Science Review* 98(2): 341-354.

Gerschenkron, Alexander. 1962. *Economic backwardness in historical perspective, a book of essays*. Cambridge, Massachusetts: Belknap Press of Harvard University Press.

Giacomello, G. 2008. *National Governments and Control of the Internet: A Digital Challenge*. London: Routledge.

Giles Ji Ungpakorn. 2007. *A coup for the rich: Thailand's political crisis*. Bangkok: Workers Democracy Publishing.

Glassman, Jim. 2011. "Cracking Hegemony in Thailand: Gramsci, Bourdieu and the Dialectics of Rebellion". *Journal of Contemporary Asia* 41(1): 25-46.

Global Voices Advocacy. 2010. "Thailand: Government shuts 43,000 more websites for lèse majesté, plans to block 3,000 more, total up to 113,000". http://advocacy.globalvoicesonline.org/2010/06/18/thailand-government-shuts-43000-more-websites-for-lese-majeste-plans-to-block-3000-more-total-up-to-113000/.

Goldsmith, Jack and Tim Wu. 2006. *Who Controls the Internet? Illusions of a Borderless World*. New York: Oxford University Press.

Gomez, James. 2002. "Think Centre: The Internet and Politics in the New Economy". *Asian Journal of Social Science* 30(2): 304-318.

—. 2004. "Dumbing down democracy: trends in Internet regulation, surveillance and control in Asia". *Pacific Journalism Review* 10(2): 130-150.

—. 2008. "Online Opposition in Singapore: Communications Outreach without Electoral Gain". *Journal of Contemporary Asia* 38(4): 591-612.

Gomez, Edmund Terence ed. 2004. *The State of Malaysia: Ethnicity, Equity and Reform*. London: RoutledgeCurzon.

Gong, Rachel. 2009. "Internet Politics and State Media Control: Candidate Weblogs in Malaysia". Paper presented at the *4th Communication Policy Research: South Conference*, Negombo, Sri Lanka, December 8.

Gooch, Liz. 2012. "Protesters in Malaysia Accuse Police of Brutality". *New York Times*. April 29. http://www.nytimes.com/2012/04/30/world/asia/malaysian-protesters-accuse-police-of-brutality.html?_r=1.

Guardian (The). 2011. "Singapore elections marked by online buzz of discontent". May 6. http://www.guardian.co.uk/world/2011/may/06/singapore-elections-internet.

Gurr, T. 1986. "Persisting Patterns of Repression and Rebellion: Foundations for a General Theory of Political Coercion". In *Persistent Patterns and Emergent Structures in a Waning Century*. M. Karns edited. New York: Praeger.

Hadiz, Vedi. 2007. "The Localization of Power in Southeast Asia". *Democratization* 14(5): 873-892.

Handley, Paul. 2006. *The King Never Smiles: A Biography of Thailand's Bhumibol Adulyadej*. New Haven and London: Yale University Press.

Hathaway, Oona. 2007. "Why Do Countries Commit to Human Rights Treaties?" *Journal of Conflict Resolution* 51(4): 588-621.

Heacock, Rebekah. 2009. "Malaysia considers, backs down from national Internet filter". *OpenNet Initiative*. http://opennet.net/blog/2009/08/malaysia-considers-backs-down-national-internet-filter.

Hewison, Kevin, Richard Robinson and Garry Rodan, eds. 1993. *Southeast Asia in the 1990s: authoritarianism, democracy and capitalism*. Allen & Unwin.

Hewison, Kevin. 1999. "Political Space in Southeast Asia: 'Asian-style' and Other Democracies". In *The Resilience of Democracy: Persistent Practice, Durable Idea*. Peter Burnell and Peter Calvert edited. London: Frank Cass Publishers.

—. 2010. "Thaksin Shinawatra and the reshaping of Thai politics". *Contemporary Politics* 16(2): 119-133.

Hicken, Allen. 2006. "Party Fabrication: Constitutional Reform and the Rise of Thai Rak Thai". *Journal of East Asian Studies* 6(3): 381-408.

—. 2008. "The Philippines in 2007: Ballots, Budgets, and Bribes". *Asian Survey* 48(1): 75-81.

Hill, David and Krishna Sen. 2005. *The Internet in Indonesia's New Democracy*. Abingdon and New York: Routledge.

Hill, David. 2006. *The Press in New Order Indonesia*. Jakarta: Equinox Publishing.

Hille, Kathrin. 2009. "Chinese bloggers hail Green Dam 'victory'". *Financial Times*. July 1. http://www.ft.com/cms/s/0/744ae9be-6639-11de-a034-00144feabdc0.html#axzz1tJk74SMt.

Holland, Lorien. 2008. "MALAYSIA: Political Tsunami". *Newsweek*. March 10.

Holmes, Len and Margaret Grieco. 2001. "The Internet, Email, and the Malaysian Political Crisis: The Power of Transparency". *Asia Pacific Business Review* 8(2): 59-72.

Honna, Jun. 2003. *Military politics and democratization in Indonesia*. London: RoutledgeCurzon.

Howard, Philip. 2010. *The Digital Origins of Dictatorship and Democracy: Information Technology and Political Islam*. New York: Oxford University Press.

Hughes, Caroline. 2009. "Cambodia in 2008: Consolidation in the Midst of Crisis". *Asian Survey* 49(1): 206-212.

Huntington, Samuel. 1991. *The third wave: democratization in the late twentieth century*. Norman: University of Oklahoma Press.

Hutchcroft, Paul. 2008. "The Arroyo Imbroglio in the Philippines". *Journal of Democracy* 19(1): 141-155.

Hutchcroft, Paul and Joel Rocamora. 2003. "Strong Demands and Weak Institutions: The Origins and Evolution of the Democratic Deficit in the Philippines". *Journal of East Asian Studies* 3(2): 259-292.

iLaw Project. 2010. *Situational Report on Control and Censorship of Online Media, Through the Use of Laws and the Imposition of Thai State Policies*. http://www.boell-southeastasia.org/downloads/ilaw_report_EN.pdf.

Indo Pacific Edelman. 2009. "2009 Indonesian Blogger Survey". http://www.slideshare.net/indopacedelman/final-report-blogger-survey-2009.

Isriya Paireepairit. 2012. *Free Space of Expression: New Media and Thailand's Politics*. Berlin: Friedrich-Ebert-Stiftung.

ITU. 2002. "Multimedia Malaysia: Internet Case Study". http://www.itu.int/asean2001/reports/material/MYS%20CS.pdf.

Jakarta Globe (The). 2011. "Indonesians Are Online and Spending". December 13. http://www.thejakartaglobe.com/business/indonesians-are-online-and-spending/484511.

—. 2011. "Tifatul Says Indonesians Not Making Most of Net". June 9. http://www.thejakartaglobe.com/indonesia/tifatul-says-indonesians-not-making-most-of-net/446060.

—. 2012. "Voters Take Jakarta Gubernatorial Election Race to the Digital Front on Twitter". September 10. http://www.thejakartaglobe.com/home/voters-take-jakarta-gubernatorial-election-race-to-the-digital-front-on-twitter/543403.

Jakarta Post (The). 2009. "Voters, elites at odds over election fairness". July 17. http://www.thejakartapost.com/news/2009/07/17/voters-elites-odds-over-election-fairness.html.

—. 2010. "PDI-P rejects multimedia regulation draft". February 16. http://www.thejakartapost.com/news/2010/02/16/pdip-rejects-multimedia-regulation-draft.html.

—. 2010. "Thai monarchy's power wanes, king still revered". May 25. http://www.thejakartapost.com/news/2010/05/25/thai-monarchy039s-power-wanes-king-still-revered.html.

Jomo, K.S. 1996. "Elections' Janus face: Limitations and potential in Malaysia". In *The politics of elections in Southeast Asia*. Robert Taylor edited. Woodrow Wilson Center Press and Cambridge University Press.

Jon Russell. 2010. "Thai government introduces Internet censorship agency". http://asiancorrespondent.com/jon-russell/2010/06/17/thai-government-introduces-internet-censorship-agency.

Jose, Lydia ed. 2011. *Civil Society Organizations in the Philippines: A Mapping and Strategic Assessment*. Quezon City: Civil Society Resource Institute.

Kalathil, Shanthi and Taylor Boas. 2003. *Open Networks, Cosed Regimes: The Impact of the Internet on Authoritarian Rule*. Washington: Carnegie Endowment for International Peace.

Kazmin, Amy. 2007. "A Setback for Thai Democracy: The Rise, Rule and Overthrow of Thaksin Shinawatra". *Asian Affairs* 38(2): 211-224.

Kengkij Kitirianglarp and Kevin Hewison. 2009. "Social Movements and Political Opposition in Contemporary Thailand". *The Pacific Review* 22(4): 451-77.

Khoo Boo Teik. 2002. "Writing Reformasi". *Kyoto Review of Southeast Asia* 1. http://kyotoreview.cseas.kyoto-u.ac.jp/issue/issue0/article_33.html.

—. 2003. *Beyond Mahathir: Malaysian Politics and its Discontents*. London: Zed Books Ltd.

—. 2010. "Cyber-networks, physical coalitions and missing links: Imagining and realizing dissent in Malaysia 1998-2008". *IDE Discussion Paper* 244.

Kim, Sedara. 2007. "From Peace-Keeping to Peace-Building: Cambodia Post-Conflict Democratization". *Political Studies Association*. http://www.psa.ac.uk/2007/pps/Kim1.pdf.

Kimura, Ehito. 2011. "Indonesia in 2010: A Leading Democracy Disappoints on Reform". *Asian Survey* 51(1): 186-195.

—. 2012. "Indonesia in 2011: A Glass Half-Empty". *Asian Survey* 52(1): 186-194.

Kingsbury, Damien. 2005. *Southeast Asia: a Political Profile* (second edition). Oxford University Press.

Kitti Prasirtsuk. 2009. "Thailand in 2008: Crises Continued". *Asian Survey* 49(1): 174-184.

—. 2010. "Thailand in 2009: Colored by Turbulence". *Asian Survey* 50(1): 203-210.

Klimburg, Alexander. 2011. "Mobilising Cyber Power". *Survival: Global Politics and Strategy* 53(1): 41-60.

Koswanage, N. 2009. "Malaysia examines Internet filter, tougher controls." http://www.reuters.com/article/companyNews/idUSSP37415 520090806.

Krain, Matthew. 1997. "State-sponsored mass murder". *Journal of Conflict Resolution* 41: 331-360.

Kraft, Herman. 2010. "The Philippines in 2009: The Fourth-Quarter Collapse". *Southeast Asian Affairs 2010*: 237-257.

Kuhonta, Erik. 2008. "The Paradox of Thailand's 1997 'People's Constitution': Be Careful What You Wish For". *Asian Survey* 48(3): 373-392.

Kuo, Eddie, Alfred Choi, Arun Mahizhnan, Lee Wai-peng and Christina Soh. 2002. *Internet in Singapore: a Study on Usage and Impact*. Singapore: Times Academic Press.

Kuppusamy, Baradan. 2010. "No funny business for Malaysian bloggers". *Asia Times Online*. http://www.atimes.com/atimes/Southeast_Asia/LJ0 8Ae01.html.

Kurlantzick, Joshua. 2011. "The long arm of China: a rising world power begins to intervene in outside governments". *The Boston Globe*. September 24.

Labovitz, Craig. 2010. "Attack Severs Burma Internet". *DDoS and Security Reports: The Arbor Networks Security Blog*. http://ddos. arbornetworks.com/2010/11/attac-severs-myanmar-internet/.

Lawson, Chappell. 2000. "Mexico's Unfinished Transition: Democratization and Authoritarian Enclaves in Mexico". *Mexican Studies / Estudios Mexicanos* 16(2): 267-87.

Lee, Edwin. 1989. "The Colonial Legacy". In *Management of success: the moulding of modern Singapore.* Kernial Sandhu and Paul Wheatley edited. Singapore: Institute of Southeast Asian Studies.

Lee, Terence. 2010. *The media, cultural control and government in Singapore*. Abingdon: Routledge.

Lee, Terence and Cornelius Kan. 2009. "Blogospheric pressures in Singapore: Internet discourses and the 2006 general election". *Continuum: Journal of Media & Cultural Studies* 23(6): 871-886.

Lee Siew Lian. 2008. "Cyberspace is now the new frontline". *New Straits Times*. March 12.

Lembaga Survei Indonesia and Goethe Institut. 2010. "MUSLIM YOUTH SURVEY 2010: Country Report of Indonesia". www.lsi.or.id/file_ download/116.

Lepawsky, Josh. 2005. "Digital Aspirations: Malaysia and the Multimedia Super Corridor". *FOCUS on Geography* 48(3): 10-18.

Lessig, Lawrence. 1999. *Code and Other Laws of Cyberspace*. New York: Basic Books.

Levitsky, Steven and Way, Lucan (2002) 'Elections without democracy: the rise of competitive authoritarianism', *Journal of Democracy*, Vol.13, No.2, pp.51-65.

Levitsky, Steven and Lucan Way. 2010. *Competitive Authoritarianism: Hybrid Regimes after the Cold War*. Cambridge University Press.

Liddle, William. 1996. "A useful fiction: Democratic legitimation in New Order Indonesia". In *The Politics of Elections in Southeast Asia.* Robert Taylor edited. Woodrow Wilson Center Press and Cambridge University Press.

—. 1999. "Indonesia's Unexpected Failure of Leadership". In *The Politics of Post-Suharto Indonesia.* Adam Schwarz and Jonathan Paris edited. New York: Council on Foreign Relations Press.

Lijphart, Arend. 1971. "Comparative Politics and the Comparative Method". *American Political Science Review* 65(3): 682-693.

Lim Hong Hai. 2002. "Electoral Politics in Malaysia: 'Managing' Elections in a Plural Society". In *Electoral politics in Southeast & East Asia.* Aurel Croissant edited. Singapore: Friedrich Ebert Stiftung.

Lim, Merlyna. 2002. "Cyber-civic space in Indonesia: From panopticon to pandemonium?" *International Development Planning Review* 24(4): 383-400.

—. 2005. "Islamic Radicalism and Anti-Americanism in Indonesia: The Role of the Internet". *East-West Center Policy Studies Series* 18.

—. 2006. "Cyber-Urban Activism and the Political Change in Indonesia". *EastBound* 1.

Loh, Deborah and Jacqueline Surin eds. 2011. *Understanding the Dewan Rakyat*. Petaling Jaya, Malaysia: ZI Publications.

Lum, Thomas. 2007. "Cambodia: Background and U.S. Relations". *CRS Report for Congress*. Order Code RL32986. http://www.fas.org/sgp/crs /row/RL32986.pdf.

Magadia, Jose. 2003. *State-Society Dynamics: Policy Making in a Restored Democracy*. Quezon City: Ateneo de Manila University Press.

Mahathir Mohamad. 1997. "On the Threshold of the Cyber Revolution". In *Mahathir Mohamad:* A *Visionary & His Vision of Malaysia's K-economy.* N. T. Chuan and D. N. Abdulai edited, 129-142. Subang Jaya: Pelanduk Publications.

Malaysian Insider (The). 2009. "PM says no plan to censor the Internet". August 8. http://www.themalaysianinsider.com/malaysia/article/PM-says-no-plan-to-censor-the-Internet/.

Mann, Tim. 2012. "Jakarta Governor's Race Goes Online, With Mixed Results for Indonesia's Democracy". *In Asia: Weekly Insight and Analysis from the Asia Foundation*. http://asiafoundation.org/in-asia/2012/09/19/jakarta-governors-race-goes-online-with-mixed-results-for-indonesias-democracy/.

Marcus, David. 1998. "Indonesia revolt was Net driven". *Boston Globe*. May 23.

Marthinus, Pierre. 2011. "Indonesia's cryptic conservatism". *The Jakarta Post*. April 1. http://www.thejakartapost.com/news/2011/04/01/indonesia%E2%80%99s-cryptic-conservatism.html.

Martinez, Patricia. 2002. "Malaysia in 2001: An Interlude of Consolidation". *Asian Survey* 42(1): 133-140.

Mathiason, John. 2008. *Internet Governance: The New Frontier of Global Institutions*. London: Routledge.

Maznah, Mohamad. 2008. "Malaysia – democracy and the end of ethnic politics?" *Australian Journal of International Affairs* 62(4): 441-459.

McAdam, Doug, Sidney Tarrow and Charles Tilly. 2001. *Dynamics of Contention*. Cambridge University Press.

McCargo, Duncan. 2005. "Network Monarchy and Legitimacy Crises in Thailand". *The Pacific Review* 18(4): 499-519.

—. 2009. "Thai Politics as Reality TV". *The Journal of Asian Studies* 68(1): 7-19.

McCargo, Duncan and Ukrist Pathmanand. 2005. *The Thaksinization of Thailand*. Copenhagen: NIAS Press.

McCoy, Alfred. 1999. *Closer Than Brothers: Manhood at the Philippine Military Academy*. Yale University Press.

McNair, Brian. 2009. "The Internet and the changing global media environment". In *Routledge Handbook of Internet Politics*. Andrew Chadwick and Philip Howard edited. Abingdon: Routledge.

Media Monitor. 2010. "Media Influencers Survey Findings 2010". http://www.mediamonitors.com.sg/insights/media-influencers-survey-findings.

Medina, Marielle. 2011. "Church, media most trusted, says survey". *Philippine Daily Inquirer*. September 17. http://newsinfo.inquirer.net/60143/church-media-most-trusted-says-survey.

Mersat, Neilson Ilan. 2009. "'Blue waves versus political tsunami': Sarawak and the 2008 Malaysian General Election". *AKADEMIKA* 77: 113-132.

Meyer, David. 2004. "Protest and Political Opportunities". *Annual Review of Sociology* 30: 125-145.

Mickey, Robert. 2011. *Paths Out of Dixie: The Democratization of Authoritarian Enclaves in America's Deep South*. Princeton University Press.

Mietzner, Marcus. 2010. "Indonesia in 2009: Electoral contestation and economic resilience". *Asian Survey* 50(1): 185-194.

Mirandilla, Mary. 2009. "Cybercampaigning for 2010: The Use and Effectiveness of Websites and Social Networking Sites as Campaign Platforms for the 2010 Philippine Presidential Election". Paper presented at the *4th Communication Policy Research: South Conference*, Negombo, Sri Lanka, December 8.

Montemayor, Carla. 2008. "Journalist-Bloggers and the Public Sphere in the Philippines: Exploratory Questions". *Journalism Studies*: 1-15. http://newpolcom.rhul.ac.uk/politics-web-20-paper-download/.

Moore, Will. 2000. "The Repression of Dissent: A Substitution Model of Government Coercion". *Journal of Conflict Resolution* 44: 107-127.

Morozov, Evgeny. 2011a. *The Net Delusion: The Dark Side of Internet Freedom*. New York: Public Affairs.

—. 2011b. "Liberation Technology: Whither Internet Control?" *Journal of Democracy* 22(2): 62-74.

Mostarom, Tuty Raihanah and V. Arianti. 2009. "Declining support for Islamist parties: exploring the Indonesian 'paradox'". *RSIS Commentaries* 43. http://www.rsis.edu.sg/publications/Perspective/RSIS0432009.pdf.

Moten, Abdul Rashid. 2009a. "2004 and 2008 General Elections in Malaysia: Towards a Multicultural, Biparty Political System?" *Asian Journal of Political Science* 17(2): 173-194.

—. 2009b. "2008 General Election in Malaysia: Democracy at Work". *Japanese Journal of Political Science* 10(1): 21–42.

Mujani, Saiful and William Liddle. 2009. "Muslim Indonesia's Secular Democracy". *Asian Survey* 49(4): 575-590.

Mujani, Saiful and William Liddle. 2010. "Voters and the New Indonesian Democracy". In *Problems of Democratization in Indonesia: Elections, Institutions and Society.* Edward Aspinall and Marcus Mietzner edited. Singapore: Institute of Southeast Asian Studies.

Muliana, Amelia. 2008. *Online Journalism in Indonesia*. MA diss. National University of Singapore.

Murdoch, Steven and Ross Anderson. 2008. "Tools and Technology of Internet Filtering". In *Access Denied: The Practice and Policy of Global Internet Filtering.* Ronald Deibert et al. edited. Massachusetts: The MIT Press.

Mutalib, Hussin. 2000a. "Malaysia's 1999 general election: Signposts to future politics". *Asian Journal of Political Science* 8(1): 65-89.
—. 2000b. "Illiberal democracy and the future of opposition in Singapore". *Third World Quarterly* 21(2): 313-342.
Mutebi, Alex. 2004. "THAILAND IN 2003: Riding High Again". *Asian Survey* 44(1): 78-86.
Mydans, Seth. 2011. "Opposition Makes Inroads in Singapore". *New York Times*. May 7. http://www.nytimes.com/2011/05/08/world/asia/08singapore.html.
Nain, Zaharom. 2008. "Regime, media and the reconstruction of a fragile consensus in Malaysia". In *Political Regimes and the Media in Asia.* Krishna Sen and Terence Lee edited. Abingdon: Routledge.
Nair, Sheila. 2007. "The Limits of Protest and Prospects for Political Reform in Malaysia". *Critical Asian Studies* 39(3): 339-368.
Najib Tun Abdul Razak. 2011. "Keynote Address at the 1st Malaysia-Asean Bloggers Forum". *1Malaysia.* April 24. http://www.1malaysia.com.my/my/speeches/1st-malaysia-asean-bloggers-forum/.
New Straits Times. 2008. "Internet served a painful lesson". March 26.
Naruemon Thabchumpon and Duncan McCargo. 2011. "Urbanized Villagers in the 2010 Thai Redshirt Protests: Not Just Poor Farmers?" *Asian Survey* 51(6): 993-1018.
Nation (The). 2006. "ARC summons media bosses to toughen controls". September 21.
—. 2006. "Community radio stations shut down". September 22.
—. 2006. "19sep.org shut down". September 22.
—. 2006. "Midnight University website shut down after protest". October 1.
Nelson, Michael. 2012. "Some Observations on Democracy in Thailand". *Southeast Asia Research Centre (SEARC) Working Papers Series* 125.
Neumayer, Eric. 2005. "Do International Human Rights Treaties Improve Respect for Human Rights?" *Journal of Conflict Resolution* 49(6): 925-953.
New York Times. 2008. "Malaysian leader admits ignoring Internet was a mistake". March 25. http://www.nytimes.com/2008/03/25/world/asia/25iht-malay.1.11396684.html.
—. 2011. "A High-Tech War Against Slights to a Centuries-Old Monarchy". Octorber 2. http://www.nytimes.com/2011/10/03/world/asia/03iht-thailand03.html?pagewanted=all.
Noman, Helmi. 2011. "In the Name of God: Faith-based Internet Censorship in Majority Muslim Countries". *OpenNet Initiative*. August 1.

Onishi, Norimitsu. 2010. "Debate on Internet's Limits Grows in Indonesia". *New York Times*. April 19.
Ooi, Yang-May. 2007. "Blogging thrives in Malaysia". *Communication World* (November-December): 37-39.
OpenNet Initiative. 2007. "Country Profiles: Singapore". http://opennet.net/research/profiles/singapore.
—. 2007. "Country Profiles: Malaysia". http://opennet.net/research/profiles/malaysia.
—. 2010. "2010: the year in review". http://opennet.net/about-filtering/2010yearinreview/.
Orren, Karen and Stephen Skowronek. 1995. "Order and time in institutional study: a brief for the historical approach". In *Political Science in History.* James Farr, John Dryzek and Stephen Leonard (eds.), 286-317. Cambridge, UK: Cambridge University Press.
Ortmann, Stephan. 2011. "Singapore: Authoritarian but newly competitive". *Journal of Democracy* 22(4): 153-164.
Ottaway, Marina. 2003. *Democracy Challenged: The Rise of Semi-Authoritarianism*. Carnegie Endowment for International Peace.
Palasri, Sirin. Steven Huter and Zita Wenzel. 1999. *The history of the Internet in Thailand*. Eugene, Oregon: University of Oregon Books.
Pan, Phatry Derek. 2011. "3 reasons why the social media movement won't come to Cambodia". *The Khmerican*. http://khmerican.com/2011/09/03/3-reasons-why-the-social-media-movement-wont-come-to-cambodia/.
Pandian, Sivamurugan. 2010. "2006 Sarawak State Elections: Issues and Electoral Results". *Canadian Social Science* 6(5): 43-48.
Pasuk Phongpaichit and Chris Baker. 2009. *Thaksin*. Chiang Mai: Silkworm Books.
Pavin Chachavalpongpun. 2010. "Thailand's Massive Internet Censorship". *Asian Sentinel.* July 22.
—. 2011. "The Necessity of Enemies in Thailand's Troubled Politics: The Making of Political 'Otherness'". *Asian Survey* 51(6): 1019-1041.
People's Daily. 2010. "Speech by Mr. Pichai Chuensuksawadi, Editor-in-Chief, Bangkok Post Newspaper, at the 4th Asean-China Media Cooperation Seminar". March 24. http://english.people.com.cn/90002/98666/6929274.html.
Pepinsky, Thomas. 2009. *Economic Crises and the Breakdown of Authoritarian Regimes: Indonesia and Malaysia in Comparative Perspective*. Cambridge University Press.
—. 2011. "*Tak Nak Mereform*: New Media and Malaysian Politics in Historical Perspective". Paper presented at the workshop *The Jasmine*

Revolution and the 'Bamboo' Firewall: The Impact of the Internet and New Social Media on Political Change in East Asia, Center for Asian Democracy, University of Louisville, August 24-25.

—. 2012. "Malaysia after regime change". *New Mandala*. March 2. http://asiapacific.anu.edu.au/newmandala/2012/03/03/malaysia-after-regime-change-thomas-pepinsky/#more-17800.

Pérez, Javier Gil. 2009. "Electoral Report: MALAYSIA/Parliamentary and State Elections". *TEIM Election Watch Analysis*.

Pereira, Anthony. 2005. *Political (in)justice: authoritarianism and the rule of law in Brazil, Chile, and Argentina*. University of Pittsburgh Press.

Pierson, Paul and Theda Skocpol. 2002. "Historical Institutionalism in Contemporary Political Science". In *Political Science: The State of the Discipline.* I. Katznelson and H. Milner edited. New York: Norton.

Pirongrong Rananand. 2003. "Internet and Democracy in Thailand". In *Rhetoric and reality: the Internet challenge for democracy in Asia.* Banerjee, Indrajit edited. Singapore: Eastern University Press.

—. 2012. "Internet politics in Thailand after the 2006 coup: regulation by code and a contested ideological terrain". In *Access Contested: Security, Identity, and Resistance in Asian Cyberspace.* Ronald Deibert et al. edited. The MIT Press.

Poowin Buyavejchewin. 2010. "Internet Politics: Internet as a Political Tool in Thailand". *Canadian Social Science* 6(3).

Privacy International. 2003a. "Privacy and Human Rights 2003: Thailand". http://www.privacyinternational.org/survey/phr2003/countries/thailand.htm.

—. 2003b. "Silenced – Thailand". http://www.privacyinternational.org/article.shtml?cmd[347]=x-347-103785.

Quimpo, Nathan. 2005. "Oligarchic Patrimonialism, Bossism, Electoral Clientelism, and Contested Democracy in the Philippines". *Comparative Politics* 37(2): 229-250.

Rawnsley, Gary. 2006. "The media, internet and governance in China". *China Discussion Paper* 12. http://www.nottingham.ac.uk/china-policy-institute/publications/discussionpapers.php.

Regan, Patrick and Errol Henderson. 2002. "Democracy, threats and political repression in developing countries: are democracies internally less violent?" *Third World Quarterly* 23(1): 119-136.

Randhawa, Sonia and Gayathry Venkiteswaran. 2010. "Civil society use of media and ICT: A case study of the SOS Selangor campaign". In *Media, Culture and Society in Malaysia.* Yeoh Seng Guan edited. Abington: Routledge.

Reporters Without Borders. 2008a, "Online newspaper editor freed on bail, pending trial on sedition charge". http://en.rsf.org/malaysia-online-newspaper-editor-freed-on-09-05-2008,26916.html.

—. 2008b. "Court orders online newspaper editor to identify visitors to website". http://en.rsf.org/malaysia-court-orders-online-newspaper-14-08-2008,28182.html.

—. 2010a. "Press Freedom Index 2010". http://en.rsf.org/spip.php?page=classement&id_rubrique=1034.

—. 2010b. "WEB 2.0 VERSUS CONTROL 2.0". http://en.rsf.org/web-2-0-versus-control-2-0-18-03-2010,36697.

—. 2011. "Many opposition and news sites brought down by cyber-attacks in election run-up". http://en.rsf.org/malaysia-many-opposition-and-news-sites-15-04-2011,40034.html.

Reuters. 2009. "Malaysia backs off Internet filter plan". August 7. http://in.reuters.com/article/2009/08/07/idINIndia-41603120090807.

Richards, David, Ronald Gelleny and David Sacko. 2001. "Money with a Mean Streak? Foreign Economic Penetration and Government Respect for Human Rights in Developing Countries". *International Studies Quarterly* 45(2): 219-239.

Riggs, Fred. 1966. *Thailand: the modernization of a bureaucratic polity*. Honolulu: East-West Centre Press.

Robison, Richard. 1988. "Authoritarian States, Capital-Owning Classes, and the Politics of Newly Industrializing Countries: The Case of Indonesia". *World Politics* 41(1): 52-74.

Robison, Richard and Vedi Hadiz. 2004. *Reorganizing Power in Indonesia: The Politics of Oligarchy in an Age of Markets*. London: RoutledgeCurzon.

Rodan, Garry. 1993. "Preserving the one-party state in contemporary Singapore". In *Southeast Asia in the 1990s: Authoritarianism, Democracy and Capitalism.* Kevin Hewison, Richard Robison and Garry Rodan edited. St Leonards: Allen & Uniwin Pty Ltd.

—. 1998. "The Internet and Political Control in Singapore". *Political Science Quarterly* 113(1): 63-89.

—. 2004. *Transparency and Authoritarian Rule in Southeast Asia: Singapore and Malaysia*. London, RoutledgeCurzon.

Rodgers, Jayne. 2003. *Spatializing International Politics: Analysing activism on the Internet*. London: Routledge.

Rosenzweig, Roy. 1998. "Wizards, Bureaucrats, Warriors, and Hackers: Writing the History of the Internet". *American Historical Review* 103(5): 1530-1552.

Rosser, Andrew. 2002. *The Politics of Economic Liberalisation in Indonesia: State, Market and Power*. Surrey: Curzon.
Roughneen, Simon. 2011. "Malaysia nips an hibiscus uprising". *Asia Times Online*. http://www.atimes.com/atimes/Southeast_Asia/MG12Ae01.html.
Sani, Mohd Azizuddin Mohd. 2009a. *The Public Sphere and Media Politics in Malaysia*. Cambridge Scholars Publishing.
—. 2009b. "Freedom of Speech and Democracy in Malaysia". *Asian Journal of Political Science* 16(1): 85-104.
Sani, Mohd Azizuddin Mohd and Knocks Tapiwa Zengeni. 2010. "Democratization in Malaysia: The impact of social media in the 2008 general election". Paper presented at the *18th Biennial Conference of the Asian Studies Association of Australia*, Adelaide, July 5-8.
Saravanamuttu, Johan. 2009. "Malaysia: Political Transformation and Intrigue in an Election Year". *Southeast Asian Affairs* 2009.
Schedler, Andreas. 2002. "The Menu of Manipulation". *Journal of Democracy* 13(2): 36-50.
—. 2006. "The logic of electoral authoritarianism". In *Electoral Authoritarianism: The Dynamics of Unfree Competition.* Andreas Schedler edited. Lynne Rienner Publishers.
Schmidt, Adam. 2010. "Indonesian's 2009 Elections: Performance Challenges and Negative Precedents". In *Problems of Democratization in Indonesia: Elections, Institutions and Society*. Edward Aspinall and Marcus Mietzner edited. Singapore: Institute of Southeast Asian Studies.
Schultz, Kenneth. 2001. "Looking for Audience Costs". *Journal of Conflict Resolution* 45(1): 32-60.
Schumpeter, Joseph. 1976. *Capitalism, Socialism and Democracy*. London: George Allen and Unwin.
Singh, Bilveer. 2009. "Malaysia in 2008: The Elections That Broke the Tiger's Back". *Asian Survey* 49(1): 156-165.
Sidel, John. 1997. "Philippine Politics in Town, District, and Province: Bossism in Cavite and Cebu". *Journal of Asian Studies* 56(4): 947-966.
Sihaloho, Markus Junianto and Nivell Rayda. 2010. "Activists Slam Indonesia Military for 'Sidelining' Papua Torture". *The Jakarta Globe*. November 22.
Sim, Soek-Fang. 2006. "Hegemonic Authoritarianism and Singapore: Economics, Ideology and the Asian Economic Crisis". *Journal of Contemporary Asia* 36(2): 143-159.
Sjöberg, Örjan and Fredrik Sjöholm. 2006. "The Cambodian economy: ready for take-off?" *The Pacific Review* 19(4): 495-517.

Slater, Dan. 2004. "Indonesia's accountability trap: party cartels and presidential power after democratic transition". *Indonesia* 78: 61-92.

—. 2008. "Democracy and Dictatorship Do Not Float Freely: Structural Sources of Political Regimes in Southeast Asia". In *Southeast Asia in Political Science: Theory, Region, and Qualitative Analysis.* Erik Kuhonta, Dan Slater and Tuong Vu edited. Stanford: Stanford University Press.

—. 2010. *Ordering Power: Contentious Politics and Authoritarian Leviathans in Southeast Asia*. Cambridge University Press.

—. 2012. "Southeast Asia: Strong-State Democratization in Malaysia and Singapore". *Journal of Democracy* 23(2): 19-33.

Smith, Clinton. 2007. *Online Contentious Politics: Internet Use in the Dynamics of Political Change in Singapore*. PhD diss. University of Oregon.

Smith, W. C. 2009. *Latin American democratic transformations: institutions, actors, and processes*. Malden, MA: Wiley-Blackwell.

Smith, Roger ed. 1974. *Southeast Asia: Documents of Political Development and Change*. Ithaca and London: Cornell University Press.

Soriano, Cheryll. 2008. "Philippine NGO Websites, Usage Patterns, and Implications to State-Civil Society Relations". Paper presented at the *3rd Communication Policy Research, South Conference*, Beijing, China, December 6.

Stallybrass, Peter and Allon White. 1986. *The politics and poetics of transgression*. Ithaca, NY: Cornell University Press.

Steele, Janet. 2009. "Professionalism Online: How Malaysiakini Challenges Authoritarianism". *International Journal of Press/Politics* 14(1): 91-111.

Steinberg, David ed. 1987. *In Search of Southeast Asia: A Modern History*. University of Hawaii Press.

Suchit Bunbongkarn. 1996. "Elections and democratization in Thailand". In *The politics of elections in Southeast Asia.* Robert Taylor edited. Woodrow Wilson Center Press and Cambridge University Press.

Sukma, Rizal. 2009. "Indonesian Politics in 2009: Defective Elections, Resilient Democracy". *Bulletin of Indonesian Economic Studies* 45(3): 317-336.

—. 2010. "Civil-Military Relations in Post-Authoritarian Indonesia". In *Democracy under Stress: Civil-Military Relations in South and Southeast Asia.* Paul Chambers and Aurel Crolssant edited. Bangkok: Institute of Security and International Studies.

Tamada, Yoshifumi. 2008. *Myths and Realities: The Democratization of Thai Politics*. Kyoto: Kyoto University Press.

Tan Jun-E and Zawawi Ibrahim. 2008. *Blogging and Democratization in Malaysia*. Petaling Jaya, Selangor: Strategic Information and Research Development Center.

Tan, Kenneth. 2012. "Singapore in 2011: A New 'Normal' in Politics?" *Asian Survey* 52(1): 220-226.

Tan Lee Ooi. 2004. "The Emerging Virtual Civil Society in Malaysia: A First Glance". Paper presented at the *4th International Malaysian Studies Conference*; Universiti Kebangsaan Malaysia, Bangi, August 3-5.

Tang, Hang Wu. 2009. "The Networked Electorate: The Internet and the Quiet Democratic Revolution in Malaysia and Singapore". *Journal of Information, Law & Technology* 2: 1-33.

Tanuwidjaja, Sunny. 2010. "Political Islam and Islamic Parties in Indonesia: Critically Assessing the Evidence of Islam's Political Decline". *Contemporary Southeast Asia* 32(1).

Tarrow, Sidney. 1998. *Power in Movement*. New York: Cambridge University Press.

Taubman, Geoffry. 1998. "A Not-So World Wide Web: The Internet, China and the Challenges to Nondemocratic Rule". *Political Communication* 15(2): 255-272.

Tedjabayu. 1999. "Indonesia: The Net as a Weapon". *Cybersociology* 5. http://www.cybersociology.com/files/5_netasaweapon.html.

Thelen, Kathleen. 1999. "Historical Institutionalism in Comparative Politics". *Annual Review of Political Science* 2: 369-404.

Thompson, Mark. 2008. "People Power Sours: Uncivil Society in Thailand and the Philippines". *Current History* (November): 381-387.

Thongchai Winichakul. 2008. "Toppling Democracy". *Journal of Contemporary Asia* 38(1): 11-37.

Tomsa, Dirk. 2010. "The Indonesian Party System after the 2009 Elections: Towards Stability?" In *Problems of Democratization in Indonesia: Elections, Institutions and Society.* Edward Aspinall and Marcus Mietzner edited. Singapore: Institute of Southeast Asian Studies.

Tomz, Michael. 2007. "Domestic Audience Costs in International Relations: An Experimental Approach". *International Organization* 61(4): 821-840.

Tong Yee Siong. 2004. "Malaysiakini: treading a tightrope of political pressure and market factors". In *Asian Cyberactivism: Freedom of*

Expression and Media Censorship. Steven Gan, James Gomez and Uwe Johannen edited. Bangkok: Friedrich Naumann Foundation.

Transparency International. 2010. "Corruption Perceptions Index 2010". http://www.transparency.org/policy_research/surveys_indices/cpi/2010 /results.

Tuaño, Philip. 2011. *Civil Society Index: Philippines – An assessment of Philippine Civil Society*. Quezon City: Caucus of Development NGO Networks.

Ufen, Andreas. 2009. "The transformation of political party opposition in Malaysia and its implications for the electoral authoritarian regime". *Democratization* 16(3): 604-627.

—. 2012. "Party Systems, Critical Junctures and Cleavages in Southeast Asia". *SEARC Working Paper Series* 129.

Um, Khatharya. 2011. "Cambodia: Hopes, Trials, and Tribulations". *Southeast Asian Affairs* 2011.

Un, Kheang. 2012. "Cambodia in 2011: A Thin Veneer of Change". *Asian Survey* 52(1): 202-209.

Wacker, Gudrun. 2003. "The Internet and censorship in China". In *China and the Internet: Politics of the Digital Leap Forward.* Christopher Hughes and Gudrun Wacker edited. London: Routledge Curzon.

Wain, Barry. 2009. *Malaysian Maverick: Mahathir Mohamad in Turbulent Times.* Palgrave Macmillan.

Washington Post (The). 2011. "Thailand warns Facebook sharing may slur monarchy". November 29. http://www.washingtontimes.com/news/ 2011/nov/29/thailand-warns-facebook-sharing-may-slur-monarchy/?page=all.

Weiss, Meredith. 2006. *Protest and Possibilities: Civil Society and Coalitions for Political Change in Malaysia.* Stanford University Press.

—. 2009. "Edging toward a New Politics in Malaysia: Civil Society at the Gate?" *Asian Survey* 49(5): 741-758.

Welsh, Bridget. 2006. "Malaysia's Sarawak State Elections 2006: Understanding a Break in the BN Armor". *Report Prepared for National Democratic Institute.*

—. 2007. "Malaysia's November 2007 Protests: Challenge to Legitimacy". *Asia Pacific Bulletin* 6: 1-2.

Whaley, Floyd. 2012. "Philippine Judge's Trial Draws Interest, and Critics". New *York Times*. January 13. http://www.nytimes.com/2012/ 01/14/world/asia/philippine-judges-trial-draws-interest-and-critics.html?_r=1.

Winters, Jeffrey. 2002. "The Political Impact of New Information Sources and Technologies in Indonesia". *International Communication Gazette* 64(2): 109-119.

Wong Kok Keong. 2001. "Unfair Coverage: A Look at the Mainstream Media's Bias in the 1999 General Election." *Aliran Monthly*. http://www.aliran.com/oldsite/monthly/2001/1b.html.

Woodier, Jonathan. 2008. *The Media and Political Change in Southeast Asia: Karaoke Culture and the Evolution of Personality Politics*. Cheltenham: Edward Elgar Publishing Limited.

World Public Opinion. 2008. "World Public Opinion on Freedom of the Media". http://www.worldpublicopinion.org/pipa/articles/btjusticehuman_rightsra/477.php.

Wu, Irene. 2004. "Canada, South Korea, Netherlands and Sweden: regulatory implications of the convergence of telecommunications, broadcasting and Internet services". *Telecommunications Policy* 28(1): 79-96.

Yacob, Imran Imtiaz Shah. 2007. "Malaysian practitioners defy police". *Asian Sentinel*. November 10. http://www.asiasentinel.com/index.php?option=com_content&task=view&id=863&Itemid=31.

Yang, Guobin. 2003. "The Co-evolution of the Internet and Civil Society in China". *Asian Survey* 43(3): 405-422.

York, Jillian. 2011. "Africa's cascade of Internet censorship". *Al Jazeera*. May 12. http://www.aljazeera.com/indepth/opinion/2011/05/2011512134039497302.html.

Yow Hong Chieh. 2010. "PR, BN say no to policed internet". *The Malaysian Insider*. http://www.themalaysianinsider.com/mobile/malaysia/article/pr-bn-say-no-to-policed-internet/.

—. 2011. "PAS on million-man march for Bersih". *The Malaysian Insider*. http://www.themalaysianinsider.com/malaysia/article/pas-on-million-man-march-for-bersih/.

Zanger, Sabine. 2000. "A Global Analysis of the Effect of Political Regime Changes on Life Integrity Violations, 1977-93". *Journal of Peace Research* 37(2): 213.

Zheng, Yongnian. 2008. *Technological Empowerment: The Internet, State, and Society in China*. Stanford: Stanford University Press.

Zittrain, Jonathan and John Palfrey. 2008. "Internet Filtering: The Politics and Mechanisms of Control". In *Access Denied: The Practice and Policy of Global Internet Filtering*. Ronald Deibert et al. edited. Massachusetts: The MIT Press.

Zuckerman, Ethan. 2010. "Intermediary Censorship". In *Access Controlled: The Shaping of Power, Rights, and Rule in Cyberspace*. Ronald Deibert et al. edited. Massachusetts: The MIT Press.

INDEX